# AQA History

## AS
### Unit 2

BOOK

Anti-Semitism, Hitler and the German People, 1919–1945

**Exclusively endorsed by AQA**

Chris Rowe
Alan Gillingham

Series editor
Sally Waller

## Nelson Thornes

Published in 2009 by:
Nelson Thornes Ltd
Delta Place
27 Bath Road
CHELTENHAM
GL53 7TH
United Kingdom

10 11 12 13 / 10 9 8 7 6 5 4 3 2

A catalogue record for this book is available from the British Library

978 0 7487 8260 4

Illustrations by David Russell Illustration

Page make-up by Thomson Digital

Printed and bound in Spain by Graphycems

# Contents

# Introduction

## Nelson Thornes and AQA

Nelson Thornes has worked in collaboration with AQA to ensure that this book offers you the best support for your AS or A Level course and helps you to prepare for your exams. The partnership means that you can be confident that the range of learning, teaching and assessment practice materials has been checked by the senior examining team at AQA before formal approval, and is closely matched to the requirements of your specification.

## How to use this book

This book covers the specification for your course and is arranged in a sequence approved by AQA.

The features in this book include:

## Timeline

Key events are outlined at the beginning of the book.

*Learning objectives*

At the beginning of each section you will find a list of learning objectives that contain targets linked to the requirements of the specification.

### Key chronology

A short list of dates usually with a focus on a specific event or legislation.

### Key profile

The profile of a key person you should be aware of to fully understand the period in question.

### Key terms

A term that you will need to be able to define and understand.

### Did you know?

Interesting information to bring the subject under discussion to life.

### Exploring the detail

Information to put further context around the subject under discussion.

### A closer look

An in-depth look at a theme, person or event to deepen your understanding. Activities around the extra information may be included.

## Sources

Sources to reinforce topics or themes and may provide fact or opinion. They may be quotations from historical works, contemporaries of the period or photographs.

### Cross-reference

Links to related content within the book that may offer more detail on the subject in question.

### Activity

Various activity types to provide you with different challenges and opportunities to demonstrate both the content and skills you are learning. Some can be worked on individually, some as part of group work and some are designed to specifically 'stretch and challenge'.

## Question

Questions to prompt further discussion on the topic under consideration and are an aid to revision.

## Summary questions

Summary questions at the end of each chapter to test your knowledge and allow you to demonstrate your understanding.

## AQA Examiner's tip

Hints from AQA examiners to help you with your study and to prepare for your exam.

## AQA Examination-style questions

Questions at the end of each section in the style that you can expect in your exam.

*Learning outcomes*

Learning outcomes at the end of each section remind you what you should know having completed the chapters in that section.

## ■ Web links in the book

Because Nelson Thornes is not responsible for third party content online, there may be some changes to this material that are beyond our control. In order for us to ensure that the links referred to in the book are as up-to-date and stable as possible, the websites provided are usually homepages with supporting instructions on how to reach the relevant pages if necessary.

Please let us know at **kerboodle@nelsonthornes. com** if you find a link that doesn't work and we will do our best to correct this at reprint, or to list an alternative site.

# Introduction to the History series

When Bruce Bogtrotter in Roald Dahl's *Matilda* was challenged to eat a huge chocolate cake, he just opened his mouth and ploughed in, taking bite after bite and lump after lump until the cake was gone and he was feeling decidedly sick. The picture is not dissimilar to that of some A Level history students. They are attracted to history because of its inherent appeal but, when faced with a bulging file and a forthcoming examination, their enjoyment evaporates. They try desperately to cram their brains with an assortment of random facts and subsequently prove unable to control the outpouring of their ill-digested material in the examination.

The books in this series are designed to help students and teachers avoid this feeling of overload and examination panic by breaking down the AQA History specification in such a way that it is easily absorbed. Above all, they are designed to retain and promote students' enthusiasm for history by avoiding a dreary rehash of dates and events. Each book is divided into sections, closely matched to those given in the specification, and the content is further broken down into chapters that present the historical material in a lively and attractive form, offering guidance on the key terms, events and issues, and blending thought-provoking activities and questions in a way designed to advance students' understanding. By encouraging students to think for themselves and to share their ideas with others, as well as helping them to develop the knowledge and skills they will need to pass their examination, this book should ensure that students' learning remains a pleasure rather than an endurance test.

To make the most of what this book provides, students will need to develop efficient study skills from the start and it is worth spending some time considering what these involve:

- Good organisation of material in a subject-specific file. Organised notes help develop an organised brain and sensible filing ensures time is not wasted hunting for misplaced material. This book uses cross-references to indicate where material in one chapter has relevance to material in another. Students are advised to adopt the same technique.

- A sensible approach to note-making. Students are often too ready to copy large chunks of material from printed books or to download sheaves of printouts from the internet. This series is designed to encourage students to think about the notes they collect and to undertake research with a particular purpose in mind. The activities encourage students to pick out information that is relevant to the issue being addressed and to avoid making notes on material that is not properly understood.

- Taking time to think, which is by far the most important component of study. By encouraging students to think before they write or speak, be it for a written answer, presentation or class debate, students should learn to form opinions and make judgements based on the accumulation of evidence. These are the skills that the examiner will be looking for in the final examination. The beauty of history is that there is rarely a right or wrong answer so, with sufficient evidence, one student's view will count for as much as the next.

## Unit 2

Unit 2 promotes the study of significant periods of history in depth. Although the span of years may appear short, the chosen topics are centred on periods of change that raise specific historical issues and they therefore provide an opportunity for students to study in some depth the interrelationships between ideas, individuals, circumstances and other factors that lead to major developments. Appreciating the dynamics of change, and balancing the degree of change against elements of continuity, make for a fascinating and worthwhile study. Students are also required to analyse consequences and draw conclusions about the issues these studies raise. Such themes are, of course, relevant to an understanding of the present and, through such an historical investigation, students will be guided towards a greater appreciation of the world around them today, as well as develop their understanding of the past.

Unit 2 is tested by a 1 hour 30 minute paper containing three questions. The first question is compulsory and based on sources, while the remaining two, of which students will need to choose one, are two-part questions as described in Table 1. Plentiful sources are included throughout this book to give students some familiarity with contemporary and historiographical material, and activities and suggestions are provided to enable students to develop the required examination skills. Students should familiarise themselves with the question breakdown, additional hints and marking criteria given below before attempting any of the practice examination-style questions at the end of each section.

Answers will be marked according to a scheme based on 'levels of response'. This means that the answer will be assessed according to which level best matches the historical skills displayed, taking both knowledge and understanding into account. All students should have a copy of these criteria and need to use them wisely.

**Table 1** *Unit 2: style of questions and marks available*

| Unit 2 | Question | Marks | Question type | Question stem | Hints for students |
|---|---|---|---|---|---|
| Question 1 based on three sources of *c.*300 – 500 words in total | (a) | 12 | This question involves the comparison of two sources | Explain how far the views in Source B differ from those in Source A in relation to … | Take pains to avoid simply writing out what each source says with limited direct comment. Instead, you should try to find two or three points of comparison and illustrate these with reference to the sources. You should also look for any underlying similarities. In your conclusion, you will need to make it clear exactly 'how far' the views differ |
| Question 1 | (b) | 24 | This requires use of the sources and own knowledge and asks for an explanation that shows awareness that issues and events can provoke differing views and explanations | How far … <br><br> How important was … <br><br> How successful … | This answer needs to be planned as you will need to develop an argument in your answer and show balanced judgement. Try to set out your argument in the introduction and, as you develop your ideas through your paragraphs, support your opinions with detailed evidence. Your conclusion should flow naturally and provide supported judgement. The sources should be used as 'evidence' throughout your answer. Do ensure you refer to them all |
| Question 2 and 3 | (a) | 12 | This question is focused on a narrow issue within the period studied and requires an explanation | Explain why … | Make sure you explain 'why', not 'how', and try to order your answer in a way that shows you understand the inter-linkage of factors and which were the more important. You should try to reach an overall judgement/conclusion |
| Question 2 and 3 | (b) | 24 | This question is broader and asks for analysis and explanation with appropriate judgement. The question requires an awareness of debate over issues | A quotation in the form of a judgement on a key development or issue will be given and candidates asked: <br><br> Explain why you agree or disagree with this view (of … in the years …) | This answer needs to be planned as you will need to show balanced judgement in your answer. Try to think of points that agree and disagree and decide which way you will argue. Set out your argument in the introduction and support it through your paragraphs, giving the alternative picture too but showing why your view is the more convincing. Your conclusion should flow naturally from what you have written |

## Marking criteria

### Question 1(a)

**Level 1** Answers either briefly paraphrase/describe the content of the two sources or identify simple comparison(s) between the sources. Skills of written communication are weak. *(0–2 marks)*

**Level 2** Responses compare the views expressed in the two sources and identify some differences and/or similarities. There may be some limited own knowledge. Answers are coherent but weakly expressed. *(3–6 marks)*

**Level 3** Responses compare the views expressed in the two sources, identifying differences and similarities and using own knowledge to explain and evaluate these. For the most part, answers are clearly expressed. *(7–9 marks)*

**Level 4** Responses make a developed comparison between the views expressed in the two sources and own knowledge is applied to evaluate these and to demonstrate a good contextual understanding. For the most part, answers show good skills of written communication. *(10–12 marks)*

## Question 1(b)

**Level 1** Answers may be based on sources or on own knowledge alone, or they may comprise an undeveloped mixture of the two. They may contain some descriptive material that is only loosely linked to the focus of the question or they may address only a part of the question. Alternatively, there may be some explicit comment with little, if any, appropriate support. Answers are likely to be generalised and assertive. There is little, if any, awareness of different historical interpretations. The response is limited in development and skills of written communication are weak. *(0–6 marks)*

**Level 2** Answers may be based on sources or on own knowledge alone, or they may contain a mixture of the two. They may be almost entirely descriptive with few explicit links to the focus of the question. Alternatively, they may contain some explicit comment with relevant but limited support. They display limited understanding of different historical interpretations. Answers are coherent but weakly expressed and/or poorly structured. *(7–11 marks)*

**Level 3** Answers show a developed understanding of the demands of the question using evidence from both the sources and own knowledge. They provide some assessment backed by relevant and appropriately selected evidence, but they lack depth and/or balance. There is some understanding of varying historical interpretations. For the most part, answers are clearly expressed and show some organisation in the presentation of material. *(12 –16 marks)*

**Level 4** Answers show explicit understanding of the demands of the question. They develop a balanced argument backed by a good range of appropriately selected evidence from the sources and own knowledge, and a good understanding of historical interpretations. For the most part, answers show organisation and good skills of written communication. *(17–21 marks)*

**Level 5** Answers are well focused and closely argued. The arguments are supported by precisely selected evidence from the sources and own knowledge, incorporating well-developed understanding of historical interpretations and debate. For the most part, answers are carefully organised and fluently written, using appropriate vocabulary. *(22–24 marks)*

## Question 2(a) and 3(a)

**Level 1** Answers contain either some descriptive material that is only loosely linked to the focus of the question or some explicit comment with little, if any, appropriate support. Answers are likely to be generalised and assertive. The response is limited in development and skills of written communication will be weak. *(0–2 marks)*

**Level 2** Answers demonstrate some knowledge and understanding of the demands of the question. Either they are almost entirely descriptive with few explicit links to the question or they provide some explanations backed by evidence that is limited in range and/or depth. Answers are coherent but weakly expressed and/or poorly structured. *(3–6 marks)*

**Level 3** Answers demonstrate good understanding of the demands of the question providing relevant explanations backed by appropriately selected information, although this may not be full or comprehensive. For the most part, answers are clearly expressed and show some organisation in the presentation of material. *(7–9 marks)*

**Level 4** Answers are well focused, identifying a range of specific explanations backed by precise evidence and demonstrating good understanding of the connections and links between events/issues. For the most part, answers are well written and organised. *(10–12 marks)*

## Question 2(b) and 3(b)

**Level 1** Answers either contain some descriptive material that is only loosely linked to the focus of the question or address only a limited part of the period of the question. Alternatively, there may be some explicit comment with little, if any, appropriate support. Answers are likely to be generalised and assertive. There will be little, if any, awareness of different historical interpretations. The response is limited in development and skills of written communication are weak. *(0–6 marks)*

**Level 2** Answers show some understanding of the demands of the question. Either they will be almost entirely descriptive with few explicit links to the question or they contain some explicit comment with relevant but limited support. They display limited understanding of different historical interpretations. Answers are coherent but weakly expressed and/or poorly structured. *(7–11 marks)*

**Level 3** Answers show a developed understanding of the demands of the question. They provide some assessment, backed by relevant and appropriately selected evidence, but they lack depth and/or balance. There is some understanding of varying historical interpretations. For the most part, answers are clearly expressed and show some organisation in the presentation of material. *(12–16 marks)*

**Level 4** Answers show explicit understanding of the demands of the question. They develop a balanced argument backed by a good range of appropriately selected evidence and a good understanding of historical interpretations. For the most part, answers show organisation and good skills of written communication. *(17–21 marks)*

**Level 5** Answers are well focused and closely argued. The arguments are supported by precisely selected evidence leading to a relevant conclusion/judgement, incorporating well-developed understanding of historical interpretations and debate. For the most part, answers are carefully organised and fluently written, using appropriate vocabulary. *(22–24 marks)*

# Introduction to this book

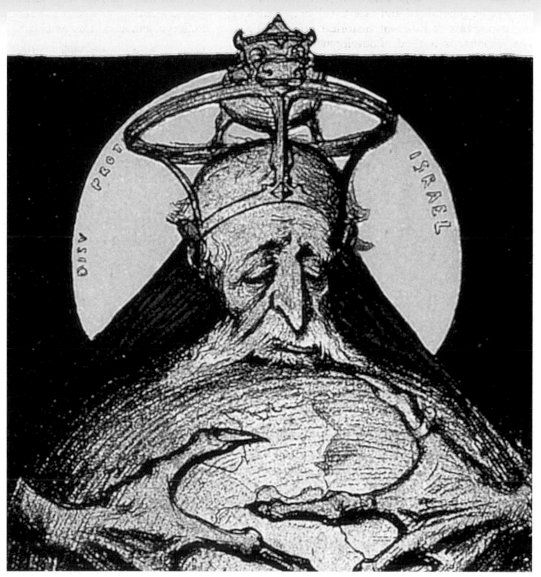

**Fig. 1** *A French cartoon of 1898 satirising the wealth of the Rothschilds*

## Studying anti-Semitism

Any study of anti-Semitism in Germany during the Nazi era is bound to raise issues of morality and involve students in the controversy that has arisen from rival historical interpretations. A study of anti-Semitism demands rigorous and objective historical enquiry, which it is not always easy to accomplish. There are three 'moral' dangers. One is of an excessively emotional reaction, for example branding *all* Germans as guilty. In the propaganda of the Second World War, and in many Hollywood films since 1945, powerful images were portrayed of sadistic Germans on the one hand and Jews as saintly victims on the other. The reality, however, was more complicated than that. There were many 'good Germans' and many other Germans who were neither good nor bad but became caught up in the Nazi regime and either remained aloof from what was happening around them, or persuaded themselves to accept it. Such moral compromises would have been felt necessary in order to survive under the dictatorship. Not all Jews were morally perfect either – there were instances of betrayal and exploitation of Jews by Jews.

Another, opposite danger is that of not being emotional enough. It is easy to accept what happened and to forget how horrific it was. Equally dangerous is the ease with which students can fall into the trap of accepting the usage of Nazi terms such as 'the Final Solution to the Jewish problem' or 'racial hygiene' or de-humanising language such as 'resettlement' instead of death camps or 'actions' instead of mass murder. Finally, the third danger, is to fall for the intellectual fascination of deciding between rival interpretations and to lose sight of the events themselves. An effective student of Nazi anti-Semitism needs to reflect on what actually happened and, as in all historical study, make personal judgements based on the evidence available to them.

## The problems of interpretation

The one incontrovertible fact about anti-Semitism and Germany is its ultimate outcome – the deaths of millions of European Jews by 1945. This knowledge can result in 'reading history backwards', seeing all the events of the 1920s only as 'clues to the future'. In this way, Jews in Weimar Germany are seen as simply waiting for the Holocaust to happen. This is not what German Jews thought at the time. They believed that Germany was the best and safest place for Jews anywhere in Europe. In the 1930s, many Jews who might have emigrated from Germany chose not to do so because they felt they faced only a temporary period of persecution before life returned to normal. Even in 1943, many people, both Jews and Germans, did not really know what was happening in the camps.

Another problem of interpretation concerns the definitions of Nazi ideology. It is possible to argue that the Jewish race was *the* most important target for the Nazis – that the other victims of Nazi extermination were somehow less significant. But there were indeed other victims of Nazi policies: mentally and physically disabled children; homosexuals; and the Roma. Proportionately, even more Roma were murdered than Jews. It is possible to see Jews as one element in the list of Nazi 'racial enemies' – the largest element, but not the only one.

There is also the problem of perception. It is easy to view the history of the Jews in Germany from 1919 as the history of victims and nothing else. Rightly, there are many memorials to the horrific fate of those who were killed – there are museums, archives and the ruins of the camps. In addition to the way they were persecuted and died, however, the Jews need also to be remembered for the way they lived. Before the Third Reich destroyed it, there was a vibrant Jewish culture in Weimar

■ **Cross-reference**

For the complexities and controversies of terms and definitions, see the Glossary.

Germany, making a massive contribution to societies in Germany and Eastern Europe.

Another problem is the issue of 'collective guilt'. Many historians have applied this concept to the German people as a whole, sometimes even to people not yet born when the persecution and Holocaust was taking place. Separating the perpetrators from 'ordinary Germans' is a difficult task. On the one hand, many decent Germans did not know the full truth and, if they did, there was little or nothing they could do about it because they were controlled by a repressive dictatorship. On the other hand, many people who claimed not to have known clearly *did* know. The 'Final Solution' could never have been carried out without the knowledge and collaboration of thousands of soldiers, railwaymen, civil servants and a host of others.

One final problem of interpretation is the issue of Holocaust denial. In recent years, far-right 'historians' have carried out a vocal campaign, claiming that the Holocaust never really happened at all. These extremists have claimed that the deaths of millions in the camps were merely the inventions or exaggerations of 'Zionist (Jewish) propaganda'. Such denial runs entirely contrary to the known facts; the topic of Holocaust denial is not history.

## ■ The wider historical context

By 1919, European anti-Semitism was already 1,000 years old. What Robert Wistrich called 'The Longest Hatred' was a feature of societies in medieval Christian Europe, including England, from before the time of the Crusades. There were **pogroms** in Norwich and York in 1189. Until modern times, European Jews knew that they were outsiders, unable to share in the legal and property rights available to Christians. Although the legal position eased in the 19th century, the undercurrent of prejudice and discrimination remained. To understand what happened in Germany after 1919, it is necessary to look at the wider historical context of anti-Semitism in Europe before the First World War.

### The different faces of anti-Semitism

**Anti-Judaism**, the religious persecution of Jews as the 'Killers of Christ', was an integral part of the ideology of the Christian churches throughout Europe from medieval times. However, anti-Judaism did not mean a campaign to exterminate Jews, but rather to isolate them and try to persuade them to convert to Christianity.

However, mixed in with this religious anti-Semitism grew economic resentment. From early medieval times, Jews, not being allowed to succeed in the normal fields of land and property or government, specialised in trade and finance. Inevitably, this involved money lending – what the medieval Church called the 'sinful practice of usury'. Jewish moneylenders became vital to rulers and noblemen who pursued glory and success through war and land and who looked down on finance. In the 15th century, for example, Jewish financiers virtually ran the economy of the Spanish Empire – it was Jewish finance that made possible the voyages of Columbus.

However, the economic success and importance of Jews aroused strong jealousies and resentment. In 1492, Spain expelled the Jews. Many Jews moved eastwards across the Mediterranean leaving the Spanish economy to stagnate. This pattern of Jewish economic success and periodic

■ Key terms

**Pogrom:** organised violence against Jews. Pogroms were a frequent occurrence in many parts of Europe, from the 12th century onwards.

**Anti-Judaism:** anti-Judaism did not only exist in Christian Europe. Hatred of the Jewish religion has appeared in many other parts of the world.

reactions against it occurred all over Europe. It became particularly prevalent from the mid-19th century as banking became even more crucial for investment and economic expansion at a time of industrial change. There was, for example, a strong economic reaction against Jews in the French Third Republic in the 1880s.

Another strand of anti-Semitism was to use the Jews as scapegoats. In times of crisis and economic hardship, there was often a tempting opportunity to channel resentment away from politicians by blaming people's misfortunes on the Jews. This was especially true in the late-19th century. One notorious example of political anti-Semitism occurred as the long-serving mayor of Vienna from 1893 to 1910, Karl Lüger, played skilfully on popular prejudices to keep himself in power. This was pure political calculation. Lüger cooperated with Jews when it suited him and once said: 'I will decide who's a Jew.'

By the late-19th century, 'biological anti-Semitism', based on the pseudo (pretend)-scientific concepts of racial inheritance and **eugenics**, began to have an influence. Unlike traditional anti-Judaism, this was based on race, not religion, and there was no escape for Jews by religious 'conversion'. The idea of 'racial hygiene' – protecting the purity of the race by eliminating inferior raccs – was not only applied to Jews. In Sweden and other Nordic countries, there was much scientific interest in birth control and other methods, such as sterilisation, to eliminate physical and mental disabilities.

By the early 20th century, all these different strands of anti-Semitism were circulating in Europe. Some were based on ignorance and violent prejudice; others were considered academically and politically respectable according to the intellectual fashions of the time. They provided the background against which the anti-Semitic ideas of Hitler and the Nazis would later develop.

## Anti-Semitism in Germany before 1914

More than half a million Jews lived in Germany before 1914. They were part of a Jewish community that had existed since before the Crusades, but it was only after 1848 that German Jews had been emancipated and granted legal equality. This emancipation was confirmed in the constitution of the new united German Empire in 1871. In the years after emancipation, German Jews became prominent in business and banking, in medicine and the law, in science and education, in culture and the arts.

Anti-Semitism continued to exist after 1848, but most Jews in Germany considered themselves lucky to be living in a country that offered better prospects for assimilation and social advancement than anywhere in continental Europe. Anti-Semitism in Imperial Germany was, for example, far less threatening than in Tsarist Russia. For most Jews, economic hardship was far less than in Austria-Hungary. There was no equivalent in Germany of the anti-Jewish rioting that took place in France in the 1890s, during the Dreyfus Affair.

Evidence that life was relatively better for Jews in Germany than elsewhere in Europe can be found in the rates of outward emigration in the years before the First World War. Between 1899 and 1914, 250,000 Jews emigrated from Austria-Hungary to the United States. The total number of Jews emigrating from the Tsarist Empire was 1.2 million and most of them passed through German seaports like Hamburg and Bremen on their way. In the same period, only 15,000 German Jews emigrated.

■ **Key terms**

**Eugenics:** the 'science' of selective breeding – applying scientific methods to improving the population. Eugenicists promote policies such as contraception and family planning, or the use of sterilisation to prevent the birth of mentally or physically-handicapped children.

■ **Exploring the detail**

**The Dreyfus Affair**

Captain Alfred Dreyfus was an officer in the French Army who was wrongly accused of espionage in 1894. The Dreyfus Affair continued to divide French politics and society for years. Although Dreyfus was a fully assimilated Jew, at the head of a Catholic family, his trial led to vicious outbursts of anti-Semitism in France. The extent of the anti-Semitism revealed by the Dreyfus trial influenced the ideas of Theodor Herzl, the founder of Zionism. Herzl's book, *The Jewish State*, was published in 1896.

Many German Jews felt they were being absorbed into German society. Many of them were intensely patriotic. During the First World War more than 70,000 Jews served in the armed forces. 12,000 were killed in action; many of those who survived the war were honoured with medals. After the war ended, Germany became a democratic republic, with a new, liberal constitution. Under the Weimar Republic, the prospects for Jews in Germany seemed even better than before.

**Fig. 2** *Between East and West – Jewish population centres in Germany and Eastern Europe, 1919*

# Timeline

| 1918 | 1919 | 1920 | 1922 | 1923 | 1923 | 1924 |
|------|------|------|------|------|------|------|
| The German Revolution and proclamation of the republic<br><br>Death of Rosa Luxemburg after Spartacus uprising | Overthrow of Kurt Eisner in Munich<br><br>Imposition of Versailles Treaty<br><br>New democratic constitution drafted by Hugo Preuss | Failure of Kapp Putsch<br><br>25-point programme of the NSDAP | Murder of Walther Rathenau | Financial crisis and hyper-inflation | (Nov) Beer Hall Putsch in Munich | Advances by anti-Semites in May election<br><br>Economic recovery and start of 'Golden Years' |

| 1932 | 1933 | 1933 | 1933 | 1933 | 1933 | 1934 |
|------|------|------|------|------|------|------|
| Nazis become the largest single party in Germany | (Jan) Hitler appointed German Chancellor | (Mar) Enabling Law passed<br><br>Opening of Dachau concentration camp | (Apr) Boycott of Jewish shops and businesses<br><br>Law for the Restoration of the Professional Civil Service | (Oct) Exclusion of German Jews from the press | (Nov) Gestapo (Secret State Police) set up by Göring | (Apr) Himmler appointed Inspector of the Gestapo |

| 1938 | 1938 | 1938 | 1939 | 1939 | 1939 | 1939 |
|------|------|------|------|------|------|------|
| *Anschluss* with Austria<br><br>German annexation of the Sudetenland | (Oct) Jewish passports stamped with a 'J' | (Nov) *Kristallnacht* pogrom | (Jan) Hitler's Reichstag speech threatening 'annihilation of the Jewish race in Europe' | (Mar) German occupation of Prague | (Aug) Nazi-Soviet Pact | (Sept) German invasion of Poland<br><br>Start of ghettoisation in Poland |

| 1941 | 1941 | 1942 | 1942 | 1942 | 1942 | 1942 |
|------|------|------|------|------|------|------|
| (Sept) Mass killings of Jews near Kiev | (Dec) German declaration of war on USA<br><br>Gassing of Jews at Chelmno | (Jan) Wannsee Conference | (Apr) Opening of Sobibor death camp | (May) Assassination of Reinhard Heydrich | Mass deportation of Jews from Western Europe to Auschwitz | (Dec) German gypsies deported to Auschwitz |

| 1925 | 1926 | 1928 | 1929 | 1930 | 1931 | 1931 |
|---|---|---|---|---|---|---|
| *Mein Kampf* published<br><br>Barmat scandal | Germany accepted into League of Nations<br><br>Fritz Lang's film *Metropolis* | Brecht and Weill's *The Threepenny Opera*<br><br>Election of Müller's coalition government | Wall Street Crash<br><br>Sklarek scandal<br><br>Heinrich Himmler appointed leader of the SS | Sternberg's film *The Blue Angel*<br><br>Big electoral gains by Communists and Nazis | (Aug) SD created under Reinhard Heydrich | SA revolt led by Walter Stennes put down by the SS |

| 1934 | 1934 | 1935 | 1935 | 1936 | 1936 | 1936 |
|---|---|---|---|---|---|---|
| (Jun) Night of the Long Knives, the SS purge the SA | (Aug) Death of Hindenburg; Hitler made head of state | (Sept) The Nuremberg Laws | (Nov) Supplementary Decree on the Reich Citizenship Law | Olympic Games in Berlin | (Jun) Göring made head of the Four Year Plan | (Autumn) SD Section of Jewish Affairs set up |

| 1939 | 1940 | 1940 | 1940 | 1941 | 1941 |
|---|---|---|---|---|---|
| (Oct) Euthanasia programme authorised | (Jan) First gassing of mental patients | (Jun) Fall of France; Vichy regime established<br><br>Start of the Madagascar Plan | (Nov) Warsaw ghetto 'sealed' | (Jun) German invasion of USSR<br><br>*Einsatzgruppen* deployed behind Eastern Front | (Aug) Euthanasia programme halted |

| 1943 | 1944 | 1945 | 1945 | 1945 |
|---|---|---|---|---|
| Warsaw ghetto uprising<br><br>End of mass killings in Chelmno and Treblinka | (Jun) Mass deportation of Hungarian Jews to Auschwitz<br><br>Allied landings in Normandy<br><br>Start of death marches<br><br>End of gassings ordered by Hitler | Liberation of Auschwitz and other camps | (Apr) Hitler's suicide | (May) German surrender |

# Anti-Semitism in Germany, 1919–30

## The Jews in Weimar Germany

*In this chapter you will learn about:*

- German society at the time of the Weimar Republic

- the social and political relationships between Jews and others within the Weimar Republic

- the contribution of Jews to cultural life in Weimar Germany

- the extent to which Jews had become assimilated by 1930.

**Fig. 1** *A contemporary view of the synagogue at Nuremberg*

**Fig. 2** *Jewish populations in Germany c.1933*

The social achievements of German Jews under the Weimar Republic were remarkable. Jews represented only 1 per cent of the total population of Weimar Germany, but they achieved a degree of influence out of all proportion to their numbers. German Jews achieved prominence in politics and the press, in business and banking, in the universities and in almost all aspects of Weimar culture. The foreign minister of the new republic from 1919 was a Jew – Walther Rathenau, the wealthy industrialist at the head of the great engineering conglomerate, AEG. Jews had huge influence in the publishing of books and newspapers. Jewish musicians were at the forefront of musical life. Jewish producers and directors dominated theatre and the new medium of cinema.

These social, political and cultural achievements encouraged the belief of assimilated Jews that Germany was the best possible homeland. Most Jews identified with the Weimar Republic and felt that they were safer there than anywhere in continental Europe. Anti-Semitism did exist but mostly on the fringes of politics. Only a small minority of German Jews favoured Zionism. Most looked forward to a continued process of assimilation. This helps to explain why, when things became dangerous after 1933, so many Jews did not take the chance to emigrate to safety; they simply could not believe that 'their' Germany would become a fatal trap.

## Jews in the Weimar Republic, 1919–30

There were more than half a million Jews living in Germany under the Weimar Republic. Eighty per cent of Jews in Germany (400,000) were urban-based and educated. Many of them felt much more German than Jewish. Most were often intensely patriotic. Many believed in **assimilation** – keeping their ethnic and cultural identity but becoming fully integrated and accepted in mainstream German society. German Jews were not, of course, one homogeneous mass. There were many differences within Jewish communities – political, religious and economic.

**Fig. 3** *Poster commemorating Jewish soldiers who died fighting for Germany in the First World War*

Politically, Jews were to be found in all parties. A number of Jews were **Communists**. At the other extreme, many Jews supported the Conservatives. Surprisingly, some Jews voted for the Zentrum (Catholic Centre Party) especially in the late 1920s. On the whole, however, Jews in Germany identified with the moderate democratic parties: the SPD (German Socialist Party) and, above all, the Liberal DDP (German Democratic Party). Most Jews were also liberal in religion. Orthodox Jews, strictly observing religious traditions, were a minority; so were

## ■ Key terms

**Zionists:** they believed in the idea of a national homeland for the Jewish people. Their dream was to create this homeland in Palestine, the historic home of Jews before they were driven out by the Romans in the 1st century AD. The founding father of modern Zionism was Theodor Herzl, the author of *The Jewish State* published in 1896.

## ■ Exploring the detail

### Jewish religious groups

Jews in Germany were divided not only by class but by their different attitudes to religion. Orthodox Jews stuck closely to traditional Judaism; they were easily recognisable by their dress. Reform Jews practised a more liberal form of Judaism and were willing to assimilate into modern German society. Zionists wanted a national homeland for the Jews, not assimilation. Secular Jews had moved away from Judaism but kept their Jewish cultural identity. Many other assimilated Jews inter-married with non-Jews, converted to Christianity and did not think of themselves as Jewish at all.

## ■ Cross-reference

For a map of Eastern Jewry, see the Introduction, page 5.

the **Zionists**. The great majority were either Liberal Jews or belonged to the group known as Neo-Orthodox. Both these groups believed in assimilation into modern German society.

Some Jews achieved greater prosperity and status than others. In his 1980 book, *The Jews In Weimar Germany*, Donald Niewyk placed Jews in four general categories:

1  At the top were Jews who had reached great wealth and influence – great industrialists, publishers, celebrities in culture and mass entertainment.

2  In the second tier were the successful Jewish middle classes – businessmen and, especially, educated professionals in the universities, medicine and the law.

3  In the third tier were small businessmen and craftsmen, people who had a stake in society but were less than prosperous.

4  All the above three groups regarded themselves as superior to those in the lower levels of society – 75,000 'Polacks', poorer, 'eastern' Jews who were less assimilated and struggled to find secure employment.

## ■ A closer look

### Jews, Germans and Germany

In explaining the position of Jews in Germany, the simplest of words can cause massive difficulties for historians. Were Jewish people born and brought up in Germany 'German Jews' or 'Jewish Germans'? Should not assimilated Jews who had married non-Jews, who did not practise the Jewish religion and who had perhaps converted to Christianity, be regarded as 'Germans of Jewish descent'? Could people who were not born or brought up in Germany, like Adolf Hitler, an obscure young Austrian deserter from military service who arrived in Munich in 1914, claim to be truly German? Definitions of both 'Jewishness' and 'German-ness' between 1919 and 1945 remain complicated and controversial, with an ever-present danger of apparently innocent words taking on unintended racist implications.

These important questions not only provide difficulties for historians, they really bothered people at the time, both Jews and non-Jews. Zionist Jews were conscious first and foremost of their Jewishness – their loyalty was not to Germany but to the national homeland for Jews they hoped to achieve one day. *Völkisch* nationalists wanted Germans to be defined by race and not citizenship – for them, Jews were 'un-German', while *Volksdeutsche*, ethnic Germans living in other countries such as Austria, Czechoslovakia, Poland, the Baltic States and Romania, *ought* to be recognised as true Germans. Liberal and assimilated Jews rejected such notions – most German Jews *felt* intensely German, proud of their German cultural heritage.

Part of the problem was the shifting historical geography of Germany. German nationalism in the 19th century was very different from nationalism in Britain or France, for example, because Germany only became a united nation in 1871. The idea of being German had to be based on something other than belonging to the state. Another problem is that the borders of Germany kept shifting. The 1919 Treaty of Versailles, for example, left Germany significantly smaller than in the days of the *Kaiserreich*. Territories populated by substantial numbers of German people were now parts of Poland, France or Czechoslovakia. The Versailles Treaty expressly prohibited union *(Anschluss)* between Germany and Austria.

After the rise of Hitler, all this changed. In 1938, many 'Lost Germans' were brought 'home': the *Anschluss* added 8 million Austrians to the Third Reich; the Munich agreement transferred 3 million Sudeten Germans from Czechoslovakia to Germany. Between September 1939 and December 1941, conquering German armies enabled millions more ethnic Germans to be incorporated into the expanding Reich. Defining who was, or was not, 'truly German' was a matter of chronology, as well as a matter of perception and opinion.

The birth of the Weimar Republic strengthened the bonds between Jews and their German homeland. Jews were predominantly **liberal** in their political outlook. It was Liberal Germany that had emancipated the Jews in 1848. It was middle-class Liberalism that enabled Jews to make such rapid progress in business and the professions in the 70 years since then. This had an important effect. In the Kaiserreich before 1914, Jews had been 'outsiders' – as were non-Jewish Liberals. Although many Jews were economically successful, they were not part of the ruling system, which was dominated by the Junker aristocracy and the armed forces.

The German Revolution of 1918 changed all this. The monarchy was abolished and the old ruling elites were pushed to the sidelines. The new ruling class was liberal, socialist and democratic. The constitution of the new Weimar Republic (originally drafted by a Jew, the interior minister Hugo Preuss) strengthened civil rights and made Jews and other minorities feel more secure. Jews were no longer outsiders – now they were 'insiders'.

## Key profile

### Hugo Preuss

Preuss (1860–1925) was a member of the Liberal DDP (German Democratic Party) that came to prominence after the First World War. He was state secretary for home affairs in the provisional government of 1918–19 and later became minister of the interior. In 1919, he was the main author of the proposals for the new constitution of the Weimar Republic. Because of his Jewish origins and because he was a democrat, Preuss was frequently attacked by the Conservative Right as 'un-German'.

## A closer look

### The Weimar Republic: a drama in three acts

*Act one: The German Revolution, 1918–23*

The Weimar Republic was born out of defeat and revolution. In November 1918, the sudden collapse of Germany's war effort led to the breakdown of order on the home front. Wilhelm II abdicated. Socialist politicians in Berlin proclaimed the birth of the republic. Power was handed to a provisional government, led by the moderate socialist, Friedrich Ebert. The government moved to the university city of Weimar because Berlin was not safe.

In 1919 an idealistic democratic constitution established the Weimar Republic – but the survival of the new government was threatened by enemies on both the Left and the Right. To save itself from the Communist Spartacus uprising in Berlin, headed by Karl

### Key terms

**Liberal:** the economic and political ideas of Liberals in Germany reflected the views of the educated middle classes. Liberalism was strengthened by the 1848 revolution. Liberals believed in democracy and the rights of the individual; they also believed in science and progress.

### Activity

**Research exercise**

Find out some background information on different elements of the Jewish community in Germany before 1918.

## Key terms

**Freikorps**: unofficial armies that were formed out of the chaos of Germany's defeat in the First World War. These 'Free Corps' were led by experienced army commanders and played a key role in suppressing left-wing uprisings in 1919 and 1920. Those who joined the Freikorps were often violently nationalist, anti-Slav and anti-Semitic.

## Cross-reference

The Spartacus uprising is outlined in Chapter 2, page 25.

The *Freikorps* is described in Chapter 2, page 27.

Liebknecht and Rosa Luxemburg, Ebert's government was forced to rely on the power of the regular army and also of the **Freikorps** (Free Corps), the unofficial armies of ex-soldiers, under individualist commanders, which played a major role in 'restoring order'.

This saved the republic from Communism but left it open to the danger of right-wing counter-revolution. In 1920, elements of the *Freikorps* tried to seize power in Berlin; in 1923 an ex-army corporal, Adolf Hitler, led a similar failed putsch in Munich. Ebert's government was also blamed for the unpopular Versailles peace treaty. Right-wing extremists carried out 2,000 political murders, including those of Matthias Erzberger in 1921 and Walther Rathenau in 1922.

From 1919 to 1923, Weimar governments had to deal with a sustained economic crisis. In 1923, there was hyper-inflation and the complete collapse of the currency, causing appalling hardship to the middle classes. Economic crisis caused political instability. All Weimar governments depended on coalitions between two or more parties; these coalitions came and went every few months.

*Act two: The 'Golden Years' 1924–9*

From 1924, Weimar Germany entered a new period of economic prosperity and political stability. Inflation was tamed by the financial reforms of Dr Hjalmar Schacht. Business and industry recovered. By 1928, industrial production and living standards were back to pre-war levels. Gustav Stresemann, foreign minister from 1923 to 1929, rebuilt Germany's relations with foreign powers. Foreign loans boosted Germany's economic recovery. Coalition governments became more stable. Cultural life flourished.

Not all historians accept that the 'Golden Years' represented genuine stability and permanence. Many claim that Weimar democracy was fragile, dependent on shallow, temporary prosperity. At the time, however, the supporters of the republic believed it was here to stay. Extremist parties were marginalised. The republic might have been able to put down deep roots; but the good years did not last. What Germany got instead was the Wall Street Crash and the Great Depression.

*Act three: The collapse of democracy*

The Wall Street Crash did not immediately lead to deep depression; it was 1932 before the economic slump was at its worst. Already in 1930, however, economic crisis was undermining support for moderate democratic parties. The Communists made big gains. By 1932, the Nazi Party was the biggest single party in the *Reichstag* (parliament). In January 1933, President Hindenburg appointed Hitler German Chancellor. In March 1933, in a 'legal revolution', the Reichstag passed an Enabling Law giving Hitler temporary dictatorial powers. The Weimar Republic was dead.

## Key profile

### Dr Hjalmar Schacht

Schacht (1877–1970) was a brilliant (and very arrogant) financier. He became president of the *Reichsbank* (Germany's national bank) in 1923, the year when there was hyper-inflation and the German currency collapsed. Schacht gained a huge reputation as the man who saved Germany's economy by introducing a new currency, the *rentenmark.* This restored stability to the German financial system. Schacht remained at the *Reichsbank* until 1929. He joined the Nazi Party in 1931 and had a key role in running the economy of the Third Reich from 1933 until 1937.

## The social achievement of Jews in Weimar Germany

### The political parties and the press

German Jews were already well established in the world of politics before 1914. Jewish publishing firms had a powerful influence in the media, with two Jewish-run newspapers in particular, the *Berliner Tageblatt* and the *Frankfurter Zeitung*, promoting Liberal political views. Theodor Wolff, editor of *Berliner Tageblatt*, was the driving force behind the moderate Liberal DDP (German Democratic Party).

**Fig. 4** *Prominent members of the Jewish community in Würzburg*

### Key profile

#### Theodor Wolff

Wolff (1868–1943) was a liberal journalist from a wealthy Jewish family. From 1887, he worked for the Mosse publishing house; in 1906 Mosse appointed him editor of the *Berliner Tageblatt,* a reformist liberal newspaper. Wolff became well known for his lengthy editorials every Monday. From 1916, Wolff and his paper came under attack for urging a negotiated peace. In 1918, he was one of the founders of the DDP (German Liberal Party). Wolff remained active and influential until 1933, when he went into exile after his books were burned by the Nazis. In 1943, Wolff was arrested in Italy and sent to a concentration camp north of Berlin, KZ Sachsenhausen, where he died.

The most important figure in the DDP and the most important Jew in early Weimar politics was the industrialist Walther Rathenau, who was appointed foreign minister in 1922.

### Key profile

#### Walther Rathenau

Rathenau's father, Emil, founded the huge electrical-engineering firm AEG. Walther (1867–1922) joined the AEG board in 1899 and became one of the leading industrialists in Germany. He was a firm believer in Jewish assimilation, convinced that anti-Semitism would gradually wither away if Jews became more integrated into German society. In the First World War, Rathenau ran much of the war economy, responsible for the vital Raw Materials department. After the war, Rathenau joined the moderate Liberal DDP. He became minister of reconstruction and then foreign minister. He was assassinated in June 1922.

■ Cross-reference

Anti-Semitic attacks on the Jewish influences in the press and media are covered in Chapter 2, pages 23–4.

■ Key terms

**Propaganda:** manipulation of information to influence public opinion. Propaganda emphasises the elements of information that support their position and plays down or leaves out bits that do not. Misleading statements and even lies may be used to create the desired effect in the public audience.

■ Exploring the detail

**The Rothschilds**

The Rothschilds were a rich Jewish banking family, with branches in Britain, France, Italy and Austria. The founder of the dynasty, Nathan Rothschild, was born in the poor Jewish quarter of Frankfurt. The family rose to prominence in the 1820s and 1830s; by the end of the 19th century, the Rothschilds were as rich as any members of the European aristocratic elite. The Rothschilds supported many charities. They were also strong supporters of Zionism. In 1940, the rise of the Rothschilds was the target of an anti-Semitic propaganda film sponsored by Göbbels and the Nazi propaganda ministry (see Chapter 6, page 83).

■ Exploring the detail

**Wertheim**

The early 20th century was the heyday of the department store. The leading Berlin store was Wertheim, in competition with its prestigious rivals Tietz and KdW. The biggest Wertheim store opened in 1896, with 83 lifts and a huge central atrium; throughout the 1920s Wertheim symbolised the glamour of cosmopolitan Weimar Berlin. The Jewish-owned family firm was 'Aryanised' by the Nazi regime after 1933, but continued to exist. In 2009, two Wertheim stores still had prime locations on Berlin's key shopping street, the *Kurfürstendamm*.

The Ullstein publishing empire produced numerous political newspapers and journals. The *Berliner Illustrierte Zeitung* (*BIZ*) had a circulation of 1.8 million by 1930. In 1923, a similar illustrated paper came out in Munich; followed by one in Cologne in 1926. Lavishly illustrated with photographs and advertisements, these papers were not directly political but reached a wide audience. The influence of Jews in publishing was strongly attacked by anti-Semites who moaned about the evil effects on public opinion of this 'monopoly of the Jewish Press'. This was typical of a widespread tendency in Weimar Germany for the extent of the wealth and influence of Jews to be grossly exaggerated; and also to be regarded as the result of a conspiracy, not a reward for hard work and a drive to succeed.

### Industry, business and banking

German Jews did achieve considerable wealth and influence in industry and commerce, although the extent of this influence was massively exaggerated by anti-Jewish **propaganda**, both at the time and afterwards. The Rathenau family controlled the huge electrical engineering firm AEG, though the firm was taken over by non-Jews from 1927. Jewish firms dominated coalmining, steelworks and the chemical industry in Silesia, but had very little importance in the western industrial areas, the Rhineland or the Ruhr. Jews were predominantly middle-class businessmen and professionals, not owners of large-scale enterprises.

Jewish banking families, such as the Rothschilds, Mendelssohns and Bleichröders, owned about 50 per cent of private banks. Jewish directors also managed several major public banks. Eugen Gutmann was director of the Dresdner Bank; Jakob Goldschmidt was director of the Darmstadt National Bank, closely involved in raising foreign loans for German firms. The huge DD Bank (a large bank created by merging the Deutsche Bank with the DiscontoGesellschaft Bank owned by Arthur Salomonsohn) helped to finance the rebuilding of German industry after the First World War. To make such a list of Jewish banking interests can be misleading, however – in the 1920s, the role of Jews in banking was actually declining. Banks owned by Jews made up about 18 per cent of the banking sector in Germany, a considerably smaller proportion than in the years before 1914.

■ Activity

**Thinking point**

Working in two groups, assemble **five** reasons why Jews held a prominent position in banking and finance in Weimar Germany. Arrange your reasons in rank order of importance.

Jews were particularly active and successful in retailing. Jews owned almost half of the firms involved in the cloth trade. Jewish firms also controlled large numbers of shoe shops. Most department stores (about 80 per cent) were owned by Jews, including famous stores in Berlin like Wertheim and the giant KdW (*Kaufhaus des Westens*) store, purchased in 1926 by the Tietz brothers, who made it into the largest in Germany. Away from the capital, the Jewish Schocken family owned a chain of more than 30 department stores.

More than 60 per cent of all Jews who were employed worked in some form of trade or commerce. The role of Jews in business and retail was much more visible, of course, in the larger cities, especially Berlin. However, one other area of business in which Jews were active was in selling agricultural equipment to farmers. By no means were all Jews well off – there were many unemployed eastern Jews even in the 'Golden Years' after 1924 – but it has been calculated that the average income of Jews in employment was more than three times the average income of the population as a whole.

Jewish success in banking and commerce led to resentment. This resentment was accentuated by high-profile scandals concerning Jewish firms. In 1925, three brothers, Julius, Salomon and Henri Barmat, were found guilty of bribing public officials to obtain state loans. Similar scandals of the time included the Kutisker case in 1927 and the Sklarek brothers in 1929. In general, German Jews were notably law-abiding (nobody criticised the Barmats and Sklareks more fiercely than their fellow Jews did), but these scandals did provoke anti-Semitic outbursts.

### The professions and the universities

Jews were immensely successful in the professions, especially law and medicine. Jews made up 1 per cent of the total population but 16 per cent of lawyers and 11 per cent of doctors. As with many other aspects of Jewish life in Germany, there were especially high numbers in Berlin. More than half of the doctors in Berlin in 1930 were Jewish; of 3,400 lawyers in Berlin, 1,835 were Jews.

In medicine, there was a surge in the numbers of Jewish doctors in the early days of the Weimar Republic. Social reforms by the new government, especially the introduction of public health insurance, meant there were many openings for young, newly-qualified doctors. Many big firms appointed so-called 'panel doctors' to look after the health of their employees. In the universities, there were openings in new special fields of research; Jewish doctors were particularly active in such new medical developments because more traditional fields were monopolised by non-Jews.

However, by the late 1920s, the medical profession had become crowded and competitive because so many new entrants were attracted into it. Many Jewish doctors were struggling financially – one estimate was that 10 per cent of them earned so little that they had no prospect of being able to marry.

Lawyers of Jewish origin had more favourable prospects. Many reached positions of wealth and influence. A few individuals became national figures, well known to politicians and journalists. Julius Magnus was the editor of the prestigious journal of the German Bar Association, *Juristische Wochenschrift* (Legal Weekly). Erich Frey became a 'celebrity' defence lawyer, famous for his flamboyant tactics in cases involving Berlin's criminal underworld. Ernst Fränkel was well known for his work on trade union law and his links with the SPD. Rudolf Olden was a lawyer and journalist who specialised in human rights law and was a colleague of Theodor Wolff at the *Berliner Tageblatt*. The most famous of all was Max Alsberg.

### Cross-reference

The Barmat, Kutisker and Sklarek scandals and the issue of economic resentment against Jewish businessmen are covered in Chapter 2, page 32.

### Activity

**Thinking point**

Historians frequently fall into the trap of describing aspects of Jewish influence in Weimar Germany as 'disproportionate'. On the surface, this seems innocent and straightforward, simply reflecting the fact that in many areas of society the number of Jews involved was much greater than the percentage of Jews in the total population. To describe this fact as 'disproportionate', however, risks giving credence to the anti-Semitic idea that the Jewish presence was something that was 'excessive' and needed to be reduced.

**Fig. 5** *Erich Frey at work in the courtroom*

### Key profile

#### Max Alsberg

Max Alsberg (1877–1933) established a successful legal practice in Berlin from 1906. In the 1920s, he got a high reputation as a criminal lawyer and worked with Erich Frey in the notorious Immertrau trial of 1928. In 1931, Alsberg defended the socialist publisher Carl von Ossietsky, on trial for insulting the German Army. Alsberg was best known for writing stage plays on legal themes: 'Preliminary Investigation' (1930) was such a hit that it was made into a film in 1931; *Conflict* was premiered in 1933. After Hitler came to power, Alsberg escaped to Switzerland, but committed suicide a few months later.

## ■ Exploring the detail

### The fate of the Jewish lawyers

All these prominent and well-established lawyers later became victims of Nazism. In 1933, Frey fled to South America, via Paris; Olden escaped to Czechoslovakia and later settled in Britain; Fränkel stayed on for a time but then got out to the United States in 1938; Julius Magnus escaped to Holland but was later captured and deported to the camps, where he disappeared some time in 1943.

## ■ Did you know?

One of the great ironies of history is that Nazi Germany later expelled large numbers of brilliant scientists and thus 'gifted' them to the enemies of the Third Reich. The team of physicists working on the Manhattan Project that produced the world's first atomic bomb in 1945 included many Jewish exiles. The 'Aryan' scientists working to develop a Nazi atomic bomb failed.

## ■ Activity

### Research exercise

Using the internet, assemble a list of 10 German-Jewish exiles who moved to Britain or the United States and later made a significant contribution to the defeat of the Third Reich.

The great majority of Jewish lawyers in Weimar Germany lived more anonymous lives than celebrities like Erich Frey and Max Alsberg, but many achieved a comfortable position in society. There were several reasons for this. Jewish cultural traditions put a high price on the value of education. Jewish family traditions fitted perfectly with the model of small legal partnerships handed down from father to son. Many young men of Jewish descent went into the legal profession because of the difficult obstacles in the way of pursuing other careers.

Jews in the professions in Germany in the 1920s almost always saw their future in continuing assimilation. Men like Rudolf Olden and Ernst Fränkel, who both served in the First World War, or Erich Frey, who was baptised as a Christian, were patriotic citizens who would never have considered themselves to be 'Jewish lawyers' but Germans who happened to be of Jewish descent. Most lawyers also regarded their position in middle-class Weimar society to be much more fortunate than the circumstances faced by Jews in other countries at that time, or in Germany in the past. This helps to explain why, in the more dangerous times after 1930, many successful professional Jews were reluctant to consider going anywhere else.

Jews also had a significant impact on the academic life of Germany. Of the 38 Nobel Prizes awarded to people working in Germany up to 1938, nine (24 per cent) were Jewish. Germany was a world leader in the physical sciences, not least because of Albert Einstein, who revolutionised theoretical physics with his work on the theory of relativity and quantum mechanics. Several German Jews were among the scientists working in the Max Planck Institute who led the way in the new field of atomic physics. Despite the high academic standing of many Jews in German universities, however, they found that gaining promotion was a slower and more difficult process than for non-Jews – relatively few full professors were of Jewish descent, for example.

### The contribution of Jews to Weimar culture

The extent of the influence of Jews in industry and commerce in the 1920s has often been overstated; but this is not true of the Jewish contribution to Weimar culture. In the 1920s, the cultural life of Germany was exceptionally rich. Berlin became world famous for its cutting-edge creativity in architecture, music, theatre and cinema. The contribution of Jews was so important in so many areas that Weimar culture could simply not have developed as it did without them.

This fact has made Weimar culture into an important historical issue. When the Nazis came to power in 1933, they launched a furious and lethal counter-attack against the modernist cultural trends that they called 'Jewish-Bolshevik filth'. Many Jewish artists found their work banned or burned. Some died in the Holocaust. Many others were forced into exile in Britain or the United States. This Nazi persecution made cultural heroes out of its victims – in the same way, those who were promoted by the Nazis found that their careers were ruined after 1945, through 'guilt by association'.

As a result, it is difficult to evaluate the true worth of Weimar culture. Was it overrated because of the halo effect provided by Nazi persecution? Or did Weimar Germany really produce a cultural Golden Age? Whatever the answer to this question, the scale of the Jewish contribution to the cultural life of Germany was undeniable: in art and architecture, classical and popular music, cinema and the theatre.

Modernist developments in architecture and art were a notable feature of Weimar Germany in the 1920s, especially the group of architects, the so-called *Bauhaus School*, founded by Walter Gropius at Dessau near Leipzig in 1919. Gropius himself was not of Jewish descent (though his wife, Alma, the widow of Gustav Mahler, was) but this did not save him from attacks by anti-modernist, anti-socialist, and anti-Jewish right wingers. Two Jewish associates of Gropius, Bruno Taut and Erich Mendelsohn, were important figures in the developments of the time. Taut was an architect and painter who specialised in designing modernist social housing projects. Mendelsohn was an architect and scientist who produced many stunning and original buildings; his Einstein Tower, at Babelsberg near Berlin, was one of the iconic buildings of the Weimar era.

## Key profile

### Erich Mendelsohn

Mendelsohn (1887–1953) had many interests beyond architecture. He was closely associated with art movements like the 'Blue Rider' school and the 'Bridge'. He was also a trained scientist – his Einstein Tower was influenced by his friend Herbert Freundlich, whose special field was chemistry. Like Bruno Taut, Mendelsohn designed modernist social housing; he was also responsible for the design of many of the shops in the Schocken chain of department stores across provincial Germany and the 77 metre-high tower for the Ullstein Press in Berlin. Mendelsohn's modernism and Jewish origins made him an obvious target for the Nazis; he moved to Britain in 1933.

**Fig. 6** *Erich Mendelsohn's Einstein Tower*

Mendelsohn was influenced by modern trends in art, including Expressionism. In the 1920s, several German artists were associated with modernism, including the surrealist painter Max Ernst and the expressionist Max Beckmann. Neither was Jewish, though both were denounced by the Nazis as 'cultural Bolsheviks'. The best-known Jewish artist was Max Liebermann, head of the Prussian Academy of Art. A number of the most influential art dealers and directors of art galleries were of Jewish origin.

In classical music, German-Jewish artists were internationally famous, including the composers Hanns Eisler and Arnold Schoenberg, orchestral conductors such as Otto Klemperer and Bruno Walter, and a large number of instrumentalists. Many Jewish violinists held posts in symphony orchestras; the great violin soloist of the age, Fritz Kreisler, was based in Berlin from 1924. The director of the Music Conservatory in Berlin was the Jewish modernist composer, Franz Schreker. There was also an explosion of interest in jazz and popular music. Weimar Berlin was full of dance halls, clubs and cabarets. Classically-trained composers like Hanns Eisler and Kurt Weill turned their hand to jazz and modern popular styles. Composers who specialised in writing songs for Weimar's naughty nightclub life included Friedrich Holländer and Mischa Spoliansky.

Many of Weimar's Jewish composers had close links to the theatre. The dominant influence over the Berlin theatre from 1905 to 1930 was the great Jewish director, Max Reinhardt, and it was from working with Reinhardt's German Theatre that Bertolt Brecht emerged as the new force in 20th-century drama. Brecht was not Jewish but he might as well have declared himself an 'honorary Jew'. He was a modernist and a committed

## Exploring the detail

**Max Liebermann**

Liebermann resigned in 1933 after seeing Nazis marching through the Brandenburg gate in Berlin to celebrate Hitler's coming to power. As he watched, Liebermann announced that it would be impossible to eat the amount of food he would like to vomit back out again.

## Activity

**Research exercise**

**Top of the Weimar Pops**

Find and download recordings of cabaret songs from the Weimar era. Play five of them in class and organise a vote to decide which song provides the most entertaining insight into Weimar culture.

Marxist. His second wife, Helene Weigel, had a Jewish mother. His most famous collaborator, Kurt Weill, was Jewish. Inevitably, right wingers and anti-Semites labelled Brecht a 'cultural Bolshevik'.

### ■ Key profile

#### Max Reinhardt

Reinhardt (1873–1943) was an Austrian from a Jewish family; his original name was Max Goldmann. From 1905, he was director of the German Theatre, which became famous for its innovative productions. Reinhardt gained a huge international reputation. In 1920, he founded the Salzburg Festival. From 1930, Reinhardt increasingly worked abroad. One of his most famous productions was Shakespeare's *A Midsummer Night's Dream*, later turned into a film version, with music by Felix Mendelssohn arranged by Erich Korngold. In 1938, after the *Anschluss*, Reinhardt settled permanently in the United States.

Brecht and Weill developed a new form of music theatre that came to symbolise Weimar Berlin, above all *The Threepenny Opera*, a savage left-wing satire that treated the respectable middle classes as villains, while making heroes out of criminals and prostitutes. The story was based in part on the sensational events of the Ringverein Immertrau trial of 1928, which had made the Jewish defence lawyers Erich Frey and Max Alsberg famous. Kurt Weill's music perfectly mirrored the cultural mood of the times; the song *Mack the Knife* has been sung all over the world for 80 years and never seems likely to go out of fashion.

### ■ Key profile

#### Kurt Weill

Kurt Weill's (1900–50) spiky, cabaret-style music provided the signature tunes for Weimar culture in the 1920s. He collaborated with Bertolt Brecht on several famous musicals, such as *The Threepenny Opera* (1928), *Happy End* (1929) and *The Rise and Fall of the City of Mahagonny*. Weill's music was a perfect match for Brecht's biting sarcasm and aggressively left-wing views. Weill's wife, the singer Lotte Lenya, had the ideal smoky voice for songs such as *Mack the Knife* and *The Song of Jenny* ('in 27 languages she couldn't say no'). Weill, Brecht and Lotte Lenya all escaped to Hollywood in the 1930s.

Jewish directors and actors were also at the forefront of new developments in cinema, both silent films and, from 1928, talking pictures. Berlin became an important centre for world cinema, developing modern techniques that would later be exploited by Nazi propaganda. Important figures of Jewish descent in the German film industry included Fritz Lang, Billy Wilder, later to become famous in post-war Hollywood, and Josef von Sternberg. It was Sternberg (whose real name was Jonas; he used the 'Josef von' name to make himself seem less Jewish and more upper crust) who directed *the* film of the Weimar era, *The Blue Angel*, starring Marlene Dietrich as Lola, the sexy singer in a sleazy nightclub cabaret who seduces the innocent old professor played by Emil Jannings.

**Fig. 7** *Poster for the 1930 film* The Blue Angel

## Key profile

### Fritz Lang

Lang (1890–1976) was an Austrian whose mother was Jewish, although she converted to Catholicism when he was a young boy. He worked at the influential UFA film studios at Potsdam, near Berlin in the 1920s. As in many other cultural fields, German cinema was strongly influenced by expressionist art and Fritz Lang was the most famous exponent of this. His two most famous films were *Metropolis* (1926), probably the most ambitious and expensive silent film ever made, and *M* (1931), a chilling psychological thriller about a child murderer. Lang moved to Hollywood in 1934, after clashing with Dr Göbbels.

The Jewish contribution to Weimar culture was wide ranging, but it should not be overstated. Later, Nazi propaganda put out the myth that everything that was modern, or 'decadent and immoral' – by which they meant pretty much everything about Weimar culture – came from and was moulded by Jews. This is not true. There would have been a thriving, forward-looking culture in 1920s Germany anyway, with or without Jewish artists. What is true is that Germany lost out culturally by driving out all those they termed 'Jewish-Bolsheviks'; in the 1930s and during and after the Second World War, cultural life in Britain and the United States benefited hugely at Germany's expense. Perhaps the most important aspect of the prominence of German Jews in Weimar culture is the fact that it seemed to demonstrate how far assimilation had progressed.

## Key terms

**Secularisation:** the process of moving away from religious observance. The majority of Jews in Weimar Germany were secular Jews, who had partly or wholly given up the outward forms of Jewish religious identity. Orthodox rabbis were very alarmed at the rate of secularisation in the 1920s, fearing that the religious core of Judaism might disappear altogether.

## The extent of Jewish assimilation by 1930

Assimilation is a two-way process. The vast majority of German Jews wished to assimilate. For many of them, the process of acculturation had gone a long way. In language, dress and lifestyle, thousands of Jews looked and acted like the Germans they lived among. Many had married non-Jewish spouses, given up religious observance, or converted to Christianity. By the late 1920s the process of **secularisation** and assimilation was far advanced. The chief factor limiting the degree of integration into German society, however, was the reluctance of many Germans to stop identifying Jews as somehow alien. There was still a significant gap between *wanting* to be completely assimilated and *feeling* the security of being completely accepted.

**Fig. 8** *Jewish New Year postcard celebrating Jewish family life*

### Hopes

The majority of assimilated Jews in Weimar Germany before 1933 felt that they had a good future to look forward to. They lived in a liberal democracy that provided greater legal protections than any European Jews had ever known before. There was a free press and a multi-party system in which Jews were able to play an influential role. Many Jews had achieved economic and social success and they expected the next generation to do even better. Most Jews identified closely with the Weimar Republic, which seemed to have settled into a pattern of economic prosperity and political stability since its turbulent early years.

There were several trends that seemed to indicate progress towards assimilation:

■ Inter-marriage was at an all-time high – in 1927, 54 per cent of all marriages of Jews were 'mixed'.

■ Many Jews were converting to Christianity, such as the famous musician Otto Klemperer. In 1927, more than 1,000 Jews lapsed from Judaism, half of them through conversion.

■ The incidence of anti-Semitism seemed to be lessening – one Jewish writer suggested in 1924 that, 'if not yet fully overcome, it is at least on its way out.'

■ Membership of the German Zionist Federation dropped to 17,000 by 1929 – in 1923 it had been 33,000. This reduction in the numbers of people supporting a national homeland in Palestine or some other faraway place seemed to show that Jews were now less afraid for their future in Germany.

---

Ernst Feder was a true representative of the urban Jewish upper middle class, a journalist on the editorial board of the *Berliner Tageblatt*. Feder knew just about everyone in public life and talked often to politicians and top civil servants. He dictated his diary to his wife every evening. Feder's diary is a combination of gossip and first-hand information, rumour and fact, and reflects opinion from all sides. Feder mentions more than a thousand names in politics, the economy, the press and the arts in the Weimar Republic. Significantly, Hitler's name does not appear for the first time until September 1930. Before then, Feder's views reflected the resurgence of the republic from 1924 and the growing hope that anti-Semitism was merely a passing phenomenon. He really believed, after all, that he was living in a civilised country.

**1**      *A. Elon, **The Pity Of It All: A Portrait of the Jews in Germany, 1743–1933**, 2002*

---

### Fears

Not all Jews were as keen to assimilate as the liberal, educated and professional majority. For some Jewish religious leaders, assimilation was a terrifying prospect – they genuinely feared that the separate Jewish identity might soon disappear entirely. There were also Orthodox and Zionist communities who were hostile to assimilation, both because they did not want it and because they were convinced it could never actually happen.

---

In Prussia, not even a single teacher is to be found in 285 Jewish communities. 219 communities have not one religious functionary of any kind. 119 Jewish communities are without religious instruction; more than 400 have no cemetery, no house of worship and none of the institutions required by religious law. These numbers plainly tell us that *Prussian Jewry is in the midst of a disaster.*

**2**      *Address to the Prussian Association of Jewish Communities, June 1925. Quoted in D. L. Niewyk, **The Jews in Weimar Germany**, 2001*

---

Despite their outward success in so many aspects of Jewish life in Weimar Germany, not even the most successful assimilated Jews could escape completely from the deep anxieties underneath the surface. There was an undercurrent of pessimism. The rates of suicide and divorce were twice as high for Jewish Germans than for the population as a whole; so was the incidence of clinical depression. Many Jews struggled to remain optimistic. Many Jews feared deep down that they lived in a kind of limbo, not fully Jewish but not allowed to be fully German.

There was also fear and uncertainty about how to respond to anti-Semitism. The overall situation in the Weimar Republic grew more stable after 1923 but there were still attacks on Jews, from insults in the street to vandalising synagogues and Jewish cemeteries. For many, the sensible Jewish response was to keep low and avoid provocation. This approach often reflected the fact that the police and the courts in Weimar Germany usually took action against the offenders – and many middle-class Jews lived in comfortable areas where such incidents were very rare anyway – but a number of Jewish organisations took action to protect Jewish interests.

Zionists tried to fight back by emphasising Jewish cultural traditions, such as encouraging more study of the Hebrew language. Zionists, of course, did not see assimilation as a goal to strive for and had less faith in the Weimar Republic than assimilated Jews did. Another active organisation was the *RjF* (National League of Jewish Frontline Veterans), which represented Jewish ex-soldiers. The *RjF* organised pamphlets and meetings and sometimes cooperated with the *Reichsbanner*, the uniformed militia of the SPD. The *RjF* also promoted Jewish 'self-discipline' – avoiding behaviour by Jews that might provoke hostility.

The largest organisation to defend Jews was the *Centralverein* (Central League for Citizens of the Jewish Faith), which had been founded in 1893. The *Centralverein* produced a regular newspaper with a circulation of about 80,000. It also gave money to help legal prosecutions of anti-Semites. On many occasions, the leaders of the *Centralverein* revealed their anxiety about the dangers facing Jews in Germany. However, the fact that membership peaked at 72,000 in 1924 but then declined steadily after that might suggest that many Jews felt safer in the prosperous 'Golden Years' of Weimar.

By 1930, despite all the turbulence of the 1920s and the underlying anti-Semitism, Jews in Germany had made enormous progress towards assimilation. Many prosperous and educated Jews regarded themselves as utterly German, fully identified with Weimar democracy. From their standpoint, assimilation was the future. As long as that future was identified with the Weimar Republic, Jewish assimilation was likely to deepen. Anti-Semitism, like right-wing extremism in general, remained on the fringes of society and politics.

Even so, Weimar democracy was still fragile. Any weakening of the republic would inevitably undermine the position of Jews in Germany. In 1930, as the effects of the world economic depression began to affect Germany, the enemies of Weimar democracy, both on the left and the right, were able to make political gains at the expense of the Liberal centre.

## Activity
### Talking point

Working in two groups, make a list of the reasons why many Jews wished to accelerate the pace of assimilation into German society; and why other Jews were anxious to preserve their separate identity.

## Activity
### Revision exercise

Working in four groups, assemble a list of 20 questions to be used as a revision quiz by the rest of the class. Be careful to choose questions that will invite brief and definite answers; but your main aim should be to select items that reveal something important about Jews in Weimar Germany, not merely facts in isolation. The four quizzes can then be used one at a time as a revision session.

## Cross-reference

The effects of the economic depression and the links between anti-Semitism and Reichstag elections are explored in Chapter 2, pages 33–6.

## Summary questions

1. Explain why Jews played such a prominent role in the cultural life of Germany in the 1920s.

2. Assess the extent to which Jews had become assimilated into German society by 1930.

# 2 The extent of anti-Semitism in Weimar Germany

*In this chapter you will learn about:*

- the extent of anti-Semitism in Weimar Germany after the First World War

- the impact of right-wing political movements and the associations between Jews and Communism

- the backlash against Jewish politicians and financiers

- the influence of anti-Semitism in election campaigns in the 1920s and in 1930.

Between 1916 and 1923, then, antisemitism had established itself as a central component of right-wing thinking in Germany, and was now taken up in the politics of mass movements, among them, of course, the still-small Nazi Party. The calmer middle years of the Weimar Republic from 1924 to 1929 flattered to deceive. The antisemitic fundamentalists had been forced out of the limelight. But they had not disappeared. And even in a pluralist democracy Jews, outside their own organisations and some liberal and left-wing circles, found few friends or defenders. Once that democracy crumbled and collapsed from 1930 onwards, opening up the path for Hitler's rise to power, increasing numbers of Germans were exposed to the full antisemitic armoury as they became drawn into the ever-expanding Nazi movement.

**1**    *I. Kershaw, Fateful Choices: Ten Decisions That Changed the World, 1940–41, 2007*

**Fig. 1** *Poster by a Jewish society protesting against Jews being used as scapegoats for 'all evils of the world', 1919*

Politically, it was very easy for lots of people to focus on the Jew. The Jew became a symbol for left-wing politics, for exploitative capitalism, for avant-garde cultural experimentation, for secularisation, for all the things that were disturbing a fairly large sector of the conservative part of the political spectrum. The Jew was the ideal political buzz word.

**2**    *Christopher Browning, quoted in L. Rees, The Nazis: A Warning From History, 2005*

The influence of anti-Semitism in the Weimar Republic is often thought of in simplistic terms:

- There was a lot of anti-Semitism in Germany.

- Hitler and the Nazis exploited anti-Semitism through their propaganda.

- Anti-Semitism helped Hitler to come to power in 1933, and to carry through his race policies after that.

This view is not only simplistic but also false. There were many other elements in extreme right-wing politics in Germany apart from the Nazis. Until 1930, almost nobody believed the Nazis would ever become a national mass movement. There were many strands of Nazi ideology apart from hatred of the Jews. Nazi propaganda in the 1920s often played down anti-Semitism and placed more emphasis on anti-Communism, or the evils of the Versailles Treaty, because anti-Semitism was more of a turn-off than an attraction for potential supporters.

The collapse of Weimar democracy might seem inevitable with perfect historical hindsight, but in the 'Golden Years' from 1924, the republic appeared to be achieving both economic prosperity and political stability. Anti-Semitism was pushed to the margins. In 1928, the Nazis made minimal impact. It was only in 1930, after the start of the world economic crisis, that the democratic centre ground of politics was weakened and there was a surge in support for extremist parties. Adolf Hitler's breakthrough into national politics provided him with the opportunity to gain respectability. Anti-Semitism started to move from the fringes to the national stage.

## The extent of anti-Semitism in Germany, 1919–30

In the difficult early years of the republic, from 1918 to 1924, there was a backlash against the threat from **'Jewish-Bolshevism'**, as perceived in events such as the Spartacus uprising in Berlin and in the breakaway regime of Kurt Eisner in Munich. Anti-Semitism was part of the violent nationalism behind right-wing movements such as the *Freikorps* and the NSDAP (National Socialist German Workers' Party) formed in 1920. There was a surge of hostility against Jewish financiers at the time of the hyper-inflation crisis in 1923.

Between 1924 and 1930, however, as Weimar Germany entered its 'Golden Years' of economic recovery and political stability, anti-Semitism was pushed to the fringes of public and political life. Nobody who did not know what these ideas led to after 1933 would waste time on them. The problem is that after 1933 the ideas of these cranks and losers were going to be put into practice by the Nazi dictatorship. That is why historians have to try to make sense of them and to explain the connections between Nazi ideology and the mass of ordinary Germans who were not cranks but who ended up accepting or supporting Hitler's rule in Germany.

### Key chronology
**The Weimar Republic, 1918–30**

**1918** The German Revolution and proclamation of the republic

**1919** Crushing of Spartacus uprising
Imposition of Versailles Treaty

**1922** Murder of Walther Rathenau

**1923** Hyper-inflation

**1924** Stabilisation of the currency under Dr Schacht

**1926** Germany accepted into League of Nations

**1928** Stable coalition government under Hermann Müller

**1930** Start of economic crisis

### Key terms

**'Jewish-Bolshevism':** term used by anti-Semites to imply that Jews and Communists were closely associated and represented a danger to German values.

**Fig. 2** *'Nothing but the Fourteen Points!' A demonstration against the Versailles Treaty*

### A closer look

#### The legacy of the past: anti-Semitism in Germany in 1918

Between 1916 and 1923, in the crisis conditions of the First World War and the German Revolution, there was a surge in anti-Semitism in Germany. By this time, Jewish assimilation had been in progress for 70 years. Jews had achieved emancipation in 1848, confirmed by the constitution of Imperial Germany in 1871. The economic and social achievements of Germany's Jews had twice before provoked a backlash: first in the financial crisis caused by the stock market collapse of 1873 and again in the 1890s. The third wave of anti-Semitism that occurred during and after the First World War went deeper.

### Cross-reference

The Spartacus uprising and the regime of Kurt Eisner in Munich are outlined on pages 25–6.

I was summoned to see the company commander. A questionnaire was lying on his desk. 'I have to take down your particulars', he said.

'Might I ask, Lieutenant, what for?'

'Well, the Minister of War … they want to know how many Jews are serving at the front.'

'And how many are behind the lines! What kind of nonsense is this? Do they want to demote us and make us look ridiculous in the eyes of the whole army? They subject us to all kinds of harassment, refuse to promote us, and then wax indignant when they catch someone watching the war from the rear!'

'Yes, you're right, but there's nothing I can do about it – so what's your date of birth?'

'Damn it to hell! So this is why we're risking our necks for this country?'

**3** *Recollections of Julius Marx. Quoted in A. Elon, **The Pity Of It All: A Portrait of the Jews in Weimar Germany, 1743–1933**, 2002*

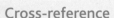

### Cross-reference

Walther Rathenau is profiled in Chapter 1, page 13.

The catalyst for this anti-Jewish backlash was the army census of October 1916. The census came about because the war minister, Wild von Hohenborn, wanted to respond to accusations that Jews were hindering the war effort. There were protests in the Reichstag and in the press; many people pointed out that 3,000 Jewish soldiers had already been killed fighting for the Reich, with 7,000 wounded. Hohenborn went ahead with the census, to discover how many Jews were serving at the front and how many in rear areas. The census proved that 80 per cent were on the front lines – but the results were not published, supposedly to 'spare Jewish feelings'.

For many German Jews, the 1916 census was a devastating blow. Hostile reactions to the census from Germans, both in the army and on the home front, seemed like a betrayal of the patriotism displayed by Jewish soldiers. Ernst Simon was so shocked he became a Zionist. Other frontline soldiers felt angry and frustrated.

Anti-Semitic journalists were quick to produce emotive and misleading reports on the 1916 census. Many Germans were ready to believe them. Many Jewish leaders rushed to proclaim how patriotic Jews really were. Other Jews kept their thoughts to themselves, believing that they now had nothing to do with this war, that its aims were totally alien to them. By the end of the war, 12,000 Jewish soldiers had died in the war.

Another persistent anti-Semitic accusation was that Jewish businessmen were profiteering from the war. Two of the most important officials managing the war effort, the industrialist Walther Rathenau and the shipping magnate Albert Ballin, were Jews; they became targets for these attacks. Apart from economic exploitation, Jews were also accused of defeatism. Hostility against Jews intensified in 1918, when 140 prominent politicians and businessmen drew up a memorandum in favour of a negotiated peace. Most of the 140 signatures came from non-Jews, but this did not stop the anti-Semitic attacks on those who favoured a 'Jew peace'.

### ■ Key profile

#### Albert Ballin

Ballin (1857–1918) was the founder and chairman of the giant Hamburg-Amerika shipping line. Until 1916, he was a key figure in the war effort and frequently consulted by the Kaiser – one result of this was that Ballin became known as a *Kaiserjude* (Kaiser Jew). Ballin became very depressed as the war turned against Germany. He committed suicide in 1918.

In November 1918, the German generals knew Germany faced total defeat. The German war effort began to fall apart, leading to outbreaks of revolution, first with the mutiny at the naval base in Kiel but then swiftly spreading across Germany – west to Cologne, south to Munich, east to Dresden. The German Revolution had begun. On 9 November, the Kaiser abdicated. The war was ended by an armistice on 11 November. Central government was close to complete collapse.

When the war ended, it came as a shock. Few people outside the army high command had realised how bad the military situation was. Thousands of frontline soldiers were astonished and embittered by the suddenness of the catastrophe. They were encouraged by their commanders to believe they had been 'stabbed in the back' by internal traitors – the pacifists, Jews and socialists they vilified as the so-called 'November Criminals'. One of the countless ordinary soldiers who felt like this was a temporarily blinded army corporal recovering in a military hospital at Pasewalk in Pomerania; his name was Adolf Hitler. Right wingers and anti-Semites had a deep psychological need to find suitable scapegoats for Germany's defeat – Jews figured high on their list.

## Key profile

### Adolf Hitler

Hitler (1889–1945) was born at Braunau-on-the-Inn in Austria. He was a fervent German nationalist and hated the multinational system of the Austro-Hungarian Empire. In 1914, Hitler moved to Munich and volunteered for service in the German Army. After the war, Hitler became active in revolutionary politics in Munich; by 1920, he had emerged as the leader of the National Socialist German Workers' Party. In November 1923, Hitler was imprisoned at Landsberg Castle in Bavaria after his failed attempt to seize power in the Munich Putsch. It was in Landsberg that he wrote his political testament *Mein Kampf*. From 1930, the Nazis gained widespread support; Hitler was appointed chancellor in January 1933.

## Jews and Communism

Left-wing political movements seized the opportunity presented by the political vacuum in Germany. The two most significant developments were the Spartacus uprising in Berlin at the end of 1918 and the separatist Republic of Councils set up by Kurt Eisner in Bavaria in January 1919. The Conservative Right was terrified at the prospect of Communist revolution being imported into Germany from Bolshevik Russia. In their minds, there was a direct link between Communism and the Jews.

### Cross-reference

The origins of Adolf Hitler's anti-Semitic views are covered in Chapter 3, pages 39–40.

**Fig. 3** *'The Danger of Bolshevisim'*

**Fig. 4** *Rosa Luxemburg speaking at a party congress in Stuttgart, 1907*

### Exploring the detail

**The Spartacus uprising of 1918**

The Spartacus movement was a Communist revolutionary group that took its name from the leader of the revolt of the slaves against the Roman Empire in AD 33. The key leaders of the uprising were Rosa Luxemburg and Karl Liebknecht. The Spartacist leaders were in direct contact with Lenin's Bolshevik regime in Russia. Right wingers in Germany saw the Spartacus uprising as 'Jewish-Bolshevism', partly because Rosa Luxemburg was Jewish.

## ■ Exploring the detail

### Eisner's separatist regime in Bavaria

Bavaria, in Catholic southern Germany, had a long history as an independent kingdom and only joined the united Germany in 1870. Even then, the Wittelsbach Kings of Bavaria continued to rule from Munich until 1918. After the collapse of the German Empire, many people hoped Bavaria might become a separate and independent state again – this was one of the aims of the left-wing regime headed by Kurt Eisner in 1919. Preventing it was one of the aims behind Hitler's Munich Putsch in 1923.

## ■ Cross-reference

The exploitation of fears of 'Jewish-Bolshevism' by Hitler and the Nazis is covered in Chapter 3.

## ■ Key profile

### Rosa Luxemburg

Rosa Luxemburg (1871–1919) was a brilliant political theorist from a Polish Jewish background. She was involved in the 1918–9 Spartacus uprising in Berlin, led by Karl Liebknecht. After the failure of the rising, Luxemburg was murdered by the *Freikorps* and her body was dumped in a canal. For both her admirers and her enemies, Rosa Luxemburg was a symbol of the link between Jews and Communism.

In addition to the Spartacus uprising and Eisner's regime in Bavaria, a number of Communist threats kept alive the sense of crisis and inflamed the fears of 'Jewish-Bolshevism'. The war between Poland and Soviet Russia in 1919 and 1920 raised the prospect of 'Red Terror' advancing westwards and spilling over into Germany. There were violent clashes in Upper Silesia as a result of the long-running dispute about the status of the area following the Treaty of Versailles. There were several left-wing revolts by industrial workers in the Ruhr.

It was simply not true that all Communists were Jews. Very few of the supposed Communist threats had any specifically Jewish connections; but right wingers in Germany made it seem so. One persistent and pervasive myth in Weimar Germany was the threat from 'Jewish-Bolshevism'. There was just enough truth in this to keep the myth alive. The founder of Communist beliefs, Karl Marx, was of Jewish origin; but the co-author of the 1849 *Communist Manifesto*, Friedrich Engels, was not. Several leaders of the Bolshevik revolution in Russia were Jews, including Leon Trotsky. Lenin, like most other Bolshevik leaders, was not. One of the leaders of the 1918–19 Spartacus uprising in Berlin, Rosa Luxemburg, was Jewish; the other, Karl Liebknecht, was not.

Few right wingers in Germany were bothered by the facts that contradicted their prejudices. They feared Communism, they were afraid of the 'Slavic hordes' to the east of Germany, they hated Jews – all three elements were woven together to make Communism and Jewishness appear inextricably linked.

## Right-wing political movements

The chaotic economic and political situation in Germany after the First World War was a breeding ground for bitterness and resentment. Much of this resentment was turned against the Jews. Right-wing political movements emerged, demanding that the 'guilty ones' should be punished for their betrayal of Germany. Communists, Jews, democrats and pacifists were lumped together and labelled the November Criminals. Anti-Semitism was a thread running through this angry backlash. Right wingers identified the Jews as the cause of the Communist threat; they identified Jewish financiers as the cause of the economic disasters afflicting ordinary Germans; and they identified Jewish politicians as the cause of everything they hated about the democratic Weimar Republic.

The largest and most powerful force in Germany between the end of the war and 1920 was the *Freikorps* (Free Corps), the unofficial armies of ex-soldiers who stayed loyal to individualist commanders and who played a big role in 'restoring order'. The officers and men in the Freikorps had many motives, but anti-Semitism was often a key factor. Many of the men who became active in right-wing political movements in the 1920s had their ideas shaped by formative experiences in the Freikorps.

**Fig. 5** Freikorps *men*

### The *Freikorps*

The *Freikorps* (Free Corps) had a special place in the violent phase of the German Revolution in 1919–20. The demobilisation of the mass army that had fought in the war was not thorough nor efficient. Large numbers of ex-soldiers kept their weapons and remained together as armed gangs or private armies. Individual commanding officers organised these armed bands into fighting units, usually named after their leader – The Maercker Brigade, the Reinhardt Brigade, and so on. Since the Versailles Treaty restricted the official German army to a maximum of 100,000 men, the Freikorps represented a powerful and dangerous military force.

Many volunteers joined the Freikorps because they had no prospects as civilians. Others joined because of ideology – responding to the appeal to 'save the Fatherland' from the threat of invasion from the East, or from Communism. The violent nationalism of the Freikorps often included anti-Semitism. The vulnerable new democratic government headed by Friedrich Ebert was forced to rely on the military strength of the regular army and the Freikorps units to defeat the Spartacist uprising in 1919. Freikorps brigades also brutally crushed Kurt Eisner's breakaway regime in Bavaria in 1920. The Freikorps were of no help at all, of course, in saving the republic from right-wing threats – the Freikorps were heavily involved in the Kapp Putsch that tried to overthrow democracy in 1920.

The Freikorps eventually disbanded as political stability returned, but they left a dangerous legacy. Reliance on the Freikorps weakened the government because it drove a wedge between the moderate socialists of the SPD and the Communists. Many violent right-wing elements drifted from the Freikorps into the *Black Reichswehr*, or the SA (*Sturm Abteilung*) that became the paramilitary wing of the Nazi movement.

### Exploring the detail

**The *Black Reichswehr***

The so-called *Black Reichswehr* consisted of the unofficial army units that continued to meet for secret military drills, even though they were not part of the regular army. Many ex-soldiers carried on with this unofficial military service even though they had been demobilised after the war and many of them held civilian jobs.

■ Cross-reference

The rise of Adolf Hitler and the NSDAP (National Socialist German Workers' Party) is covered in Chapter 3, page 41.

■ Cross-reference

Alfred Rosenberg is profiled in Chapter 3, page 42.

■ Key terms

**Völkisch:** this term means literally 'of the people', but the German word *Volk* implies much more than the people. Germany did not become a united state until 1871 and the idea of belonging to the German *Volk* involved deep feelings about national and racial identity.

**Aryan race:** this term referred to people of 'pure' Nordic origins, supposedly superior to 'lesser' racial types such as Jews.

**SS:** (*Schutzstaffel*, or Protection Force) this was a paramilitary organisation linked to the Nazi Party and led by Heinrich Himmler. Originally, the SS was only a small part of the SA, the main Nazi uniformed militia, but the SS steadily grew in power and influence until it took over from the SA after the Blood Purge of 1934.

■ Cross-reference

Eckart, Feder, Streicher and Heydrich are profiled on pages 42, 43, 47 and 86 respectively.

■ Cross-reference

The 25-Point Party Programme is detailed on page 42.

Fig. 6 *1924 election poster for the BVP (Bavarian People's Party)*

1918 was the year of the breakdown. I lost my job. On a billboard in Berlin, I saw the inscription:

WHO WANTS TO SAVE THE FATHERLAND?

JOIN THE LÜTZOW FREIKORPS!

I joined. The commander, Major Hans von Lützow, sent me to Linz in Austria to recruit volunteers. What political wisdom had I gained by the time of my discharge in March 1920? Following the course of political and anti-Semitic lectures held by the Lutzow Freikorps, I came to the conclusion that German working men were deliberately deceived by so-called labour leaders (Jews, of course) to prevent a union of all people of German blood, irrespective of class, from coming together.

| 4 | *Quoted in T. Abel,* **Why Hitler Came Into Power,** *1938* |

Most of the right-wing movements of the early 1920s were small and ineffectual. Some gained prominence for a short while, but then saw their followers dwindle when the immediate post-war crisis eased and normal conditions started to return. Many of these groups disbanded and disappeared; several were incorporated into Hitler's National Socialist movement as it grew stronger in the later 1920s.

Figure 7 provides a short selection of these movements; there were dozens of others.

| | |
|---|---|
| **Stahlhelm** | The **Stahlhelm** (Steel Helmet) was also known as the League of Frontline Soldiers. It was founded at the end of 1918, based in Magdeburg and led by Franz Seldte. The *Stahlhelm* was totally hostile to the Weimar Republic; many of its followers were monarchists, usually with anti-Semitic views as well as their hatred of Socialism and democracy. The *Stahlhem* allied with the NSDAP from 1929 and was completely taken over by the Nazis in 1934. |
| **Bayrische Einwohnerwehr** | The **Bayrische Einwohnerwehr** (Bavarian Citizens Guard) was a volunteer army formed in Bavaria in 1919 to fight against Communism and the left-wing regime in Munich led by Kurt Eisner. Its aims and right-wing attitudes were very similar to those of the *Freikorps*. |
| **Thule Gesellschaft** | The **Thule Gesellschaft** (Thule Society) was a **völkisch** nationalist and anti-Semitic group in Munich, influenced by belief in the occult – the Thule Society was closely linked to the German Order of the Holy Grail. 'Ultima Thule' was the legendary land in the far north from which the **Aryan race** was supposed to have come. Alfred Rosenberg was a key member. The Thule Society sponsored the Nazi Party in its early months and bought a newspaper, The *Münchener Beobachter*, which later became the *Völkischer Beobachter* (People's Observer), the official Nazi newspaper. <br>*Thule Society emblem* |
| **Deutsch-Völkische Freiheitsbewegung** | The **Deutsch-Völkische Freiheitsbewegung** (German People's Freedom Movement) appealed to traditional right-wing Conservative values, with a strong element of anti-Semitism. The movement got financial support from the Wulle brewery in Stuttgart and from the *Schutz- und Trutzbund* (German People's Protection and Trust League). Its most famous personality was the former chief of the Army High Command, General von Ludendorff. |
| **Schutz- und Trutzbund** | The **Schutz- und Trutzbund** has been described as the largest and most virulent anti-Semitic organisation in post-war Germany. Founded in 1919, the league quickly gained several hundred thousand members. Its chairman was Konstantin von Gebsattel, a notoriously anti-Semitic army general from Bavaria who had promoted the idea of an 'ethnic German empire' in a memorandum he sent to Wilhelm II in 1913. Many *Trutzbund* members later became prominent Nazis, including Dietrich Eckart, Gottfried Feder, Julius Streicher and Reinhard Heydrich. |
| **National Socialist German Workers' Party** | The National Socialist German Workers' Party (NSDAP) was originally the German Workers' Party, founded in 1919 by Anton Drexler before Adolf Hitler took over as leader. The NSDAP produced its 25-Point Party Programme in 1920 – its ideology mixed left-wing socialist ideas with right-wing Nationalism and anti-Semitism. <br>*NSDAP emblem* |
| **Hawks and Eagles** | The Hawks and Eagles was a youth group, founded by a nationalist poet, Wilhelm Kotzde-Kottenrodt. The ideology of 'Blood and Soil' was a key theme of the Hawks and Eagles, encouraging close ties to the land through volunteer work on traditional farms and completely rejecting urban, 'cosmopolitan' (i.e. Jewish) values. The movement was later swallowed up by the League of Artam. |
| **Artamane** | The **Artamane** (League of Artam) was another back-to-the-land nationalist youth movement driven by the ideology of Blood and Soil. The group was particularly strong in East Prussia, where there were 2,000 members by 1929. Important members of the Artamane included the head of the **SS**, Heinrich Himmler, the agricultural policy expert, R. W. Darre, and the future SS commandant at Auschwitz, Rudolf Höss. From 1933, many aspects of the Hitler Youth were modelled on the *Artamane*. |

**Fig. 7** *Right-wing political movements in Germany in the 1920s*

**Activity**

**Group activity**

Working in four groups, design four propaganda posters, appealing for new members to join your right-wing, anti-Semitic political movement. Make sure that the slogans you choose are attention-grabbing, but use the fewest words possible.

In 1921 I joined the Hawk and Eagle youth group. Its ideals were national defence, race and nationalism, with an absolute rejection of the poisons of 'civilisation' and the proprieties of a society infected by the virus of alien thought. In 1924 Professor Willibald Hentschel issued a call to the agricultural high school movement, the nationalist youth, and the national defence movement, to form a volunteer corps to halt the flight from the land, and to defend German soil against the aliens from the east, by settling in the eastern provinces. He called this volunteer corps 'Artam', from the Aryan. I was one who heeded the call. I persuaded my father to let me join the Artamane group in Saxony. In summer, we lived in simplicity and cultivated the soil. In winter, we were free to attend classes at the agricultural high school, and Artamane leadership courses. A number of prominent men were connected with the Artamane, including Heinrich Himmler and R. W. Darre.

> **5**
> *Quoted in T. Abel, **Why Hitler Came Into Power**, 1938*

My observations convinced me that our honest and upstanding German people had been poisoned to the marrow by alien Jews. Jewish literature and the Jewish press dragged everything through the mud. Not even the most sacred feelings were spared. What did they make of theatre, films, art and literature? A stinking sewer filled the German land with pestilence. They corrupted the youth. In the tents of the youth organisations there were Jewish leaders who slept with golden-haired girls. They declared it was 'the freedom of the individual' but they soon disappeared if children resulted.

> **6**
> *Oral recollections quoted in T. Abel, **Why Hitler Came Into Power**, 1938*

**Key chronology**

**The backlash against Jewish politicians and financiers, 1919–29**

| | |
|---|---|
| 1919 | Overthrow of Kurt Eisner in Munich |
| 1920 | Failure of Kapp Putsch |
| 1922 | Murder of Walther Rathenau |
| 1924 | Advances by anti-Semites in May election |
| 1925 | Barmat scandal |
| 1929 | Sklarek scandal |
| 1930 | Nazi breakthrough in Reichstag election |

To make a list of all the right-wing and anti-Semitic elements in German society in the early 1920s can have a misleading effect – it looks as if huge numbers of Germans were involved. In reality, even in the disturbed conditions from 1918 to 1923, such elements were always in the minority. Once economic prosperity and political stability began to take root from 1924 onwards, the extremists had even less influence.

## The backlash against Jewish politicians and financiers

Anti-Semites in post-war Germany repeatedly hammered away at one theme – that all Germany's miseries had been caused by Jewish politicians and financiers, that ordinary soldiers, workers and farmers were victims of a Jewish financial conspiracy. This idea was central to almost all the right-wing political movements that emerged in the crisis years from 1919 to 1923. Another obsession of anti-Semites was *völkisch* Nationalism and the urgent need to protect true German values from 'alien' Jewish influences. This idea was a powerful recruiting agent for right-wing political movements and it fuelled a violent backlash against the supposed dominance of Germany by Jewish politicians and financiers.

The most prominent victim of the anti-Jewish backlash after the founding of the Weimar Republic was Kurt Eisner, the leader of the so-called Republic of Councils that was established in Bavaria. Contrary to the right-wing propaganda of the time, Eisner was not a revolutionary

**Cross-reference**

The ideological motives behind this backlash are covered in Chapter 3, pages 45–9.

socialist ideologue; his aims were certainly left wing but also idealistic and democratic. In the eyes of his opponents, however, Eisner represented 'Jewish-Bolshevism', just as much as the Spartacus uprising in Berlin at the end of 1918.

Eisner's regime lasted only a few months before it was crushed by the *Freikorps* and more than 220,000 armed volunteers of the Bavarian Citizens Guard. (As it happened, they need not have bothered – Eisner was planning to step down voluntarily anyway.) It would be a mistake to assume that the primary motive for crushing Eisner's regime was anti-Semitism. The forces that crushed Eisner were driven above all by anti-Communism and the determination to stop Bavaria breaking away from the rest of Germany. However, anti-Semitism was a key element underpinning anti-Communism, and in the anti-republican attitudes that motivated so many of the volunteers.

Gustav Noske, the hardline minister of the interior in the Ebert government, eagerly supported the use of force by right-wing militias to bring down Eisner, but these forces had no loyalty to the 'Jewish Republic' they were saving from revolution. In 1920, units of the *Freikorps* were at the forefront of the Kapp **Putsch**, a military revolt in Berlin intended to overthrow Weimar democracy. In 1923, there was a less dangerous putsch in Munich, led by Adolf Hitler and his allies, among ultra-Conservatives in Bavaria.

▪ **Cross-reference**

Kurt Eisner's Bavarian regime and the Spartacus uprising of 1918 are outlined on pages 25–6.

▪ **Key terms**

**Putsch:** an attempt to seize power by force. The two best-known examples in the early years of the Weimar Republic were the Kapp Putsch in 1920, when elements of the *Freikorps* attempted to take over in Berlin, and Hitler's so-called Beer Hall Putsch in Munich in 1923. Hitler's putsch got its name from the fact that its leaders launched their revolt from a large *Bierkeller* (beer-cellar) in the centre of Munich.

**Fig. 8** *Nazis demonstrating in Munich at the time of Hitler's 1923 putsch*

▪ **Activity**

**Research exercise**

Find out how the Munich Putsch was memorialised by the Nazi movement after 1923, turning a small-scale fiasco into a legend of romantic heroism.

These right-wing revolts failed but they revealed both the extent of the dangers from the anti-Semitic, anti-democratic Right and the weakness of the support for the Weimar Republic during the early years of economic crisis and political instability. In these years, political murders were a common occurrence – there were more than 2,000 such murders, mostly committed by right-wing nationalists, who were rarely caught and usually got light sentences if they were. In 1921, Matthias Erzberger, a Catholic politician, was assassinated for the 'crime' of having signed the Versailles peace treaty. The assassination in 1922 of the Jewish industrialist and foreign minister of the Weimar Republic, Walther Rathenau, was perhaps even more significant.

### ■ Cross-reference

Walter Rathenau is profiled in
Chapter 1, page 13.

**Fig. 9** *Nazi propaganda poster from
September 1930 elections 'LIST 9'.
The blood-red words oozing from
the snake are: Usury; Versailles;
Unemployment; The War Guilt
Lie; Marxism; Bolshevism; Lies and
betrayal; Inflation; Locarno; Dawes
Plan; Corruption; Barmat; Kustiker;
Sklarek; Prostitution; Terror;
Civil War.
[Note the Red Star of David at the
point where the sword is plunged
into the snake]*

### ■ Activity

**Thinking point**

Examine the Nazi poster in Figure
9. Identify how many individual
features of this poster carry an
anti-Semitic message:

**a** directly

**b** by implication.

### ■ A closer look

**The assassination of Walther Rathenau**

Before, during and after the First World War, Rathenau was one of the
richest and most influential politicians and businessmen in Germany.
His family founded and owned the huge engineering firm AEG
(*Allgemeine Elektrizitäts Gesellschaft*). Rathenau had a key role in
running the war economy from 1915 to 1918; after the war he became
minister of reconstruction. He became foreign minister in 1922.

Rathenau was a realist in foreign policy. He strongly supported
the policy of 'fulfilment' (German acceptance of the terms of the
hated Treaty of Versailles) as the only way Germany would be able
to achieve economic recovery and rebuild Germany's trade position.
Rathenau was also responsible for negotiating the 1922 Treaty of
Rapallo with Communist Russia. As a result, Rathenau became
the target of attacks by right-wing nationalists. They hated him for
being part of the 'Jewish-Communist conspiracy', for being part of
the democratic Weimar government, for being rich (and also because
of rumours that he was a homosexual). In June 1922, two extreme
nationalist army officers murdered Rathenau, by machine-gunning
his car on its way into Berlin. In 1933, after Hitler came to power,
the assassins were declared to be national heroes and the day of the
murder became a national holiday.

From 1924, as the economic and political situation of Weimar Germany
began to improve, there was a reduction in extreme political activity.
There was still fierce opposition to perceived Jewish influence, however,
with frequent accusations of corruption and exploitation by Jewish
bankers and businessmen. Three scandals in the later 1920s provided
ammunition for such anti-Semitic attacks. The most sensational was
the Barmat scandal of 1925. The Barmat brothers, Julius, Salomon and
Henri, were Jewish businessmen who had immigrated from Galicia
in Poland just after the war. After a high-profile court case, they were
convicted of having bribed public officials to obtain loans from the
Prussian State Bank and the National Post Office. Julius and Salomon
were eventually sentenced to 11 months in jail.

The Barmat case had other ramifications apart from fuelling anti-Semitic
attacks on Jewish financiers. Opponents of the Weimar Republic used the
case as an excuse to attack President Ebert for failure to prevent corruption
– some contemporaries claimed that the stress of the Barmat affair helped
to cause Ebert's premature death later in 1925. Many assimilated Jews
turned against the Barmats, criticising them as 'eastern Jews' who had
undermined the position of German Jews by inviting hostile criticism.

Not long after the Barmat scandal, another Galician Jewish businessman,
Alexander Kutisker, and his colleagues Baruch and Holzmann, were
found guilty on very similar charges concerning corrupt loans worth
14 million Reichsmarks from the Prussian State Bank. In 1929, another
sleazy scandal dragged Jewish businessmen and the municipal authorities
in Berlin into the political dirt. The Sklarek brothers ran a wholesale
clothing business and used gifts of fur coats to bribe officials into paying
for goods that were never delivered. The political fall-out from the affair
was significant because two of the Sklarek brothers had joined the SPD in
1928. Anti-Semitic right wingers had a field day; the scandal is credited
with taking votes away from the SPD in the 1930 elections.

# The importance of anti-Semitism in Reichstag elections to 1930

Students of history need to remind themselves that events often seem different afterwards than they did at the time. There were indeed many right-wing political movements in Germany in the 1920s and there was indeed a considerable undercurrent of anti-Semitism in Weimar society. But the electoral impact of anti-Semitism was small. One reason why right-wing political movements made so much noise is the fact that they were on the losing side. Anti-Semitism played a part in the flurry of support for anti-republican parties in the special circumstances of the May 1924 election, but this trend did not last. From 1924, Weimar Germany began to experience a greater degree of economic and political stability. Only in 1930, when the world economic depression began, did the extreme right achieve a breakthrough in a **Reichstag** election.

## Reichstag elections, 1919–24

In the early years of the Weimar Republic, politics was very volatile. There were many small political parties and many shifts in public opinion. After the first Reichstag elections in 1919, the situation appeared quite favourable for the main democratic parties. The moderate socialists of the SPD had 165 seats, the Liberal DDP (strongly supported by assimilated Jews) had 75 seats and the Catholic Centre Party had 91. Extremists and anti-Semites got little support. In the 1920 elections, however, there was a notable shift away from the democratic centre. The left-wing Independent Socialists (forerunners of the German Communist Party) made big gains at the expense of the SPD. The DDP lost half of its seats, while the Conservative and nationalist parties, the DVP and the DNVP, made big gains. It appeared that the Weimar Republic was 'a democracy without enough democrats'.

After the chaotic years of post-war crisis and runaway inflation, there was so much political instability that there were two elections for the Reichstag in 1924. The results of the May election showed a dramatic rise in support for anti-democratic parties.

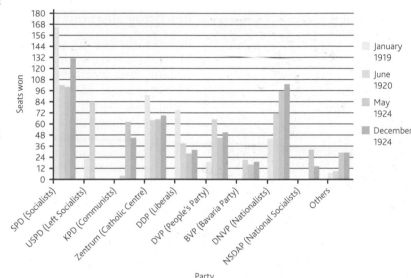

**Fig. 10** *Reichstag election results, 1919–24*

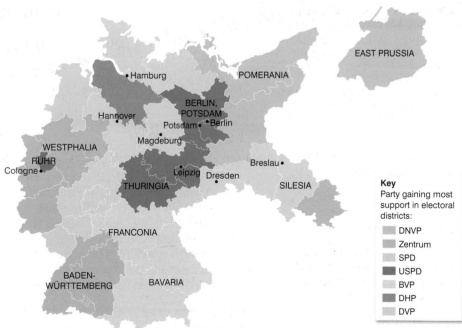

**Fig. 11** *Voting patterns in the Reichstag election, 6 June 1920*

33

On the Left, the Communist KPD did well; on the Right the DNVP made big gains and the Nazis came from nowhere to win 32 seats. The Liberal DDP now had only one-third of the seats it held in 1919. In the improved economic conditions of December 1924, the moderate parties made a slight recovery; the Nazis, with Hitler now imprisoned in Landsberg Castle, fell back to only 14 seats. Even so, the political developments of 1924 showed the democratic parties to be struggling to govern Germany effectively. Anti-republican parties were in a position to do a lot of political damage.

How much of the support for extremism was due to anti-Semitism is very difficult to measure – people have all sorts of reasons for deciding how they will vote, and very few people seem to have made up their mind purely because of anti-Semitism.

### Reichstag elections of 1928 and 1930

By 1928, the Nazi Party was well established as a national organisation. Many smaller right-wing movements had been swallowed up as the NSDAP. Party membership was steadily increasing: 27,000 in 1925, 49,000 in 1926, 72,000 in 1927. Hitler was well established as party leader, even though he had to get around the problem that in several parts of Germany there were legal bans against him speaking in public. By 1928, Hitler, Gregor Strasser and Josef Göbbels had also become skilful propagandists, far more skilful and more confident than in the amateurish early days. Nazi propaganda posters were frequently striking and colourful. Careful tracking of public opinion made the Nazis very slick in tailoring their message to mood and grievances of a specific area.

### Key profiles

#### Gregor Strasser

Strasser (1892–1934) was a Bavarian ex-soldier who was Hitler's main ideological rival within the Nazi movement. Strasser had great organising ability. He stressed the radical, left-wing elements of Nazism and worked closely with Josef Göbbels until the 'Little Doctor' switched his allegiance to Hitler in 1926. Strasser led the Nazis while Hitler was in prison and was responsible for the Nazi success in the elections of May 1924. Strasser played a leading role in the NSDAP until 1932 when he was sidelined after a party split. He was murdered on Hitler's orders in the Purge of June 1934.

#### Josef Göbbels

Dr Göbbels (1897–1945) was the chief propagandist of the Nazi movement from 1928 to 1945. He could claim to be an intellectual, having gained a PhD at Heidelberg in 1921, and had a superb speaking voice. He was originally a keen supporter of Gregor Strasser, but became fanatically loyal to Hitler from the mid-1920s. He was **Gauleiter** (Nazi Party leader) of Berlin and founded his own newspaper there, *Der Angriff* (The Attack). Göbbels played a key propaganda role in the Nazi rise to power and became minister of propaganda in 1933. He committed suicide in 1945, shortly after Hitler's death.

### Key terms

**Gauleiter:** the Nazis divided Greater Germany into 32 large administrative districts, known as a Gau – the leader of each Gau was a Gauleiter. Eleven more districts were added as the Reich expanded from 1938. These senior party bosses had considerable autonomy and reported directly to Hitler. Martin Bormann became Reichsleiter in 1941.

Despite all these favourable factors, however, the Nazis made little impression on the national political scene in 1928. The Nazi share of the vote went down even lower than where it had slipped in December 1924 – at 2.6 per cent of the vote, winning 12 seats, the NSDAP trailed behind obscure minor parties such as the Bavarian People's Party and the Reich Party of the German Middle Class. The previously unheard-of Christian-National Peasants' and Farmers' Party did almost as well as the Nazis, winning nine seats.

Hitler was now nearly 40 years of age; he seemed to have achieved next to nothing, destined to remain a minor nuisance on the fringes of Germany's political life. Although Hitler and the Nazis were better than ever at promoting their anti-Semitic ideology, most of the German people were apparently not listening. Yet two years later, in September 1930, the Nazis made their big breakthrough, shooting upwards to nearly 20 per cent of votes cast and winning 107 seats. Now, large numbers of the German people *were* listening, and voting. Why? And how much of this was due to the appeal of anti-Semitism?

The chief reason for the surge in support for the Nazis was economic. By the autumn of 1930, the world depression was already beginning to hit Germany hard, though there was still, of course, a long way down for the German economy to go. Much of the Nazi propaganda campaign stressed economic issues and it seems unarguable that this was the main cause of their increased voting support (and of the gains made by the nationalist and Conservative DNVP, led by Alfred von Hugenberg).

■ Activity

**Statistical analysis**

Study Figure 12. Compare the Reichstag election results of 1930 with those of 1928.

1 Make a list of the three parties that made the most significant gains.

2 Make a list of the three parties that lost the most ground.

3 Using the evidence of these results and the evidence in this chapter, suggest three reasons why Jews in Germany would have regarded the 1930 election result as a dangerous development.

## Key profile

### Alfred von Hugenberg

Hugenberg (1865–1951) was leader of the traditional Conservative Party the DNVP (German National People's Party). He was a multi-millionaire who owned a string of newspapers and magazines; he also owned Germany's biggest film studios, UFA. Hugenberg despised Hitler as an upstart from the lower classes, but needed Hitler's ability to attract political support. Hitler despised Hugenberg, calling him 'that old woman' in private, but was careful to treat him with great respect in public. Hugenberg played a key role in persuading President Hindenburg to make Hitler chancellor in January 1933.

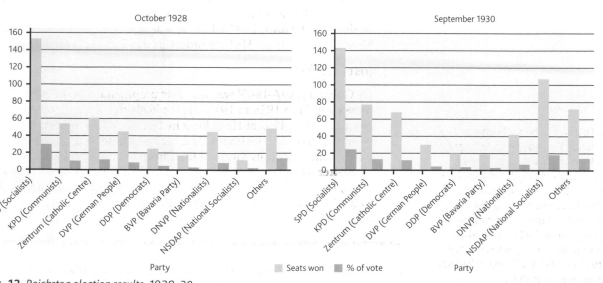

**Fig. 12** *Reichstag election results, 1928–30*

There is also powerful circumstantial evidence that anti-Semitism was not a major factor in winning votes. Yes, the Nazis did indeed hammer away at their anti-Semitic message, both through literal attacks on Jewish 'Capital' and through all kinds of indirect, implicit anti-Semitism, but they had done all that, skilfully and thoroughly, in 1928. To believe that the Nazis got nearly 10 times as many seats because of their anti-Jewish ideology would suppose that they became nearly 10 times better at selling their ideology through propaganda and that simply is not believable. It was not the message that changed, but the new political context caused by economic hard times.

And yet it may still be true that anti-Semitism *was* an important secondary factor. In exploiting the economic crisis the Nazis played on fears of unemployment, fears of Communism and contempt for the failed policies of the democratic parties in Germany. All of these issues had been relentlessly linked to anti-Semitism by the Nazis, ever since the formation of the NSDAP in 1920. The economic crisis decided the way most people voted in 1930, but many of those people had been conditioned over many years to at least half-believe there was a 'Jewish problem' and that it was time to listen to the party that had warned about it for so long.

### Cross-reference

A Nazi propaganda poster from September 1930, listing all the issues the Nazis wished to draw attention to, appears earlier in this chapter on page 32.

Rumours spread by the Right reinforced the prejudice that the Jews were behind all that was wrong in Germany – that they had shirked their war service, and that it was a Jew in the government, Walther Rathenau, who had deviously inspired the humiliating armistice. Even now, so the lies continued, German Jews were selling the country out as part of a worldwide conspiracy by international Jewry. These lies were effective, partly and ironically, because there were so few Jews actually living in Germany. In 1933 they made up only 0.76 per cent of the total population and unlike the Jewish populations of other European countries they were relatively assimilated into the general population. Paradoxically, this worked in the German anti-Semites' favour: in the absence of large numbers of flesh-and-blood Jews, a fantasy image of Jewishness could be portrayed in which the Jews became symbolic of everything the Right disliked about post-war Germany.

7

*L. Rees, The Nazis: **A Warning From History**, 2005*

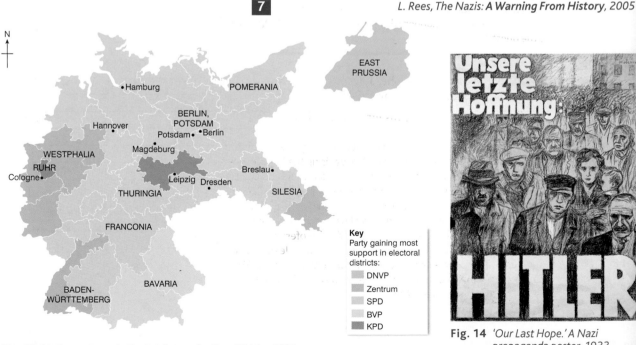

Key
Party gaining most support in electoral districts:

▢ DNVP
▢ Zentrum
▢ SPD
▢ BVP
▢ KPD

**Fig. 14** *'Our Last Hope.' A Nazi propaganda poster, 1932*

**Fig. 13** *Voting patterns in the Reichstag election, 20 May 1928*

### Activity

**Revision exercise**

Using the evidence in this chapter and the evidence in Chapter 1, write a paragraph explaining the reasons why many ordinary Germans were more receptive to Nazi electioneering in 1930 than in previous elections in the 1920s.

*Learning outcomes*

Through reading this section you have gained an understanding of the position of Jews in Germany under the Weimar Republic. You have examined the contribution made by Jews to German society and culture; and how far the assimilation of Jews into German society had progressed by 1930. You have also gained an understanding of the nature of anti-Semitism in Germany after the First World War, how this ideology influenced the rise of right-wing political extremism and the reasons why that extremism was increasing by 1930.

 Examination-style questions

(a) Explain why Walther Rathenau was assassinated in 1922.

*(12 marks)*

The key to answering this question is an explanation of a range of reasons why the event happened; narrative description is not the way to go about it! Try to provide some comment on the relative importance of your reasons, not just a list. You might also think about why the murder happened when it did – the date 1922 is part of the question.

(b) 'Under the Weimar Republic, Jews had established a secure position in German society by 1928.'

Explain why you agree or disagree with this view.

*(24 marks)*

The key to answering this question is a balanced argument, showing awareness of the alternative views and recognising the importance of the key date 'by 1928'. There are lots of reasons to disagree here – many poor Jews faced discrimination and even some assimilated Jews had many anxieties about anti-Semitism in Germany. On the other hand, there were indeed many Jews who prospered in Weimar Germany, especially in business and the professions, and German Jews thought they were much better off than Jews in other European countries. It is not enough to describe this evidence. You have to make an assessment: which side of the argument do you find to be more convincing? Why?

# 3 The development of Hitler's ideology

**Fig. 1** *Adolf Hitler with leading Nazis. Rudolf Hess is second from left*

*In this chapter you will learn about:*

■ the origins of Hitler's anti-Semitic ideas

■ the influence of anti-Semitism on the key themes in Nazi ideology: Social Darwinism; the *Volksgemeinschaft;* and *Lebensraum*

■ the development of Hitler's ideology by the late 1920s.

### Key chronology

**Hitler's career, 1918–30**

**1918** In military hospital at Pasewalk when war ended

**1919** Political activist in the pay of the German Army

**1920** Leader of the NSDAP
25-Point Nazi Party Programme

**1923** Failure of Munich Putsch

**1924** Imprisoned at Landsberg Castle

**1925** First edition of *Mein Kampf* published

**1926** Re-established as leader of NSDAP

**1928** Limited Nazi impact in Reichstag elections

**1930** Political breakthrough of NSDAP

When Adolf Hitler arrived in Munich in 1914, he was a 25-year-old nobody, wanted by the authorities in Austria-Hungary for failing to report for compulsory military service. He fought as a German frontline soldier through the First World War and was in a military hospital near Stettin in November 1918 when the stunning news of Germany's surrender broke. By that time, Hitler already had strong opinions on race and politics but only a few passing acquaintances were interested in them. He was not worth even a footnote in history. During the next 12 years, Hitler became a national figure on the right wing of German politics, shaping the anti-Semitic ideology and propaganda of the emerging Nazi movement. In those years, Hitler developed his ideas, wrote his political testament *Mein Kampf* and led the NSDAP (National Socialist German Workers' Party) to second place in the Reichstag election of September 1930. Hitler's peculiar personality was crucial to his rise to prominence; it is essential to trace where his ideas came from and how they influenced those who came under his spell.

## The origins of Hitler's views

There were three phases in the shaping of Adolf Hitler's anti-Semitic philosophy. The first phase was Austrian: Hitler's Catholic upbringing in Upper Austria and his formative years as a failed artist in Vienna, which was a hotbed of anti-Semitic prejudices in the years before 1914. The second phase was Bavarian: Hitler's experiences as a soldier in the German Army and his early political activism in Munich during the turbulent post-war years to the failed Munich Putsch in 1923. The third phase was on the fringes of national politics: Hitler's recovery of authority as leader of the growing NSDAP after his release from prison and the political campaigning that led to the Nazis making an electoral breakthrough in the Reichstag elections of September 1930.

**Fig. 2** *A face in the crowd. Adolf Hitler in Munich at the announcement of war*

All three phases were significant in the emergence of Nazi ideology, but it was above all the Munich phase that moulded Hitler's anti-Jewish obsessions into coherent form, culminating in the publication of *Mein Kampf* in 1925. Hitler was part and parcel of the great wave of anti-Semitism that washed over Germany between 1916 and 1923, the traumatic years of defeat, revolution and social displacement. Hitler's anti-Semitic ideas were one element in the wild backlash against the German Revolution and the new democracy that resulted from it. However, there was much more to the rise of Nazism than anti-Semitism.

Hitler was the guiding force behind Nazi ideology, but he did not operate in a vacuum and his ideas were not completely original. Between arriving in Vienna as a raw teenager in 1907 and writing *Mein Kampf* during his prison sentence in 1924, Hitler picked up many different ideas and influences from a variety of sources. Hitler had a quick but undisciplined mind, grabbing hold of instant passing insights and adapting them to his own special world view. This process was mostly complete by the time Hitler wrote *Mein Kampf*, but the book is not always a reliable guide to the development of his ideas. By 1924, Hitler was already creating his own myth, making his early life seem like the apprenticeship of a great leader, working out his philosophy almost single-handedly, as only a genius could. The reality was different. Hitler and Nazism did not come from nowhere.

Hitler and his disciples were men who were born and grew up before 1918. Much German anti-Semitism can be traced back to forerunners such as the composer Richard Wagner, the historian Adolf Stöcker, or the racial theorist Houston Stewart Chamberlain. Nazi ideologists followed in the footsteps of 19th-century nationalists who had promoted the ideals of *Blut und Boden* (Blood and Soil), an idealised view of peasant life and its old-fashioned values, before those values were 'poisoned' by modernism, Communism and the Jews. Hitler was a German-Austrian, influenced by his years in Vienna before 1914. Hitler's special gift was to weld these influences together into a distinctive overarching philosophy with anti-Semitism as a special unifying force.

### Cross-reference

Adolf Hilter is profiled in Chapter 2, page 25.

The Munich Putsch of 1923 is outlined in Chapter 2, page 31.

The Nazis' electoral breakthrough in September 1930 is the subject of Chapter 2, pages 34–6.

Anti-Semitism played a very important part in Hitler's propaganda right from the beginning, in his Munich days, and those who followed him disliked or hated Jews. But his followers had many other motivations – extreme nationalism, resentment of defeat in the war and the Versailles Treaty, fear of Bolshevism, the mystic belief in the unity of the people and the Hitler cult. It is next to impossible to establish exactly the specific weight of anti-Semitism in this mixture of motives. It is known that among Hitler's very early followers in Munich, only about one-fifth said anti-Semitism was the most important single factor in their decision to join the Nazi movement. But Hitler's continual, relentless and effective anti-Semitic propaganda fell on fertile ground.

**1**    *W. Laqueur, **The Changing Face Of Antisemitism**, 2006*

■ Exploring the detail

Two historians have made key contributions to explaining Hitler's ambivalent relations with Jews in pre-1914 Vienna: the Austrian historian Brigitte Hamann, in *Hitler's Vienna* (1999), and Sir Ian Kershaw, in the first volume, *Hubris*, of his definitive biography of Hitler (2000). Descriptions of Hitler's life in Vienna by earlier historians should always be checked against Hamann and Kershaw.

■ A closer look

## Austrian beginnings

Almost all historians agree that Hitler's Austrian origins moulded many of his ideas and prejudices. Hitler came from a very Catholic background in Upper Austria. In his youth, he was a choirboy at Lambach Abbey church. Although Hitler later became very hostile to Catholicism, he absorbed a lot of traditional Austrian anti-Judaism. Hitler had met few, if any, 'eastern' Jews before coming to Vienna, but he reacted strongly against their presence in the city when he got there in 1907. There were nearly 2 million Jews living in pre-war Vienna and anti-Semitism was a major factor in society and politics. Several extracts from *Mein Kampf* seem to demonstrate how Hitler's anti-Semitic ideas resulted from his time in Vienna.

It is easy to assemble a mass of evidence about Austrian anti-Semitism and to make direct connections to Hitler's lifelong professions of hatred for all things Jewish. It is clear, for example, that some of Hitler's ideas came directly from Georg von Schönerer, the leader of the Austrian Pan-German movement. The ideas of the Pan-Germans, who were hostile to the non-German nationalities in the Austria-Hungarian monarchy, fitted closely with Hitler's own views. Anti-Semitism was a key element of extreme nationalism. Another influence was a former monk, Lanz von Liebenfels, who published a few editions of a magazine called *Ostara*, full of unorthodox and extreme theories about race. Both Schönerer and Lanz were extremely anti-Semitic. Hitler also expressed admiration for Karl Lüger, the long-serving mayor of Vienna from 1893 to 1910. Lüger was a cunning populist who skilfully exploited the economic resentments of the lower-middle classes against Jewish businesses. Hitler often spoke admiringly about Lüger's effectiveness in manipulating political anti-Semitism.

But Hitler's attitudes towards Jews during his years in Vienna were complex and what Hitler said in later life was not necessarily the whole truth. Many things Hitler did and said in his Austrian youth might seem surprising in the light of his later life. The family doctor who cared for Hitler's mother, Dr Bloch, was Jewish – yet Hitler accepted and trusted Dr Bloch. When Hitler was struggling to make ends meet by selling his paintings in Vienna, it was a Jewish art dealer, Moritz Rosenthal, who arranged the sales and sometimes lent him money. According to his friend August Kubizek, Hitler rarely showed blatant anti-Jewish feelings. The composer and conductor Gustav Mahler, for example, a Jew who converted to Catholicism, was viciously attacked by the Nazi regime after 1933 for 'Jewish decadence' but in 1910, when Mahler was at the height of his fame in Vienna, Hitler attended many of his concerts. According to Kubizek, Hitler was impressed by Mahler and rarely mentioned his Jewish origins.

This does not prove that Hitler was not already a committed anti-Semite before 1914 – other evidence proves clearly that he was. Hitler may well have concealed his true opinions about the Jewish art dealer because of the pragmatic consideration that he needed his help. Even so, there was more to Hitler's anti-Semitism than the ideas he picked up in his Austrian youth.

## Key profiles

### Lanz von Liebenfels

Jorg Lanz (the von Liebenfels was a fake claim to noble birth) (1874–1954) was a racist ideologue and editor of the occasional political journal, *Ostara,* published in Vienna in the early 1900s. Lanz was a disgraced priest who considered himself to be an intellectual. It is known that Adolf Hitler read at least some issues of *Ostara,* but the extent to which Hitler's ideology was influenced by this is debatable – claims that Hitler adopted Lanz's ideas wholesale are not supported by convincing documentary evidence.

### Georg von Schönerer

Schönerer (1842–1921) founded the Austrian Pan-German League in 1889. His ideas were dominated by Austrian-German Nationalism; they were also riddled with anti-Semitism, although this was not Schönerer's main obsession. Hitler claimed in *Mein Kampf* that his thinking was influenced by Schönerer's Pan-Germanism, though there is no record of the two men ever having met.

## The NSDAP

### Hitler in Munich: the rise of the NSDAP

It is clear that, in the same way as millions of Germans, many of Hitler's ideas were shaped by the radicalising effect of his war experiences and the chaotic conditions that prevailed in Munich during the German Revolution.

Hitler served bravely throughout the First World War, which he ended at a military hospital at Pasewalk in Pomerania, recovering from war wounds and temporary blindness. After the war, Hitler was employed by the army to report on left-wing political agitation in Munich – this is how he first discovered his considerable talents for public speaking and political action, leading to his involvement in the new German Workers' Party in 1919. This was the organisation that grew into the National Socialist German Workers' Party (NSDAP) – the 25 points of the NSDAP Party Programme in 1920 provided the first organised overview of Nazi ideology.

**Fig. 3** *Hitler at a party rally in Nuremberg, 1923*

Anti-Semitism had received a sharp boost from 1916 onwards, but from about the middle of 1919 it is possible to detect a further intensification of hostility to Jews in Germany. After the true consequences of the German defeat had come to light in Versailles, after the revolution had been put down by violence and the republican forces were on the defensive, there was talk of a 'wave from the right' whose most important indicator was anti-Semitism. From then on, the political Right made 'the Jews' responsible for well-nigh every glitch in the development of Germany. Being 'liberated' from the Jews meant redemption from the greatest evils. With the help of anti-Semitism, the radical Right had created a new political agenda.

**2**

P. Longerich, ***The Unwritten Order: Hitler's Role In The Final Solution,*** 2001

### Exploring the detail

#### Hitler as 'police spy'

Hitler was paid small sums of money by an army political affairs expert, Captain Karl Mayr, to report on political activity in post-war Munich. It was as part of his role as a 'police spy' that Hitler attended meetings of Anton Drexler's German Workers' Party in 1919.

4. Only he who is a folk comrade (*Volksgenosse*) can be a citizen. Only he who is of German blood, regardless of his church, can be a folk comrade. No Jew, therefore can be a folk comrade.

23. We demand:

(a) that all editors and contributors of German-language newspapers be folk comrades

(b) that non-German investment in or influence on German-language newspapers be legally forbidden and punished by the immediate expulsion of the non-Germans involved.

> **3** *From the 25-Point Party Programme of the NSDAP (1920). Quoted in B. Miller Lane and L. Rupp (eds.), **Nazi Ideology Before 1933**, 1978*

### The 25-Point Party Programme of the NSDAP

The ideology of the Nazi Party involved much more than anti-Semitism. It was a left-wing revolutionary ideology, appealing to the 'have-nots' and attacking the Conservative upper classes. It was also a right-wing ideology, stressing the importance of Nationalism and the need to fight against the hated Versailles Treaty imposed on Germany by the allies in 1919. These nationalist ideas, however, were seen in racist terms. It was not possible for the German people to be truly German unless alien, un-German elements were removed.

When the party launched its 25-Point Party Programme in 1920, only two of the 25 points were specifically anti-Jewish – but they both carried a powerful message. Point 4 directly demanded the exclusion of all Jews from German citizenship on the grounds of race; Point 23 implicitly rejected everything about Jewish culture. In 1920, these anti-Jewish elements were overshadowed by the rest of the revolutionary party programme but, by 1930, they had become the core aims of the Nazi movement.

Hitler contributed many ideas to the emerging Nazi ideology, but he was also influenced by other theorists in the formative stages of his career. Three right-wing ideologists in particular moulded the thinking of Hitler and the Nazis in the formative stages: Dietrich Eckhart; Alfred Rosenberg; and Gottfried Feder. Eckhart was a nationalist poet motivated by fanatical hatred of the Jews. Rosenberg was a leading member of the Thule Society, which took inspiration from the myths of the German past and occultism. His writings spelt out his mystical ideas about the German *Volk* and the deep psychological differences between the Aryan race and those of 'Asiatic-Jewish blood'. Feder fancied himself as an economic expert and was obsessed with what he called 'the slavery of interest', the way Jewish capitalists ruined the lives of honest workers and small businessmen.

### ■ Key profiles

#### Dietrich Eckhart

Eckhart (1868–1923) was a nationalist poet (and an alcoholic) who joined the German Workers' Party in 1919 and had strong anti-Semitic views. Eckhart was 20 years older than Hitler and had considerable influence over his thinking, at least at first. It was Eckhart who introduced Hitler to General von Ludendorff; and also Eckhart who provided the money for purchasing the *Völkischer Beobachter* as party newspaper. Eckhart took part in the 1923 putsch and was imprisoned with Hitler at Landsberg, but was given early release on compassionate grounds when it became clear he was dying.

#### Alfred Rosenberg

Rosenberg (1893–1946) was a **Volksdeutsche**, born in Reval (now Tallinn) in Estonia, then under Russian rule – he fought for Russia in the First World War. Rosenberg had a reputation as an intellectual and wrote extensively on the ideology of Nationalism and race; his 1930 book, *The Myth of the Twentieth Century*, was considered to be a major statement of Nazi ideology. Rosenberg continued to be an influential Nazi theorist after 1933, but had little or no practical power, despite his grandiose title of 'minister for the eastern occupied territories' from 1941. He was executed for war crimes in 1946.

### ■ Key terms

**Volksdeutsche**: racially pure Germans who lived outside the Reich, for example in Poland, Romania or the Baltic States. Part of Nazi Germany was to bring these people back 'home to the Reich', giving them the lands and homes that became available when territories were 'Germanised' by expelling Jews and Slavs to the East.

## Gottfried Feder

Feder (1883–1941) was a founder member of the German Workers' Party, formed in 1919, and was responsible for devising much of the 25-Point NSDAP Programme in 1920. Feder's particular obsession was with economic issues and the 'interest slavery of finance capital' – his ideas had many similarities with those of Gregor Strasser. Feder took part in the 1923 Beer Hall Putsch and continued to have influence within the party until 1933, when he was sidelined in favour of Dr Schacht.

Even in the early years of crisis and instability, the impact of anti-Semitism on the German people should not be exaggerated. The 25-Point Nazi Programme (Source 3) reached only a small proportion of the population. The pamphlets and speeches of theorists like Eckhart, Rosenberg and Feder set out general themes, such as race, Nationalism, 'Jewish-Bolshevism', or the evils of 'Jewish Loan Capital'. However, they were very 'intellectual' and often almost unreadable. When collected together by academic historians, these ideas might seem to add up to an ideology; but most people at the time thought they were wild ideas put about by cranks and misfits.

To all people who work! To all reasonable people!

One thing is never mentioned today – and there is nothing in the world that is such a curse on humanity: LOAN CAPITAL! Listen well! Loan capital brings in money without work. Without lifting a finger, the capitalist increases his wealth by lending money. It grows by itself, to infinity. In 1806 the house of Rothschild began its lending business with about 10 million marks. Today it amounts to 40 billion!

THE HOUSE OF ROTHSCHILD OWNS FORTY BILLION!

If it continues the same way, they will own 80 billion in 1935, 160 billion in 1960 and 320 billion in 1965. But who provides them with these billions? You do, nobody but you! That's right, it is your hard-earned money that is sucked into the coffers of these insatiable people. You could gather together all the farmers of the entire world and their total wealth would not equal the 49 billion of this one family of Rothschilds. But we have a great number of such lending houses: the Mendelssohns, the Bleichroeders, the Warburgs, to name only a few. There is a conspiracy to prevent us from seeing this greatest of evils, the all-consuming evil of Jewish loan capital.

**4** *Dietrich Eckhart, 'To All Working People!' (1919). Quoted in B. Miller Lane and L. Rupp (eds.), **Nazi Ideology Before 1933**, 1978*

In all of Europe, only National Socialism has really taken seriously the idea of the *völkisch* state and fought against not only the results of Marxism and parliamentary democracy but also the causes – the weak-kneed teachings of democracy and the greedy spirit of the Jews. By recognising race as a motive force, the idea of the *völkisch* state results in the rejection of today's concept of citizenship. One may only become a citizen in the new Germany if he is free from Asiatic-Jewish blood.

**6** *Alfred Rosenberg, 'The Völkisch Idea Of State' (1924). Quoted in B. Miller Lane and L. Rupp (eds.), **Nazi Ideology Before 1933**, 1978*

Loan interest is the evil invention of big capital. It alone makes possible the lazy, parasitic life of a handful of financially powerful people at the expense of productive workers. Loan interest has led to class hatred and civil war. The only cure is to break free from the slavery of interest. Where must breaking the slavery of interest begin? WITH LOAN CAPITAL!

**5** *Gottfried Feder, 'Manifesto For Breaking the Slavery of Interest' (1919). Quoted in B. Miller Lane and L. Rupp (eds.), **Nazi Ideology Before 1933**, 1978*

### Activity

#### Source analysis

Read Sources 4, 5 and 6. Analyse the various aspects of anti-Semitism they reveal and answer the following:

1 What sections of society were being targeted?

2 Which of these sources do you consider would have been most persuasive in convincing its readers? Why?

■ Cross-reference

The Munich Putsch of 1923 is outlined in Chapter 2, page 31.

**Fig. 4** Mein Kampf, *1925*

■ Exploring the detail

*Mein Kampf*

The first volume of *Mein Kampf* was published by Max Amann in 1925. A second volume was added in 1926. Hitler later wrote a sequel, his so-called *Second Book*, though this was never published until after 1945.

> We have no intention of being emotional anti-Semites intent on creating the atmosphere of a pogrom; instead our hearts are filled with an inexorable determination to attack the evil at its core and to extirpate it root and branch. In order to achieve our goal, every possible means will be justified, even if we have to make a pact with the devil.

**7**  *Hitler speaking to an NSDAP meeting, 6 April 1920. Quoted in E. Jäckel and A. Kuhn* **Hitler: Sämtliche Aufzeichnungen 1905–1924**, *1980*

During the early years of political activity, Hitler's ideology began to take shape. By the time of the failed Munich Putsch in 1923, Hitler had discovered his talent for political leadership and his charisma enthused the followers of the Nazi Party. The failure of the putsch also taught him valuable lessons and he became more certain of his own judgement, less likely to rely on the conservative allies he felt had let him down in 1923. He then used his 11 months of imprisonment to consolidate his ideas and to write *Mein Kampf*.

### Mein Kampf

Hitler's *Mein Kampf* (My Struggle) is frequently misunderstood. It was not strictly speaking a book written by Hitler, more a lengthy conversational monologue, transcribed by the faithful Rudolf Hess during Hitler's time in prison in 1924. This helps to explain the book's rambling structure. After 1933, *Mein Kampf* became the 'Bible' of the Third Reich. Almost every adult in Hitler's Germany possessed a copy; a few of them even read it all the way through, though its turgid and repetitive style makes this a difficult task.

■ Key profile

**Rudolf Hess**

Hess (1894–1987) was deputy leader to Hitler, but people who did not understand the true sources of power in the Third Reich tended to overstate his importance. Hess was with Hitler during his imprisonment and it was Hess who took dictation of Hitler's musings to write *Mein Kampf*. However, Hess was a man of limited ability who had much less impact on the Nazi dictatorship than Nazi barons like Göring, Göbbels and Himmler. In 1941, Hess flew to Britain on a solo mission to negotiate peace, but was arrested and spent the rest of his life in prison. He committed suicide in 1987.

The anti-Semitic message running through *Mein Kampf* was consistent with ideas Hitler had been developing since his earliest speeches. The themes running through Sources 7 and 8 show clearly Hitler's fixation on the idea of struggle and life-or-death conflict. There is no compromise possible, simply destroy or be destroyed.

> The Jewish people are incapable of establishing their own state. The very existence of the Jews becomes parasitic on the lives of other peoples. The ultimate goal of the Jewish struggle for survival is therefore the enslavement of productive peoples. The weapons the Jew uses for this are cunning, cleverness, subterfuge, malice, etc., qualities that are rooted in the very essence of the Jewish ethnic character. They are tricks in his struggle for survival, like the tricks used by other peoples in combat by the sword. The end of the Jewish struggle for world domination therefore will always be bloody Bolshevism.

**8**  *A. Hitler,* **Mein Kampf**, *1925*

In 1925, when Hitler was released from Landsberg prison after serving barely a year of his lenient five-year sentence, his political career was in trouble. The economic and political situation had settled down since November 1923 – one of the reasons why Hitler was released so early was that the authorities regarded him as only a minor nuisance who had had his day. In the meantime, the NSDAP had moved on without him and fought two elections in 1924. It was by no means certain that Hitler would win back his place as unchallenged leader.

It took a long struggle for Hitler to regain his political and psychological dominance over the Nazi movement, even in northern Germany and Berlin, where he had previously made little impression. He defeated the challenge from Gregor Strasser and the left-wing radicals. He won back the unquestioning support of key Nazi leaders such as Hermann Göring, Josef Göbbels and Heinrich Himmler. Nazism became completely identified with Hitler and his particular brand of anti-Semitism. By then, even though the Nazis were still a long way from power, Hitler's ideological development was substantially complete.

**Activity**

**Thinking point**

How would you explain the fact that Hitler was given such a lenient sentence after the Munich Putsch?

**Cross-reference**

Gregor Strasser and Joseph Göbbels are profiled in Chapter 2, pages 34.

## Key profiles

### Hermann Göring

Göring (1893–1946) was a flamboyant, larger-than-life character, who had been a war hero as a fighter pilot in the First World War. His military contacts and his aristocratic wife made him very useful to the Nazis in the early stages. He was wounded in the 1923 Munich Putsch but recovered to become one of the key Nazi deputies in the Reichstag from 1928. He played a leading role in carrying out the murders on the Night of the Long Knives in 1934. From 1935, he was Commander-in-Chief of the Luftwaffe and head of the Four Year Plan from 1936. He was also deeply involved in race policy and the launch of the 'Final Solution'. He committed suicide in his cell at Nuremberg in 1946.

### Heinrich Himmler

Himmler (1900–45) was *Reichsführer* of the SS from 1929 until the end of the Third Reich. He was involved in various anti-Semitic right-wing groups including the *Artamane* in the early 1920s and participated in the 1923 Munich Putsch. Himmler led the SS (*Schutzstaffel*) from its formation in 1925. It was Himmler's bureaucratic organising skills that enabled the SS to become more powerful than the SA and to control all police and security in the Reich by 1937. Himmler was a fanatic racist and played a central role in race policies and the implementation of the 'Final Solution'. He committed suicide in 1945 after his arrest by British forces.

For the rest of his life, Hitler's tactics changed often but his core ideas, his 'world view', hardly changed at all. In 1919, Hitler already had a number of fixed ideas about politics and race in his head, but nothing like a final overall philosophy. By 1924–25, however, Hitler had made up his mind – the ideas he set out in *Mein Kampf* were to be his guiding principles for the rest of his life. What he said later, for example, in his *Table Talk*, during the Second World War shows a remarkable consistency with what he had been saying in the 1920s.

## The ideology of Nazism

Hitler's ideology was not a detailed philosophy; *Mein Kampf* was too vague and incoherent to be the Bible of Nazi doctrine. Hitler's ideas were more a 'cosmic vision', with broad themes. Among the main themes were Social Darwinism and race; the *Volksgemeinschaft* (community of the true people); and the drive to provide the German people with *Lebensraum* (living space) in the East. Anti-Semitism was a crucial element in all three.

## Social Darwinism and race theory

Hitler's view of race was obsessed with conflict – an all-out struggle between the true Germanic *Volk* and the impure blood of inferior races that threatened to 'infect' ethnically pure Germans. Social Darwinism was a theory that was widely discussed in 19th-century Europe. It was based on Charles Darwin's theory of evolution and natural selection, put forward in his great book *The Origin of Species* in 1859. Social Darwinists adapted Darwin's scientific principles of natural biological selection ('the survival of the fittest') to rather unscientific theories about human society in order to justify ideas of racial superiority and the theory of eugenics.

In the late 19th and early 20th centuries, many Social Darwinists put forward theories designed to justify European imperialism, by arguing that 'advanced' Europeans had the right and the responsibility to rule over 'inferior' or 'backward' colonial peoples. In Sweden, there was an influential group of scientists seeking to eliminate disabilities through population planning and birth control. Many of these ideas were incorporated into Nazi ideology.

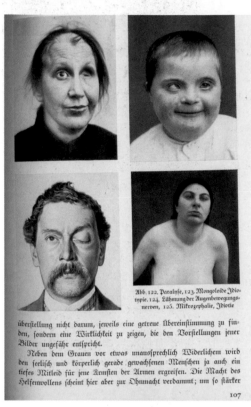

*Abb. 122. Paralyse, 123. Mongoloide Idiotypie, 124. Lähmung der Augenbewegungsnerven, 125. Mikrozephalie, Idiotie*

überstellung nicht darum, jeweils eine getreue Übereinstimmung zu finden, sondern eine Wirklichkeit zu zeigen, die den Vorstellungen jener Bilder ungefähr entspricht.

Neben dem Grauen vor etwas unaussprechlich Widerlichem wird den seelisch und körperlich gerade gewachsenen Menschen ja auch ein tiefes Mitleid für jene Ärmsten der Armen ergreifen. Die Macht des Helfenwollens scheint hier aber zur Ohnmacht verdammt; um so stärker

107

**Fig. 5** *'Racial degenerates.' From the book Art and Race, 1928*

Hitler was obsessed with the idea of struggle, and the idea of a ferocious, everlasting biological struggle between different races appealed strongly to him; it also fitted naturally with his view of the Jews. Another key Nazi idea was the need to 'purify' the stronger races by eliminating the 'germs' that threatened to poison them through inter-marriage with so-called 'degenerate' races. Source 9 outlines Hitler's views in a speech to a Nazi meeting at Salzburg in Austria in August 1920.

Do not imagine that you can combat a sickness without killing what causes it, without annihilating the germ; and do not imagine that you can combat tuberculosis without taking care to free the people from the germ that causes racial tuberculosis. The effects of Judaism will never wane and the poisoning of the people will never end until the cause, the Jews, are removed from our midst.

**9** *Hitler speaking to an NSDAP meeting, 6 April 1920. Quoted in E. Jäckel and A. Kuhn **Hitler: Sämtliche Aufzeichnungen 1905–1924**, 1980*

### Did you know?

The German word for remove is *entfernen* – literally 'to send into the distance'. Hitler's frequent use of the word carried the connotation of drastic action with terrible consequences.

### Key terms

**Gypsies (Roma):** travelling communities of gypsies had been a prominent feature of life in central and Eastern Europe for centuries. Like Jews, and for similar reasons, they were often the victims of discrimination and persecution. Twenty thousand died in the Holocaust.

Hitler's concept of Social Darwinism was, therefore, on an all-or-nothing basis. Biologically and culturally, the Jews were to be treated as posing a deadly threat to the survival of the German *Volk*. There could be no compromises and no exceptions. Conversion to Christianity could make no difference; nor could medals won in the First World War. The germ had to be eliminated. This is why Himmler, in a notorious speech to high-level Nazis in 1943, emphasised the rightness of killing women and children as well as men.

In the same way, the Nazi principles of 'racial hygiene' justified the sterilisation (or eliminating altogether) of the mentally and physically disabled, the **gypsies** and other 'racial undesirables' such as homosexuals, pacifists and Jehovah's Witnesses. The same theme of eradication of racial enemies ran through much of the more extreme Nazi propaganda of the 1920s put out by racists like the 'Jew-baiter of Nuremberg', Julius Streicher.

## Key profile

### Julius Streicher

Streicher (1885–1946) was a fanatical anti-Semite who was editor of the racist and pornographic Nazi journal *Der Stürmer*. Streicher was also Gauleiter (Nazi Party boss) of the Franconia region, with his headquarters in Nuremberg. His racist views were too violent and extreme even for many Nazi leaders, who considered him to be an embarrassment. Hitler remained loyal to Streicher, however, as one of his 'old comrades' – he was not dismissed from his post until 1940. He was executed as a war criminal in 1946.

**Fig. 6** *Julius Streicher*

Nazi race theories in the 1920s were a driving force behind the ideology of the SS and had a direct link to the later policies of the Third Reich. In the late 1930s, and especially during the war years, the SS put Social Darwinist ideas into horrific practice:

- The policy of sterilisation was implemented against those (such as the disabled) who were deemed a threat to racial purity; and also against 'social deviants'.
- *Aktion T4* carried through the programme of so-called mercy killings of the disabled, including the first experiments with gas chambers.
- The extensive *Lebensborn* programme organised the mass kidnapping of 'Aryan' children from their parents in the conquered territories, so that they could be given to childless couples in Germany. The *Lebensborn* programme also provided lavish maternity services for unmarried girls to give birth and 'donate a child to the Führer'.
- The gruesome medical experiments conducted by SS doctors under the direction of Josef Mengele at Auschwitz from 1942 were designed to advance the 'science' of racial selection.

## The *Volksgemeinschaft*

The dream of the *Volksgemeinschaft*, or community of the true German people, was a key feature of Nazi propaganda in the 1920s and in the early years of the Nazi regime after 1933. Outwardly, the *Volksgemeinschaft* was an inclusive idea, promising a classless society and national unity. Many of the early proponents of the idea were left-wing radicals such as the **Strasserites** and the SA. In the early days after the Nazis came to power in 1933, the new regime spent a lot of time and effort promoting ideas such as workers and bosses eating together, merging the trade unions into the one big German Workers' Front, and so on.

In reality, Hitler's concept of the National People's Community was not inclusive at all. In a way that was typical of many other aspects of Nazi ideology, the concept of the national community was twisted by anti-Semitism and racial thinking. The key word was the *Volk*. To qualify as a member of the Volk it was essential to be a true German, both in terms of loyalty and of racial purity. To protect the Volk, it was essential to ruthlessly eliminate all un-German elements, especially the Jews – so that the best way of defining the Volk came through identifying the racial enemies to be excluded from it, rather than the people who naturally belonged to it.

### Cross-reference

*Aktion T4*, the programme of 'mercy killings' for the disabled, is described in Chapter 7, pages 95–9.

The sterilisation programme is discussed in Chapter 6, pages 82–3.

More detail on the experiments of Josef Mengele can be found in Chapter 9, page 121.

### Key terms

**Strasserites:** the supporters of Gregor Strasser (profiled in Chapter 2, page 34) and his younger brother, Otto. The Strassers generally believed in the radical left-wing aspects of Nazi ideology. Strasserites tended to be concentrated in northern Germany and were not always happy with Hitler's personal domination of the NSDAP. They also tended to emphasise economic issues more than race.

### Cross-reference

The implementation of the Nazi ideal of the *Volksgemeinschaft*, including the marginalising and legal discrimination against 'un-German' elements, is covered in Chapter 5, pages 60–7.

The purge of the SA in 1934 is outlined on page 54.

■ **Activity**

**Group activity**

Working in two groups, devise a list of points for use in a pro-nationalist German newspaper article intended to show approval for the idea of the *Volksgemeinschaft*:

**a** basing the appeal on economic issues

**b** emphasising race and nationalism.

The negative and racist aspects of the *Volksgemeinschaft* did not become obvious until the Nazis were in power. In the 1920s, greater emphasis was placed on the idea of social unity and a classless society. Much of Nazi ideology was influenced by left-wing ideas and beliefs. It was only after the elimination of Gregor Strasser late in 1932 and the purge of the SA (*Sturm Abteilung*) in June 1934 that these left-wing elements in Nazi ideology were pushed aside.

### Lebensraum

The Nazi ideal of *Lebensraum* (living space) was yet another example of an ideological concept being twisted by anti-Semitism. Like Social Darwinism, the idea of Lebensraum was not new, nor originated by Hitler and the Nazis. In the later 19th century, many European thinkers had proposed opening up space for the expanding populations of the superior white race. The settlement of Australia by the British was one example; the opening up of the American West was another. In each case, supposedly 'backward' indigenous peoples had, rightfully it was thought at the time, been displaced or killed to make way for civilisation and progress.

These ideas were also influential in Germany. In the 1880s and 1890s, pressure groups such as the Colonial League and the Navy League promoted German colonial expansion in Africa and south-east Asia. After its publication in 1926, a book by Hans Grimm, *People Without Space*, became hugely popular in Germany. There was widespread support for the idea that Germany was already over-populated and that industrious German farmers needed more land.

One of Grimm's key themes was the idea that Germany's destiny lay in the East, conquering the supposedly inferior Slav peoples of Poland and the former Russian Empire. Many nationalist historians stressed the glories of past history, when German crusaders had 'Germanised' the Eastern territories in the 13th and 14th centuries. Other people emphasised the dangers of Russian Bolshevism and the need to win back the former German lands in the East that had been stripped away by the Treaty of Versailles. Some economic theorists believed in *autarky* (the idea that Germany should be economically self-sufficient and not dependent on imported food and raw materials) and saw expansion to the East as a way of achieving this.

Nazi ideology fitted in smoothly with these ideas about Germany's destiny to expand eastwards, but Hitler's concept of Lebensraum had a particular focus on race. The theories of Professor Karl Haushofer did much to influence this. Lebensraum would not only allow for the 'Germanisation' of the eastern lands and bringing the 'Lost Germans' back to the Reich – more importantly it would provide the battleground for a war of racial annihilation, wiping out the inferior Slav races and smashing Bolshevism in Russia.

■ **Exploring the detail**

**The SS and 'race and space'**

Himmler and the SS were enthusiastic supporters of these ideas about 'race and space'. A special SS department, the RSHA, was set up in 1931 to plan for the resettlement of 'true' Germans on the lands that would one day be conquered in the East. Its activities between 1939 and 1941 are outlined in Chapter 8, pages 102–3.

■ **Key profile**

### Karl Haushofer

Haushofer (1869–1946) was a career soldier who became a racial theorist and an influential professor at Munich University. He was a friend of Rudolf Hess (he relied on Hess to protect him from trouble over his half-Jewish wife) and played a key role in giving the Nazi ideology of living space its especially racist emphasis. Haushofer was acquitted of war crimes at Nuremberg but committed suicide, together with his wife, in 1946.

*Lebensraum* was an idea that became more important to Hitler in the later 1920s, especially in 1927 and 1928. At this time, Hitler's anti-Semitism was becoming more and more influenced by his anti-communist beliefs. In *Zweites Buch* (Second Book), a follow up to *Mein Kampf* dictated by Hitler in 1928, the themes of Social Darwinism and Lebensraum were hammered out over and again.

- Germany is short of space for economic growth.
- This territory can only be gained by the use of force.
- It is 'an iron principle that the weaker must fall so that the stronger can live'.
- The Aryan race faces a deadly threat from 'Jewish Marxism'.
- Germany must one day soon expand eastwards.

These ideas can clearly be linked to Nazi policies later in the war in the East and the Holocaust. However, in the 1920s, Hitler's ideas were still rather vague and there seemed no practical possibility of them ever being put into action (Source 10).

> In the mid-1920s, *Lebensraum* was probably little more than a militant slogan for Hitler's audiences – though it was more than that for Hitler himself. Even regarding the Jews, the real aim was still fuzzy. Hitler talked about 'chasing that pack of Jews from our fatherland with an iron broom' but the first vital step towards achieving *Lebensraum* – the establishment of a racially pure *Volksgemeinschaft* in Germany was, at that time, nothing more than a utopian vision that nobody but absolute fanatics could have thought possible.

**10** *I. Kershaw, **Hitler, The Germans and the Final Solution**, 2008*

By the time of the 1928 Reichstag elections, Hitler's anti-Semitic views were fixed. So was his control over the political and ideological direction of the Nazi movement. But the NSDAP secured only 12 seats in 1928; Hitler was still far from having any hopes of power. Between 1929 and 1933, however, the economic and political situation changed dramatically. The Nazi Party emerged as a nationwide mass movement. As it did so, there were many twists and turns and political compromises. Hitler and the Nazi leadership frequently made contradictory promises and frequently concealed their true intentions. It can be argued, however, that Hitler's core ideology rarely, if ever, changed. The tactics might be new, but not Hitler's 'world view'.

### Activity

**Group activity**

Working in three groups, draw up a two-columned table listing the sections of society who would be included within the *Volksgemeinschaft* according to Nazi ideology, alongside those who would be excluded. In a brief plenary session, compare the findings of the groups.

### Cross-reference

The links between *Lebensraum* and Nazi foreign policies 1939–41 are covered in Chapter 8, pages 101–3.

### Cross-reference

The impact of Nazi ideology on the Reichstag elections of 1928 and 1930 is discussed in Chapter 2, pages 34–5.

### Activity

**Talking point**

Consider the view that '*Mein Kampf* provides an unreliable guide to Adolf Hitler's true beliefs'. Write a speech either supporting or disagreeing with this view. When several members of the group have delivered their different speeches, you could take a class vote as to whether or not you feel this statement is fair.

### Summary questions

**1** Examine the extent to which Hitler's anti-Semitic views were shaped by outside influences in the early 1920s.

**2** To what extent was Nazi anti-Semitism in the 1920s motivated by economic factors?

# 4 Anti-Semitism and the rise of Nazism, 1930–33

*In this chapter you will learn about:*

- the extent of anti-Semitism in Germany after the onset of the Great Depression
- Hitler's personal role in the spread of anti-Semitism to 1933
- the importance of anti-Semitism in Reichstag elections to 1933
- the attitudes of Jews in Germany to the new Nazi regime.

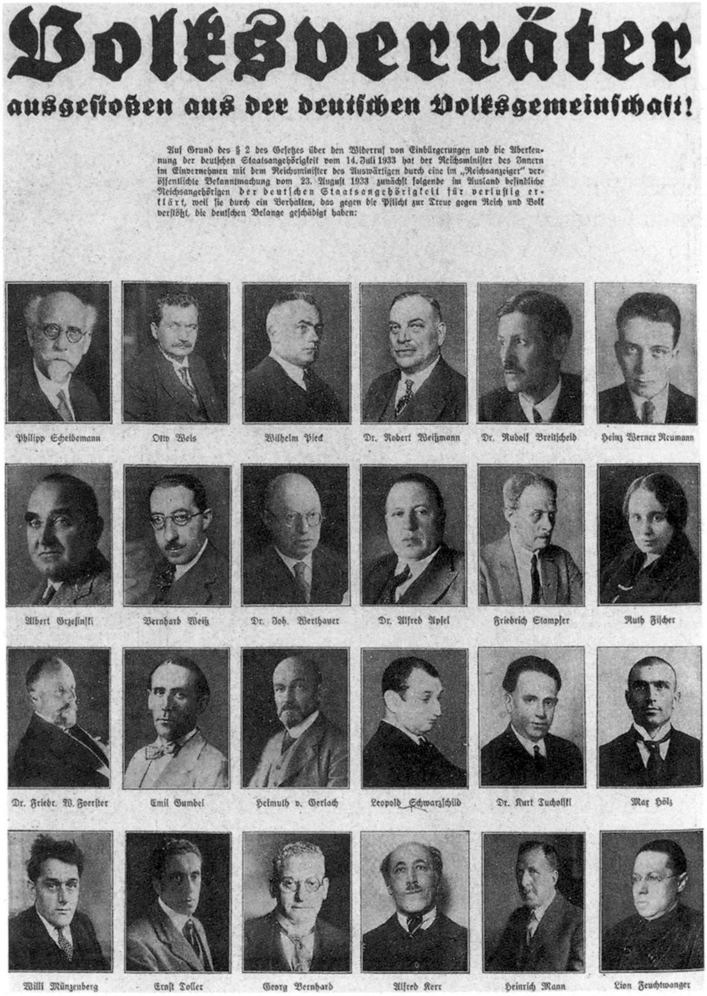

**Volksverräter**

**ausgestoßen aus der deutschen Volksgemeinschaft!**

Auf Grund des § 2 des Gesetzes über den Widerruf von Einbürgerungen und die Aberkennung der deutschen Staatsangehörigkeit vom 14. Juli 1933 hat der Reichsminister des Innern im Einvernehmen mit dem Reichsminister des Auswärtigen durch eine im „Reichsanzeiger" veröffentliche Bekanntmachung vom 23. August 1933 zunächst folgende im Ausland befindliche Reichsangehörigen der deutschen Staatsangehörigkeit für verlustig erklärt, weil sie durch ein Verhalten, das gegen die Pflicht zur Treue gegen Reich und Volk verstößt, die deutschen Belange geschädigt haben:

Philipp Scheidemann · Otto Wels · Wilhelm Pieck · Dr. Robert Weißmann · Dr. Rudolf Breitscheid · Heinz Werner Neumann

Albert Grzesinski · Bernhard Weiß · Dr. Joh. Werthauer · Dr. Alfred Apfel · Friedrich Stampfer · Ruth Fischer

Dr. Friedr. W. Foerster · Emil Gumbel · Helmuth v. Gerlach · Leopold Schwarzschild · Dr. Kurt Tucholski · Max Hölz

Willi Münzenberg · Ernst Toller · Georg Bernhard · Alfred Kerr · Heinrich Mann · Lion Feuchtwanger

**Fig. 1** *'Betrayers of the people.' Twenty-four opponents of the Nazis shown on the front page of the* Illustrierte Zeitung*, 1933*

The Reichstag elections of September 1930 were disastrous for the democratic parties. Extremist parties made huge gains: the Communists won 77 seats and the NSDAP shot up from 12 seats to 107. This meant that 184 of the deputies sitting in the new Reichstag were hostile to the very existence of the republic. Another 52 seats went to the right-wing nationalists of the DNVP. Jews recognised that this powerful political backlash against Weimar democracy was a grave threat to their social position. The Jewish longing for assimilation had to be matched by acceptance from mainstream society. After the 1930 elections, the prospects of such acceptance receded sharply.

This was Hitler's breakthrough into national politics, providing him with an opportunity to gain respectability. Anti-Semitism started to move from the fringes of politics to the centre of the national stage – but anti-Semitic ideas were still hedged around with concealment and compromise. Not until *Kristallnacht* (the Night of Broken Glass) in November 1938 would the full force of Nazi anti-Semitism be unleashed.

## Exploring the detail

### The DNVP

The DNVP (German National People's Party) represented the traditional Conservative Right in Germany. Its leader was the press magnate, Alfred von Hugenberg. The DNVP despised the Nazis as a low-class rabble and the Nazis regarded the DNVP as weak and old fashioned – but at a meeting at Bad Harzburg in 1931 the two parties made a temporary political agreement not to attack each other.

## The spread of Nazi anti-Semitism to March 1933

In the crisis years of the Great Depression from late 1929 to 1932, Hitler was able to gain political momentum and to emerge as a national figure. Many moderate Germans who had previously ignored and despised Nazism began to think differently because the economic problems were so serious and because the main democratic parties of the Weimar Republic appeared to be unable to cope. The Nazis started to gain support for their backlash against the threat from 'Jewish-Bolshevism', as perceived in the rising support for the Communists.

In this process, the direct effects of anti-Semitism should not be exaggerated. Voters who considered the Jews to be the most important problem in Germany were clearly in the minority – at the very most about 15 per cent – and they had probably already voted Nazi in 1928 anyway. The vast majority of new voters won over by the Nazis between 1930 and 1933 switched their votes on economic grounds, or because they feared Communist revolution. Hitler well understood this. The nearer he came to power, the more Hitler toned down the extreme racism and violence of the movement in an attempt to reassure members of respectable mainstream German society that they could trust the Nazis to act responsibly.

### Hitler's personal role

By 1930, Adolf Hitler was fully established as leader of the Nazi movement. He was the Nazi Party's trump card – a controversial personality who grabbed attention and a magnetic speaker who could be relied upon to pull in the crowds. Nazi propaganda posters made the most of Hitler's starring role. As the Nazis gained wider support in 1931 and 1932, Hitler's charisma was a key factor – without his high public profile, Nazi political campaigning would have had much less impact.

Hitler's role was also vital in deciding Nazi political strategy. Many radicals in the movement, especially in the SA, were eager for violence and the 'Brown Revolution', but Hitler was more realistic and more cautious. He knew that the Nazis were not strong enough to take on the forces of law and order and seize power by violent revolution. Hitler remembered how his Munich Putsch had turned into a fiasco in 1923 and how his career might easily have ended before it had really begun.

Hitler knew that he must not frighten away the middle-class voters who were beginning to come over to the Nazis. He needed to reassure them by keeping up a respectable image. In the same way, Hitler hoped to get the backing of influential conservative elements in society, such as businessmen, politicians and army officers. To do this, Hitler had to appear to be in control of Nazi 'extremists' in order to convince people that he would bring order out of chaos. This often meant watering down the anti-Semitic messages in Nazi propaganda.

Hitler, therefore, had to appear both safe and reassuring – the man who would save Germany from the dangers of economic collapse, block the rise of Communism and, at the same time give enough encouragement to the radicals in the Nazi Party and in the SA to keep them supportive and optimistic. Hitler coped well. He was a clever and flexible politician and his leadership proved crucial in the rise of the Nazis.

### Key chronology

**The rise of Hitler and the Nazis, 1930–33**

**1930**

| | |
|---|---|
| July | Nazi breakthrough in Reichstag election |

**1932**

| | |
|---|---|
| April | Surge of support for Hitler in presidential election |
| July | Peak of support for Nazis in Reichstag election |
| November | Dip in support for Nazis in Reichstag election |

**1933**

| | |
|---|---|
| January | Hitler appointed chancellor by Hindenburg |
| March | 43 per cent of votes in Reichstag election won by NSDAP |
| May | The Burning of the Books in Berlin |

### Cross-reference

The impact of anti-Semitism on the elections of 1928 and 1930 is covered at the end of Chapter 2, pages 34–5.

**Fig. 2** *Hitler at Braunschweig, 1931*

■ **Cross-reference**

Strasser, Göbbels and Göring are profiled on pages 34 and 45 respectively.

■ **Cross-reference**

President Hindenburg is profiled on page 54.

■ **Exploring the detail**

**The Wall Street Crash**

The Wall Street Crash of October 1929 was the sudden collapse of the stock market in New York after a long period of rising prosperity and overconfidence by investors. The crash of 1929 was a financial crisis that did not immediately lead to a general economic crisis – it took more than two years for the downturn of the Great Depression to reach the bottom, with industrial stagnation and mass unemployment as well as the banking crisis. Businesses in Germany were badly hit by the collapse of the Creditanstalt Bank in Austria in 1931.

■ **Did you know?**

In 1930, 15 per cent of the German workforce was unemployed; in 1932 this had risen to 30 per cent. The usual estimate of the peak level of unemployment is 6 million, but recent research indicates that the real number was probably 8 million.

However, it was never a one-man show. Hitler faced many challenges and made many mistakes. He depended on support from loyal lieutenants such as Göbbels and Göring. He had to fight off criticism from powerful rivals such as Gregor Strasser. Even late in 1932, some people thought it was possible that Strasser might take over as leader.

Nor was it certain that the Nazis would ever come to power. Many influential people, including President Hindenburg, tried hard to keep Hitler out. It was only in January 1933, after complicated negotiations with other politicians that Hitler was appointed chancellor. Hitler's personal role was obviously important for the Nazi rise to power, but he could never have achieved success simply by his own actions. For the Nazi Party to come from the fringes of German politics to the centre of the stage, there had to be favourable circumstances: the world economic crisis from 1929 and the collapse in support for German democracy and the mainstream parties.

## Links between economic depression and rising anti-Semitism

It is a mistake to assume that the 1929 Wall Street Crash had an instant impact on Germany. The onset of the Great Depression was gradual and cumulative. Already in 1930, there were business failures and increases in unemployment. The growing economic crisis helped to bring about the collapse of Müller's coalition government and enabled both the Nazis and the Communists to make gains in the Reichstag elections in September – but it was in 1931, and especially in 1932, that economic conditions became desperate. As the crisis worsened, the democratic political system was weakened and extremist politics gained support.

Part of this shift was a rise in anti-Semitism. The economic crisis had widespread effects: rising unemployment of both skilled and unskilled workers, a serious banking crisis and intensified pressures on small farmers, who had already been in trouble before 1929. It was easy for Nazi propaganda to exploit the fears of farmers who were deeply in debt to banks and unable to pay back the loans. Many shopkeepers and small businesses were more receptive to the idea that their problems were caused by 'Jewish Capitalism'. Many people who had previously kept their anti-Semitic views quiet were now willing to express them more freely.

The most important effect, however, was probably indirect. Many ordinary Germans were still unwilling to go along with openly anti-Semitic propaganda, but they were so preoccupied with immediate economic hardships that they heard the messages they wanted to hear. Their previous disapproval of Nazi extremism faded as they focused on Nazi promises to provide work and bread. Many people who voted Nazi in 1932 did so in spite of anti-Semitism, not because of it.

Nazi propaganda was frequently adapted according to the audience and to local circumstances. In January 1932, for example, Hitler addressed 650 businessmen at the Industry Club in Düsseldorf – he did not make even a single mention of the Jews in the whole two-and-a-half-hour speech. Many of the people who joined the growing Nazi Party at this time had no particular feeling about the 'Jewish question'. In 1931, a brilliant young university lecturer, the mathematician and would-be architect, Albert Speer, attended a meeting in Berlin because his students had told him he must go and hear Hitler speak. Speer instantly came under Hitler's spell and was 'converted' to Nazism. Later, he became one of the most powerful Nazi leaders, running Hitler's war economy from 1942 – but anti-Semitism had nothing to do with this, according to Speer (Source 1).

I was carried along on the wave of enthusiasm that swept Hitler onwards from sentence to sentence. Finally, Hitler no longer seemed to be speaking to convince; rather, he seemed to feel that he was expressing what the audience, by now transformed into a single mass, expected of him. Here, it seemed to me, was hope. Here were new ideals, a new understanding, new tasks. The peril of Communism, which seemed unstoppable, could be checked, Hitler persuaded us, and instead of hopeless unemployment Germany could move towards economic recovery. He had mentioned the Jewish problem only in passing. But such remarks did not trouble me even though I was not an anti-Semite and had Jewish friends from my school and university days, just like everyone else.

| 1 | |
|---|---|
| | *A. Speer, Inside The Third Reich, The Memoirs of Albert Speer, 1970* |

> ■ Activity
>
> **Source analysis**
>
> Read Source 1. Select **five** reasons why historians might regard this source as valuable evidence about rising support for Hitler and the Nazis in 1931.

At the same time, there were many meetings attended by people lower down the social scale where Nazi speakers openly encouraged hostility against Jews by accusing them of being the cause of the economic troubles of those in the audience. The rapid expansion of the SA also encouraged radical anti-Semitism – *Juda verrecke* ('Down with the Jews') was a favourite chant of the Brownshirts, who often beat up Jews in the street. On the other hand, many men were attracted into the SA because of anti-Communism, or comradeship in the pub, or because membership of the SA was a meal ticket. Anti-Semitism was rarely the main motive for joining the SA.

## A closer look

### The rise of the SA

The SA (*Sturm Abteilung*) was the paramilitary wing of the Nazi movement, first formed in 1921 and led by Ernst Röhm. From 1930, SA membership increased dramatically. The brown uniforms of the SA were seen everywhere. Pitched battles between SA men and Communists or the socialist *Reichsbanner* became a common occurrence. Many people were beaten up by SA gangs; or else intimidated by the general atmosphere that marching SA men created. By the end of 1932, SA membership was more than 400,000 (four times as many men as the regular army). The police were often intimidated by the sheer size and aggression of the SA – street violence and petty crimes committed by SA men were rarely prosecuted.

**Fig. 3** *SA rally outside Communist Party HQ in Berlin, January 1933*

Hitler had to steer a careful course in dealing with the SA – he relied on them to intimidate political opponents and to pose as protectors against Communism; but the violence and extremism of the SA was very frightening to the traditional elites, especially the regular army. Hitler often had to restrain the SA to prevent an anti-Hitler backlash.

The radicals in the SA dreamed of a '**Brown Revolution**', or 'revolution from below' – a social revolution that would destroy the old conservative elites, replace the regular army and enable the 'ordinary men' of the SA to enrich themselves at the expense of the middle classes and the rich. For many in the SA, the aim was for an

> ■ Key terms
>
> **Brown Revolution:** this was so-called because of the brown uniforms of the SA. Many leaders of the SA were impatient to let loose a 'revolution from below' that would overthrow the army and the ruling elites, paving the way for social revolution.

## ■ Exploring the detail

### The Night of the Long Knives

The Night of the Long Knives (otherwise known as the Röhm Purge) was a calculated burst of violence launched by Hitler on 30 June 1934 to eliminate or to intimidate any possible challenge to his dictatorship. The main targets were Ernst Röhm and other SA leaders. In a second category, many Conservative and Catholic politicians were killed, including a former chancellor, General von Schleicher. In a third category, Hitler took revenge against people who had opposed him in the past, such as Gregor Strasser. The undisciplined power of the SA was replaced by the more streamlined SS.

**Fig. 4** *SA stormtrooper. The poster reads: 'The SA man is the ever-ready power of the Nazi movement'*

economic revolution more than a political one. After Hitler came to power in January 1933, it was not clear whether Hitler would be able, or would want, to bring the SA under control. The question was eventually settled on the night of 30 June 1934, when many SA leaders including Ernst Röhm, were murdered in the 'Night of the Long Knives' or 'Blood Purge'.

## ■ Key profile

### Ernst Röhm

Röhm (1887–1934) was the leader of the *Sturm Abteilung* (SA) – the paramilitary wing of the Nazi movement. Röhm was a brilliant organiser and had been close to Hitler since 1921. Röhm had radical aims: he wanted his SA to take over from the regular army as the main fighting force in Germany; he also wanted radical social change through a 'Brown Revolution'. He was very impatient with Hitler's cautious political tactics in 1932 and 1933. He was murdered, on Hitler's orders, during The 'Night of the Long Knives' in June 1934.

### *The political appeal of anti-Semitism in the elections of 1932*

1932 was a year of elections in Germany:

- March/April: The presidential election (Hindenburg had been elected in 1925 and his seven-year term of office was up). The main candidates were President Hindenburg, Adolf Hitler, and the Communist candidate Ernst Thalmann.
- April: Prussian provincial election.
- July 1932: Reichstag elections called after the chancellor Heinrich Bruning resigned because his coalition government could not carry on.
- November 1932: New Reichstag elections called because all attempts to form a government without Nazi participation had failed.

The Nazis gained support throughout the first half of 1932. Hitler became a national figure, gaining huge publicity from his campaign in the presidential elections in April, when he won 11 million votes, only 2 million fewer than Hindenburg. Nazi fundraising was very successful, both from business and from individual donations, so that the Nazis were able to spend huge amounts on propaganda. Many small parties were eclipsed altogether as their voters were swallowed up by the Nazis.

## ■ Key profile

### Paul von Hindenburg

Field Marshal Paul von Hindenburg (1847–1934) was a man who lived too long for his own good. Hindenburg had fought against the Austrians at Sadowa in 1866 and became a war hero in 1914 after the Battle of Tannenberg. When he was elected president in 1925, he was already 78 years old; when he appointed Hitler as chancellor in 1933, Hindenburg was 87, a well-meaning figurehead approaching senility. His handshake with Hitler on 'Potsdam Day' in March 1933 was vital in giving Hitler the appearance of legitimacy. After Hindenburg died in August 1934, Hitler took over the role of head of state.

Widening the support for Nazism meant winning over people the Nazis had not previously targeted. This meant emphasising issues the Nazis had previously neglected. Most Nazi propaganda in 1932 had little or nothing to do with anti-Semitism. In January 1932, there was a coordinated sequence of 16 mass meetings, all on the issue of unemployment. In the election campaign against Hindenburg, many posters stressed Hitler's record as a frontline soldier, with slogans like: 'Give your vote to the Man of Strength!' Posters for the Prussian elections in April focused on 'Work, Freedom and Bread!'

The anti-Semitic theme was overshadowed, but was not totally neglected. Posters for meetings by old-style Nazis like Julius Streicher still screamed 'The Jews are our misfortune!' – other posters played on the theme of anti-communism with the not so hidden message that Jews and Bolsheviks came down to the same thing.

## ■ Activity

### Statistical analysis

Study Figure 6 showing the Reichstag election results for 1932. Compare them with the results for 1928–30 on page 35.

Working in three groups, analyse:

**a** Which parties made big gains.

**b** Which parties suffered big losses.

**c** Which parties retained fairly consistent support.

In each case, using the evidence in this section, suggest **three** possible reasons to explain the trends.

**Fig. 5** *President Paul von Hindenburg. A portrait by Max Liebermann*

## ■ Cross-reference

Julius Streicher is profiled in Chapter 3, page 47.

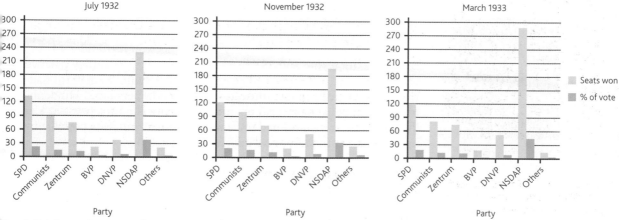

**Fig. 6** *Reichstag election results, 1932–33*

Reaching a judgement about the political appeal of anti-Semitism is extremely difficult. Millions of people voted for the NSDAP who had never done so before. It is likely that only a small minority of these new voters had anti-Semitism as a main motive, or were influenced by it in any way at all. A statistical analysis of Nazi propaganda posters and campaign speeches in 1931 and 1932 shows an overwhelming concentration on economic issues with very little emphasis on the anti-Semitic ideology of 'race and space'.

## The influence of anti-Semitism in Hitler's coming to power in 1933

There were many factors behind Hitler's dramatic rise to power. Hitler clearly benefited from economic circumstances; without the appalling

**Fig. 7** *'Vote List 1.' NSDAP election poster, 1932*

### Activity

**Thinking point**

Working in three groups, compose letters from people previously opposed to the Nazis, explaining why they are thinking of voting for the Nazi Party in future.

### Exploring the detail

**The legal revolution**

It is wrong to talk, as many people do, about the 'Nazi seizure of power'. Hitler was too afraid of the risks to launch a violent revolution. He came to power legally, in accordance with the Weimar constitution. (Göbbels called this 'using democracy in order to destroy democracy'.) President Hindenburg allowed himself to be persuaded to appoint Hitler as chancellor on 30 January 1933. In the months that followed, Hitler took a number of steps that legally gave him dictatorial powers.

impact of the world depression he would never have gained the mass support he did. Hitler also needed political help; without the weaknesses of the democratic parties and the willingness of Conservative politicians to collaborate with him he would never have become chancellor. It is important to remember that Hitler came to power in a legal revolution. He did not grab power by violent revolution. He was not voted into power by an electoral majority. He had to wait to be *given* power, legally, by President Hindenburg.

On the one hand, anti-Semitism obviously played a part, both in the long-term weaknesses of the Weimar political system and in the short-term surge of support for the Nazis between 1930 and 1933 – but it was far from being the most important cause. On the other hand, anti-Semitism had been promoted so relentlessly for so long by the Nazis that it was associated, indirectly, with many factors that were not obviously to do with the 'Jewish problem'. Anti-communism was linked to the Jews; so was disillusionment with the 'System' (Weimar democracy) and the economic worries of groups like the unemployed and struggling small farmers. Nazi anti-Semitism was so integrated and wide-ranging that it is difficult to know precisely how far and when voters were influenced by it.

When Hitler was appointed chancellor in January 1933, he was far away from being a dictator. In many ways he was in a vulnerable position, dependent upon a fragile alliance with Conservative politicians he did not like and who did not like him. Hitler knew he had to move very quickly to consolidate his power before events could turn against him, but he was determined to do this by legal means, at least on the surface. He held the SA on a tight leash, wanting to avoid uncontrolled violence. He immediately called new elections for the first week in March, hoping to exploit the propaganda opportunities and win a decisive working majority in the Reichstag.

This plan did not give Hitler what he really wanted. Even with the advantages provided by the Reichstag fire a week before the election, the NSDAP fell short of a majority. The Nazis won just under 44 per cent of the total vote and 288 seats. This was more than they had ever won before, but not enough to give Hitler a free hand. Hitler still had to tread very carefully in case the old Conservatives persuaded Hindenburg to throw him out of power. This meant that, for the time being at least, Nazi anti-Semitism still had to be toned down as much as possible in order for Hitler to present an image of respectability.

**Fig. 8** *Watching the Reichstag fire, 27 February 1933*

Hitler's desire for respectability was very evident on 'Potsdam Day', 21 March 1933. On this day, a solemn ceremony was held at the historic Garrison Church in Potsdam near Berlin. Potsdam Day was intended to celebrate the 'marriage of the old and the new Germany'. Its highlight was a handshake at the tomb of Emperor Frederick the Great, between Hitler, the new chancellor, and President Hindenburg, the symbol of past greatness. The occasion was a propaganda coup for the Nazis. It was notable that there was no sign of SA intimidation and no Nazi uniforms to be seen – Hitler, Göring and Göbbels turned up in formal morning dress with top hats, looking like in-laws at a wedding. Violence and anti-Semitism were invisible for the day.

Two days later, the Nazis showed a different face in the Reichstag when the Enabling Law was passed, giving Hitler temporary dictatorial powers. Inside the Reichstag chamber, Nazi deputies aimed a stream of abuse at the SPD and anyone else minded to vote against the Enabling Bill. Outside, a threatening mob of SA men shouted: 'Give us the Bill or else fire and murder!' Many Reichstag deputies were intimidated into staying at home. The Nazis followed a twin-track strategy in the consolidation of power – mixing respectability with menacing anti-Communist and anti-Jewish propaganda. There were many warnings of the persecution that was to come in the 1930s.

In March 1933, the first regular concentration camp was opened at Dachau, near Munich. On 1 April, the SA enforced a boycott of Jewish shops and businesses. On 10 May, the Nazi regime organised the Burning of the Books. Anti-Semitism and Nazi radicalism were held on a tight rein until the consolidation of power was safely completed, but already, in the first few months of Hitler's rule, there were more than enough indications of Nazi intimidation.

## A closer look

### The Burning of the Books

On 10 May 1933, in the cobbled square next to the opera house on Unter den Linden in Berlin, Josef Göbbels took the microphone to announce that 'the Age of **Jewish materialism** is ended!' Near to Göbbels a huge fire was set alight; organised gangs of SA men came forward to throw into the fire the books of authors deemed by the Nazi regime to be 'un-German'. At the same time, similar book-burnings were taking place in university towns all over Germany. Not all the books were by Jews – they included works by socialists, pacifists and modernists – but there was no doubt about the main target.

As the books flew into the flames, SA men read out 'incantations' to justify the destruction:

1 'Against class struggle and materialism; for the national community and an idealistic outlook.' Karl Marx; Karl Kautsky.

4 'Against the debasing exaggeration of man's animal nature; for the nobility of the human soul.' Sigmund Freud; the Freudian school.

**Fig. 9** *The Burning of the Books. Berlin, May 1933*

■ **Exploring the detail**

**The Reichstag Fire**

On the night of 27 February 1933, a week before the Reichstag election, the Reichstag building was sensationally destroyed by fire. The Nazis moved quickly to blame the fire on a Communist plot. President Hindenburg was pressured into passing emergency laws banning the Communist Party and giving extra powers to the police.

■ **Activity**

**Revision exercise**

Use the evidence in this chapter and in Chapter 2 to write an assessment of the impact of anti-Semitism on public opinion in Germany between 1928 and early 1933.

■ **Cross-reference**

The persecution that was to come in the 1930s, including the concentration camps and the Nazi boycott of Jewish shops and businesses, is described in Chapter 6, pages 75–80.

■ **Key terms**

**'Jewish materialism'**: the accusation that Jews lacked true spiritual values and were undermining German society through their influence over business and finance.

6 'Against alien journalism of a democratic-Jewish stamp; for responsible participation in national reconstruction.' Theodor Wolff; Georg Bernhard.

Not all, or even most, of these books were by Jewish authors; the targets included Communists, pacifists and social democrats. Yet the message was unmistakable. The Nazi regime had declared war on 'Jewish materialism' and everything 'un-German'.

Less than five years earlier, the Nazis had been no more than a violent nuisance on the fringes of German society. Now the capital of Germany was witnessing a public demonstration of Nazi ideology and how it would be put into action. Few people knew for certain what this meant. Many decent Germans, including many who had voted for Hitler in recent elections, were horrified by this cultural barbarism; they hoped it would be merely part of a temporary wave of 'excesses' before the new regime settled down. In reality, the Burning of the Books was indeed an awful warning of what was to come. In 1831, the great German-Jewish poet, Heinrich Heine, had written: 'Where they burn books, there, sooner or later, they burn people.' Heine was right – but many people could not bring themselves to believe this until it was much too late.

Very few observers anywhere in the world seem to have understood what the burning of the books and the expulsions of Jewish writers actually mean. As the smoke of our burned books rises into the sky, we German writers of Jewish descent must acknowledge above all that we have been defeated. Have German writers of Jewish extraction – in fact *any* German writers – ever felt at home in the German Reich? There is a sense that German writers, Jewish or not, have at all times been strangers in Germany, immigrants on home ground, full of longing for their real fatherland even when they were within its borders.

**2**

*J. Roth, 'Look Back in Anger' (September 1933). Article taken from **What I Saw: Reports From Berlin 1920–33**, 2003*

As the Nazi regime tightened its grip on Germany in the early months of 1933, even the most patriotic and assimilated Jews were bitterly disillusioned. The journalist Joseph Roth had lived and worked in Berlin from 1920 to 1933 – the articles he wrote in exile from Paris in the autumn of 1933 revealed the extent of this fear and disillusionment (Source 2).

*Learning outcomes*

Through reading this section you have gained an understanding of the nature of Hitler's anti-Semitic views, the influence of other theorists on Hitler's thinking and how Hitler's views were developed into a fixed ideology during the 1920s. You have examined the rise of right-wing political movements and the extent to which they challenged democracy in Germany. You have looked at some of the reasons why Hitler and the Nazis gained political support in the 1920s, and the extent to which economic conditions in Germany after 1929 enabled Hitler to make a breakthrough as a national politician by the time of the 1930 Reichstag elections.

 Examination-style questions

Study the following source material and answer the questions that follow.

After my chance meeting with something in a long caftan with black hair locks, I began to concern myself with the Jewish Question. Vienna appeared to me in a different light than before. Wherever I went in Vienna, I began to see Jews. The Inner City swarmed with a people who had no resemblance, even outwardly, to Germans. This was not very attractive but it became positively repulsive when, in addition to their physical uncleanliness, you discovered the moral stain on this 'chosen people'. Was there ever any form of filth, especially in cultural life, without at least one Jew involved in it? Gradually, I began to hate them.

**A**

*A. Hitler, **Mein Kampf**, 1925. Taken from B. Hamann, **Hitler's Vienna: A Dictator's Apprenticeship**, 1999*

Hitler's acquaintances in Vienna, such as Reinhold Hanisch, Dr Bloch, August Kubizek, his former fellow residents in the men's hostel, and his schoolmates in Linz were all astonished by Hitler's political career in Germany after 1919. Not one of them would have considered anything like it to be possible. They understood even less why the same person who had got along with Jews especially well was now all of a sudden supposed to be a leading anti-Semite. Hitler left Vienna in 1913 with a rag-bag of ideas that was preserved in his excellent memory. It was only in Germany that all these pieces fell into place to form a world view based on racial anti-Semitism.

B. Hamann, *Hitler's Vienna: A Dictator's Apprenticeship*, 1999

GERMAN FARMERS

Farmers, it's a matter of your house and home!

Factories, forests, railways, taxes and the state's finances have all been robbed by the Jew. Now he's stretching his greedy fingers towards the last German possession -the countryside. Jewish race-lust and fanaticism are the driving forces behind this devilish attempt to break Germany's backbone through the destruction of the German farming community.

Huge imports of frozen meat and frozen grain, at lowest prices, undercut you and push down your earnings. It won't be long before the greater part of the land-owning farmers will be driven from their farms and homes by Jewish money-lenders.

Help us build a new Germany that will be

NATIONALIST AND SOCIALIST

C

*Adapted from a Nazi leaflet distributed in 1929*

a)  Explain how far Source B differs from Source A in relation to the origins of Hitler's anti-Semitic ideas. Use Sources A and B and your own knowledge.

*(12 marks)*

Part a) The key to answering this question is to *explain* how far the sources differ. This usually means: 'up to a point but ...' – in other words an assessment of both differences and similarities. In this case the differences are pretty obvious, the similarities less so, but they are there if you look! Be sure to explain why the sources are different as sources, don't just describe what the words say. Remember that 'own knowledge' here does not mean extraneous factual material, but an understanding of the context.

b)  Use Sources A, B and C and your own knowledge. How important was anti-Semitism in attracting support for Nazism by 1929?

*(24 marks)*

Part b) The focus of this question is on the relative importance of anti-Semitism compared with other factors. Decide at the beginning *how* important it was – if your decision is 'very', then perhaps most of the evidence you use in the answer will be on anti-Semitism. However, if your view is 'not so much', then you would include a lot of evidence about other factors as well as anti-Semitism. Remember that using the sources is not optional. It's an order!

## 5 Legal discrimination and propaganda

*In this chapter you will learn about:*

- anti-Semitic legislation including the Civil Service Laws (1933) and the Nuremberg Laws (1935)

- the intensification of discrimination through the Decrees of April/November 1938

- the impact of Nazi propaganda through education and the media, especially the press and cinema.

**Fig. 1** *The Poisonous Mushroom* (Der Giftpilz)

This international unrest in the world unfortunately seems to have given rise to the view amongst the Jews within Germany that the time has come openly to oppose Jewish interests against those of the German nation. From numerous places vigourous complaints have been received of the provocative action of individuals belonging to this people.

The only way to deal with the problem which remains open is that of legislative action. The German Government is motivated by the hope that it may still be possible to create a level ground on which the German people may find a tolerable relationship with the Jewish people. Should this hope not be fulfilled and the Jewish agitation within Germany and abroad continues, then the problem must then be handed over by law to the National-Socialist Party for a final solution.

Behind all three laws there stands the National-Socialist Party and with it and supporting it stands the German nation.

| 1 | *Hitler's speech in the Reichstag on passing the Nuremberg Laws, September 1935. Taken from N. H. Baynes (ed),* **The Speeches of Adolf Hitler, I,** *1942* |

### Activity

**Source analysis**

Study Source 1 and look back to Chapter 4, in particular the section on the burning of the books on pages 57–8.

Using this evidence and the evidence elsewhere in Chapter 5, make a list of **five** factors that enabled the Nazi regime to implement its anti-Semitic policies in 1933–35.

Between 1933 and 1939 the Nazi regime began an intensive campaign of persecution and legal discrimination against Jews in Germany. To carry out Nazi policies towards the Jews, Hitler needed to steer a careful course, emphasing legality. In the years from 1933 to 1939, Hitler and the Nazi leadership set about a scheme of anti-Semitic legislation. At the same time, a relentless propaganda campaign was launched to 'educate' the German people about the need to purge Jewish influences from German society.

How far the Nazis went with their anti-Semitic legislation depended on the circumstances at different times. At first, Hitler was anxious to reassure mainstream political and public opinion in Germany and abroad. He kept the radical and violent elements in the Nazi movement mostly on a tight leash. As time went on between 1933 and 1939, the anti-Semitic legislation became more extreme. This was accompanied by relentless propaganda, attacking 'Jewishness' and promoting 'pure' German values. By late 1938, the ground had been prepared for much more intense anti-Jewish persecution than had been politically possible in 1933.

▪ **Cross-reference**

Nazi persecution and the 'revolution from below' are covered in more detail in Chapter 6.

## ▪ A closer look

### The political context of Nazism, 1933–39

The Nazi regime could not act just as it wished. Nazi ideological aims could only be implemented when it was politically possible. This political context of Nazism in the years 1933 to 1939 went through three distinct phases.

*Act one: The legal revolution, 1933–34*

Hitler was not a dictator when he came to power on 30 January 1933. He depended on political allies and he had to avoid frightening them into turning against him. Hitler could not completely prevent violence by the radicals in the SA, but he controlled it as much as he could. Hitler consolidated his power by legal means: the Enabling Act of March 1933; laws to muzzle the press and the trade unions; legally taking over as head of state after President Hindenburg died in 1934. Even Hitler's most violent action, the Blood Purge against the SA in 1934, was carried out to keep Nazi extremism under control.

▪ **Cross-reference**

For the Enabling Act of 1933 and the Blood Purge of 1934, look back to Chapter 4, pages 57 and 54 respectively.

*Act two: The new Germany, 1934–37*

By August 1934, the Nazi regime was secure, but Hitler still did not have a free hand. He worried about public opinion both at home and abroad. One example of this was the Olympic Games in Berlin in 1936. Before and during the Games, Nazi anti-Semitism was put under wraps while Nazi propaganda projected the image of Germany as a civilised society. Between 1934–37, Hitler avoided offending powerful groups like the army or the churches; he also knew that Germany was not yet ready for a war, whatever the propaganda said.

*Act three: Radicalisation, 1938–39*

By the end of 1937, the Nazi regime was far stronger than in 1933. The economy had recovered. The police system was completely controlled by the SS. Hitler felt Germany was militarily ready for war. In 1938 and 1939, therefore, the Nazis took bold steps they would not have dared to earlier. Hitler took control of the army, sacking its two most important commanders, Blomberg and Fritsch. He pushed through the *Anschluss*, union with Austria, and the annexation of the Sudetenland from Czechoslovakia. He also let loose radical persecution of his 'racial enemies' through the *Kristallnacht* pogrom of 1938, the Aryanisation of Jewish businesses and the start of the T4 euthanasia programme in 1939.

▪ **Cross-reference**

The *Kristallnacht* pogrom and the Aryanisation of Jewish businesses are discussed in Chapter 6, pages 78–81, and the T4 euthanasia programme in Chapter 7, pages 95–9.

## ■ Anti-Semitic legislation, 1933–38

### ■ Key chronology

**Anti-Semitic legislation, 1933–38**

| | | |
|---|---|---|
| **1933** | | |
| | April | Boycott of Jewish shops and businesses |
| | | Law for the Restoration of the Professional Civil Service |
| | | Law against Overcrowding of German Schools and Universities |
| | October | Exclusion of German Jews from the press |
| **1935** | | |
| | September | The Nuremberg Laws |
| | November | Supplementary Decree on the Reich Citizenship Law |
| **1938** | | |
| | April | Registration of Jewish assets over 5,000 marks |
| | October | Jewish passports stamped with a large 'J' |
| | November | Jews forbidden to visit theatres etc. |
| | | Expulsion of all Jewish pupils from schools |
| | December | Compulsory sale of all Jewish businesses |

Nazi ideology promoted the myth of a worldwide Jewish conspiracy that would undermine the rebirth of German values. It was the mission of National Socialism to smash 'Jewish-Bolshevism' and prevent the destruction of Germany. The Nazis also wanted to prevent inter-marriage between Jews and Aryans in order to protect the 'purity of German blood'. These beliefs provided the thrust behind anti-Semitic legislation after 1933.

The economic conditions in Germany in 1933 were terrible. There was mass unemployment, small farmers were struggling and large numbers of businesses were going bankrupt. Nazi propaganda exploited these hardships to convince many people that the economic crisis should be blamed on Jewish domination of banking and finance. Many Germans were receptive to this message. In rural areas, many small farmers believed the Nazi claims that Jewish bankers were to blame for the loss of their farms. The Nazis also played on the widespread belief that there was a disproportionately high number of Jews in the professions and in the civil service.

### Cross-reference

Links between economic depression and anti-Semitism are explored in Chapter 4, pages 52–3.

### ■ Exploring the detail

#### Jews and emigration

Jews in Germany decided against emigration for different reasons. Many believed the Nazis were just playing to the mob and the wave of anti-Semitism would calm down. Others simply felt unable to leave even if they had wanted to – because of age or family ties, or because they did not want to lose the business they owned, or they lacked the money or the skills they would have needed to move to another country. Many Jews were also unwilling to leave for cultural reasons, because they felt they belonged in Germany and only spoke German.

### The Civil Service Laws, 1933

In April 1933, the Nazi regime introduced the Law for the Restoration of the Professional Civil Service, requiring Jews to be dismissed from the civil service. This was not as straightforward as the Nazis hoped. There was no objective, scientific definition of who was racially Jewish, according to physical characteristics or blood group. Under the 1933 law, people were considered 'non-Aryan' if either of their parents or either of their grandparents were Jewish. Another difficulty was that President Hindenburg insisted on exemptions for German Jews who had served in the First World War and for those whose fathers had been killed in the war. Hitler reluctantly accepted this as a political necessity; the exemption was kept in place until after Hindenburg's death. The amendment lessened the impact of the law because it applied to up to two-thirds of Jews in the civil service.

The Civil Service Law had a devastating economic and psychological impact on middle-class Jews in Germany; it contributed to the increasing levels of Jewish emigration – 37,000 Jews left Germany in 1933. Most Jews, however, stayed behind. At that time, they could not know how much worse the persecution would become.

## *Further anti-Semitic legislation in 1933*

Similar laws were passed after the Law for the Restoration of the Professional Civil Service, aimed at excluding Jews from the professions. These measures were not as effective as the Nazis would have hoped, partly because there were exemptions for those who had fought in the First World War and partly because Jews in medicine, the law and education were numerous and well established, so it was not feasible to remove them all at once.

Jewish lawyers made up about 16 per cent of Germany's legal profession, often working in family firms. Of the non-Aryan lawyers practising in 1933, 60 per cent were able to continue working in spite of the new regulations. In the years that followed, the regime introduced stricter regulations to try to close these 'loopholes'. The exclusion of lawyers was a gradual process over several years.

More than 10 per cent of German doctors were Jews. They were attacked by Nazi propaganda as 'a danger to German society'. Nazi officials at local government level and in private associations initiated their own anti-Semitic measures. Some local authorities started removing Jewish doctors from their posts. Anti-Semitic propaganda against Jewish doctors treating Aryans was laced with lurid stories about inappropriate and malicious actions supposedly carried out by Jewish doctors. The Nazi regime was pushed along by these local initiatives. The regime announced a ban on Jewish doctors in April 1933. In theory, Jewish doctors could now treat only Jewish patients, but many Jewish doctors carried on their normal practice for several years after 1933.

Also in April 1933, the Law against Overcrowding of German Schools and Universities restricted the number of Jewish children who could attend state schools and universities. It was promoted on the basis that Aryan students would receive more resources and attention, instead of wasting time and money on pupils who would 'grow up to be enemies of Germany'. Nazi propaganda stressed the danger that a well-educated Jew would be a greater threat to Germany than an uneducated one. German children were being told that their former friends and classmates were unworthy of being in the same schools as them and were a burden and threat to Germany.

### Cross-reference

For the relative success and prosperity of the Jews in the 1920s, and the jealousy it could arouse, look back to Chapter 1.

**Fig. 2** *Children at a Jewish school, 1934*

> When Hitler came to power things changed. We had teachers at school who were very pro-Nazi – they went to the Nuremberg Rally each year – and I was the only Jewish girl in this high school. One particular teacher made my life a misery; she told the girls not to talk to me, and the girls with whom I used to go to school in the mornings and met afterwards suddenly ignored me because of their fear of this one teacher. She arranged that I would sit right at the back of the class; two rows were left vacant and I sat against the wall. Then there came a law – more or less at the same time as the Nuremberg Laws came out – that all the Jewish children would be expelled from German schools and universities.

**2**      *The recollections of Ruth Foster, a Jewish girl at a school in the town of Lingen in Lower Saxony. Quoted in L. Smith, **Forgotten Voices of the Holocaust**, 2005*

Not all Jewish children were forced out of state schools at this point – the process was not completed until 1938. Jewish children could also still attend private education and Jewish schools (which were one of the few places Jewish teachers could find work). These schools had many problems in gaining funding and in maintaining academic standards, but Jewish children were not yet completely denied an education. The key aim of the Nazis, of course, was the segregation of Jewish children from Aryan children.

In the universities, many Jewish professors came under pressure from students and local government officials. Many lost their jobs. German academics willingly seized the opportunity to replace them.

> Of an estimated eight hundred Jewish academics in Germany – including men and women of major international reputation – two hundred left the country in 1933 alone. Twenty of these people were Nobel laureates; the eleven physicists included Albert Einstein. Since any artistic activity depended upon membership of the new Chambers of Culture, which was withheld from 'non-Aryans', this haemorrhaging of talent was soon evident in cinema, journalism, literature, music, painting and theatre.

**3**                         *Taken from M. Burleigh, **The Third Reich: A New History**, 2001*

In October 1933, the Reich Press Law enabled the regime to apply strict censorship and to close down publications they disliked. Jews had had a prominent role in journalism and publishing in Weimar Germany and the Press Law effectively silenced the large number of Jewish journalists and editors, many of whom were forced to leave the country. The closing down of the free press was not only a matter of laws and regulations; there were also many instances of violence and intimidation.

Many Germans were in favour of these laws. Even the main Church leaders did not voice objections. A combination of underlying anti-Semitism, effective propaganda, fear, jealousy and self-interest meant that anti-Semitic policies met with little opposition. The Nazis also wanted to demonstrate their concern for marginalised and unemployed Germans. There was a great deal of enthusiasm for the new legislation at grass-roots level in the Nazi movement.

■ **Cross-reference**

The manipulation of culture and the arts by Nazi propaganda in the 1930s is covered later in this chapter, pages 70–2.

## The Nuremberg Laws, 1935

**Fig. 3** *Front page of* Völkischer Beobachter, *16 September 1935, with publication of Nuremberg Laws*

In 1935, the Nazi regime extended the anti-Semitic legislation through the Nuremberg Laws, so called because they were announced at the annual party rally at Nuremberg. By 1935, many fanatical anti-Semites in the Nazi movement were restive because they believed Nazi persecution of the Jews had not gone far enough. They urged Hitler to move further and faster. These radicals became the driving force behind the demands for anti-Jewish legislation. At the Nuremberg Party Rally in 1935, Hitler announced that the Communist International had declared war on Fascism and that it was time to 'deal once and for all with Jewish-Bolshevism'.

It is a matter of debate whether the Nuremberg Laws were the logical next stage in a carefully made plan to deal with the 'Jewish question' or a short-term concession by the leadership to prevent grass-roots violence from boiling over. By 1935, many ordinary Germans were becoming uneasy about the increasing levels of violence and disorder.

The Nuremberg Laws can be seen as a tactic to replace random violence with controlled legal discrimination. Taking action on issues such as inter-marriage and Jewish citizenship might have seemed an ideal solution to please the radicals, but also to keep them under control.

It is equally possible that the Nuremberg Laws were a deliberate next step in Hitler's planned campaign to remove Jewish influence from German life and move towards creating his 'master race' through the 'purification' of German blood. Ideologically, the Nuremberg Laws were fully consistent with Hitler's long-held anti-Semitic ideas; in many of his earlier speeches, Hitler had certainly expressed the desire to remove citizenship from the Jews and to ban inter-marriage.

On 15 September, the Nuremberg Laws were introduced: the Reich Citizenship Law and the Law for the Protection of German Blood and Honour.

■ The Reich Citizenship Law meant that someone could be a German citizen only if they had purely German blood. Jews and other non-Aryans were now classified as subjects and had fewer rights than citizens.

■ The Law for the Protection of German Blood and Honour outlawed marriages between Aryans and non-Aryans. It was made illegal for German citizens to marry Jews. It was also illegal for Jews to have any sexual relations with a German citizen.

The laws made the enforcing of anti-Semitism the major concern of civil servants, judges and the **Gestapo**.

> Entirely convinced that the purity of German blood is essential to the further existence of the German people, and inspired by the uncompromising determination to safeguard the future of the German nation, the Reichstag has unanimously resolved upon the following law:
>
> Section 1
> Marriages between Jews and citizens of German or kindred blood are forbidden.
>
> Section 2
> Extramarital sexual intercourse between Jews and subjects of the state of Germany or related blood is forbidden.
>
> Section 3
> Jews will not be permitted to employ female citizens of German blood under the age of 45 as domestic workers.
>
> Section 4
> Jews are forbidden to display the Reich and national flag or the national colours.

**4**      *'The Law For the Protection of German Blood and Honour'. Taken from J. Noakes and G. Pridham, **Documentary Reader: Nazism 1919–45, Volume 2, State, Economy and Society 1933–1939**, 1984*

The law was later extended to cover almost any physical contact between Jews and Aryans. The mere fact of an allegation was enough to secure a conviction. Aryan women were pressured to leave their Jewish husbands, on the grounds that men who lost their jobs through anti-Semitic legislation would be a burden on their partners. Although some relationships continued, there was a high risk of being denounced to the Gestapo. Punishments were harsh and Jewish men convicted under

### Exploring the detail
**The Nuremberg Laws**

It has been claimed that the Nuremberg Laws were a short-term, improvised measure in the fact that Hitler needed something 'big' to announce at the 1935 Nuremberg Rally. He had intended to announce an impressive foreign policy success, but could not do so. This is why Hitler had to rush out new laws against the Jews as an attention-grabbing substitute. This claim is supported by the fact that the printers were still busy producing copies of the laws even after Hitler had begun his speech.

### Key terms

**Gestapo:** the *Geheimstaatspolizei* (Secret State Police). Formed in 1933, the Gestapo was originally controlled by Hermann Göring. In 1934, it was taken over by Heinrich Himmler and the SS.

### Activity
**Revision exercise**

Make a list of the reasons why some sections of the German people would have supported the anti-Semitic laws brought in by the Nazis in between 1933 and 1935. Rank the reasons in order of importance.

*Mischlinge:* a person of 'mixed race', who faced lesser discrimination than 'full Jews'. *Mischlinge* were defined as either 'half breeds of the 1st degree' (two Jewish grandparents), or 'half breeds of the 2nd degree' (one Jewish grandparent).

the terms of the Law for the Protection of German Blood and Honour were often re-arrested by the Gestapo after being released and sent to concentration camps.

In November 1935, the First Supplementary Decree on the Reich Citizenship Law defined what constituted a 'full Jew' – someone who had three Jewish grandparents, or who had two Jewish grandparents and was married to a Jew. 'Half Jews' were labelled **Mischlinge**. The law was difficult to interpret as the definition of a Jew was based on the number of Jewish grandparents. In many cases, Jews or their Jewish parents had converted to Christianity. This confused situation meant that legal classifications were often arbitrary and inconsistent.

The position of Jews without the rights of citizenship left them with obligations to the state, but with no political rights and powerless against the Nazi bureaucracy. Possessing documentary proof of a person's ancestry became a high priority for many people. Many non-practising Jews attempted to prove their Aryan ancestry; some acquired falsified documents on the black market. There was further discrimination by local authorities and private companies who would not employ Jews, although *Mischlinge* were able to continue relatively 'normal' lives and could even serve in the lower ranks of the military.

The race laws deepened the influence of anti-Semitism in society. The Nazi radicals were delighted. Many otherwise moderate Germans did not see the measures as being too extreme. On the one hand, some claimed that discrimination in public areas through signs such as 'Jews not wanted here' was little different from segregation in the southern states of the USA. On the other hand, many Germans were troubled by the anti-Semitic legislation. Evidence from both Gestapo records and the reports written from inside Germany to the SPD (the socialist party in exile) suggests that German public opinion was not fully in support of the Nuremberg Laws. There was no public outcry, but this probably owed more to passivity, fear and propaganda than any great enthusiasm for the laws.

Hitler knew that restraint was still a political necessity. He explained the situation to a meeting of party leaders (Source 5).

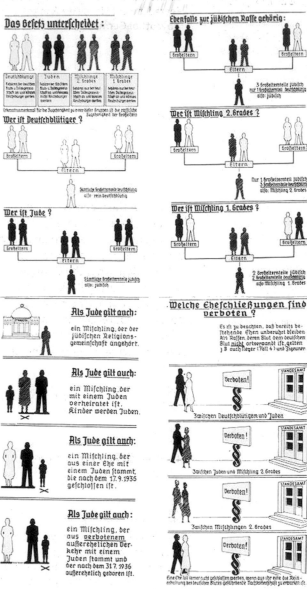

**Fig. 4** *'Scientific' chart showing Nazi classification of racial characteristics*

■ Activity

**Source analysis**

Read Source 5 on page 67.

1. In his speech to party leaders, what is Hitler trying to stop?

2. According to the source, why were the Nuremberg Laws needed?

At this meeting the Führer emphasised the importance of the new Laws by pointing out that National-Socialist legislation offered the only possibility of achieving a tolerable relationship with the Jews living in Germany. The Führer emphasised especially that, in accordance with these Laws, Jews in Germany were offered opportunities of living their own national (*völkisch*) life in all areas, as they had never been able to do in any other country. With a view to this the Führer reiterated his order to the Party to avoid all individual actions against Jews.

> **5** *Account of Hitler's speech to Nazi leaders about the Nuremberg Laws. Taken from M. Domarus (ed), **Reden und Proklamationen 1932–1945** (Speeches and Proclamations 1932–1945), 1962*

In 1936, anti-Jewish discrimination was actually reduced as preparations for the Olympic Games in Berlin were stepped up. The Nazi regime was able to put on an impressive show for the world, with the dark shadow of anti-Semitic violence hidden, for the time being, from public view. After this lull, discrimination intensified.

## A closer look

### The Nazi regime and the 'gypsy question'

Jews were not the only victims of the intensification of Nazi race policies after 1935. There was also growing persecution of Germany's 30,000 gypsies (Roma people), known in Germany as *Zigeuner*. Gypsies had been subjected to legal discrimination well before 1933. Local authorities frequently harassed them into moving away. The Nazis made the persecution much more systematic.

In 1935, Nazi legal experts ruled that the Nuremberg Laws applied to gypsies, even though they were not specifically mentioned in the laws. In 1936, the SS set up a new Reich Central Office for the Fight Against the Gypsy Nuisance. A university psychologist, Dr Robert Ritter, became the expert 'scientific adviser' to the SS and the Ministry of Health. Using Ritter's criteria, the SS began the process of locating and classifying gypsies; the centralised files they collected were essential to facilitate police action against them. In December 1938, Himmler issued a directive on the Fight Against the Gypsy Nuisance, ordering the registration of all gypsies.

Himmler's directive revealed the ideological nature of the drive against 'racial degenerates' (Source 6).

## Anti-Semitic decrees, April–November 1938

By 1938, Hitler no longer depended on compromises with traditional Conservatives. Dr Hjalmar Schacht, the minister of economics, was forced out in November 1937. In February 1938, Hitler purged the army high command and made himself head of Germany's armed forces. In March 1938, the *Anschluss* with Austria took place without any intervention by the western powers. In September, the Munich Conference handed the Sudetenland region of Czechoslovakia over to Germany. The population of the Third Reich swelled by 11 million. This also increased the Jewish population of the Reich and prompted demands from Nazi radicals for further action to deal with the 'Jewish question'.

### Exploring the detail

**Disapproval of the Nuremberg Laws**

In his 2005 book *The Third Reich in Power*, Richard Evans states that four-fifths of the population in the Palatinate region in south-west Germany disapproved of the Nuremberg Laws. Evans states that the working classes rejected Nazi anti-Semitism and the middle classes feared it would lead to a foreign boycott of German goods.

The aim of the measures taken by the State to defend the homogeneity of the German nation must be the physical separation of Gypsydom from the German people and the regulation of the Gypsy way of life. The necessary legal foundation can only be created through a Gypsy Law which prevents further intermingling of blood.

> **6**  *Directive by Himmler*

### Cross-reference

Dr Hjalmar Schacht is profiled in Chapter 1, pages 12–13.

### Did you know?

At the end of 1937, there were approximately 350,000 Jews in Germany – a drop of about 150,000 since 1933 as a result of Jewish emigration. After the Anschluss, 190,000 Austrian Jews came under Nazi rule, followed by 28,000 Jews in the Sudetenland in September 1938. This meant that after the territorial expansion of 1938, there were more Jews under Nazi rule than when Hitler came to power in 1933.

In April 1938, the Decree of Registration of Jewish Property provided for the confiscation of all Jewish-owned property worth more than 5,000 marks. This was the starting point for the **Aryanisation** of Jewish property and businesses. In April 1938, there were roughly 40,000 Jewish-owned businesses in Germany; a year later only around 8,000 had avoided being closed down or 'Aryanised'.

Further legislation banned Jews from work as travelling salesmen, security guards, travel agents and estate agents – 30,000 Jewish travelling salesmen lost their jobs. In 1938, Jews also lost their entitlement to public welfare. The increasing number of unemployed and poor Jews depended completely on the charities set up by the Jewish community, such as the Central Institution for Jewish Economic Aid.

From October 1938, the passports of German Jews had to be stamped with a large 'J'. The drive to make Jews easily identifiable and, at the

**Fig. 5** *Jewish passport stamped with 'J'*

same time, strip them of their individuality led to a new law in 1939 compelling all Jewish men to adopt the additional first name of 'Israel'; all Jewish women took the additional first name 'Sarah'. At this stage, Hitler turned down the suggestion of making all Jews wear a yellow star in public – this did not come into practice within the Reich until 1941.

On the night of 9/10 November, during *Kristallnacht* (the Night of Broken Glass), the Nazi regime authorised a vicious wave of violence against Jewish people and property. In the aftermath of the pogrom, the Nazi regime seized the opportunity to push forward with more anti-Semitic legislation. Göring, however, was very unhappy about the events of Kristallnacht. The destruction of businesses and property was a massive blow to his **Four Year Plan**, which was devised to prepare Germany for war. He demanded a greater say in Jewish policy and that it was carried out to benefit the economy, not damage it.

The most important measure was the Decree Excluding Jews from German Economic Life, but the regime took the opportunity to tighten up in other areas, too. Jews were forbidden to visit theatres, cinemas, concerts and other cultural events. There was further pressure to expel Jewish pupils from schools. In spite of the Law against Overcrowding of German Schools and Universities of April 1933, some Jewish parents had managed to keep their children in state schools. After November 1938, this was, however, no longer possible.

By the end of 1938, Nazi anti-Semitic legislation since 1933 had now almost completely isolated the Jewish population. Many had emigrated. Those who stayed were not only subject to ever-harsher legislation; they also faced the full force of anti-Semitic violence and propaganda.

## Nazi propaganda

Propaganda was the key to spreading Nazi anti-Semitic beliefs. It played a key role in dehumanising and demonising Jews. The German people were subjected to a constant barrage of negative images and stereotypes of Jews: in children's books; feature films; radio programmes; mass rallies; and the written press. Much of this was produced under the direction of Dr Josef Göbbels who was the Minister for Public Enlightenment and Propaganda. The Nazis were not the first to use anti-Semitic propaganda, but they were able to exploit the possibilities of powerful new techniques of mass communication.

### Education and conformity

The Nazi regime placed enormous emphasis on the indoctrination of youth. The Nazis concentrated a great deal on the young as they saw them as the future generation that could be moulded into committed Nazis; and believed that by indoctrinating youth, Nazi ideology would live on into the future. The constant repetition of the anti-Semitic messages was, therefore, central to the education and training of Germany's youth.

The coordination of education was a lengthy process. The Nazi regime was reluctant to antagonise parents, especially in Church schools. Local activists, however, interfered with the selection of textbooks and the purging of libraries. Anti-Semitic propaganda permeated school textbooks and children's stories. There was particular pressure on subjects such as biology and history. Propaganda encouraged pupils to disobey or denounce 'unreliable' teachers. Pro-Nazi teachers slanted their lessons towards the historic 'crimes' and 'inferiority' of Jews; this was sometimes accompanied by the deliberate isolation and humiliation of Jewish pupils.

There were similar trends in the universities. 'Jewish science' was denounced and pro-Nazi student groups organised heckling of 'un-German' professors. The Burning of the Books on 10 May 1933 was an example of the pressure Nazi propaganda placed on intellectuals to conform. A large number of academics chose to emigrate and many others adopted a low profile. The effects on the quality of university education were very harmful.

To achieve their aims of instilling ideology and race consciousness, it was not enough to take over the schools; the regime also wanted to mould the future generation by total immersion through uniformed youth groups. This led to a drive to coordinate all youth groups into the Hitler Youth, though it took several years to undermine church youth organisations.

Boys were absorbed into the Hitler Youth (*Hitlerjugend* or HJ) – girls were pressured to join the League of German Maidens (*Bund deutscher Mädel*, or BdM). Along with other Nazi ideological

### Exploring the detail

**The Decree Excluding Jews from German Economic Life**

The Decree Excluding Jews from German Economic Life of 12 November 1938 ordered the compulsory closure and sale of all Jewish businesses. The decree also ordered a final end to the part the remaining Jews played in professions such as law and medicine. The policy was popular with those German people who were able to profit from the seizure of Jewish assets. Some of the biggest winners were big industrial enterprises such as IG-Farben, Flick and Krupp. A lot of the confiscated assets went straight into funding Göring's Four Year Plan.

### Cross-reference

For more on emigration, look ahead to Chapter 6, pages 83–6.

### Cross-reference

Dr Josef Göbbels is profiled in Chapter 2, page 34.

### Cross-reference

To recap on the Burning of the Books, look back to Chapter 4, pages 57–8.

**Fig. 6** *Hitler Youth gathering in a German town, c.1935*

## Exploring the detail

The Nazi indoctrination of youth often led to clashes between the generations. In *Through Hell For Hitler* (1990), Henry Metelmann recalled his life in Hamburg in the 1930s, when the author was an enthusiastic member of the Hitler Youth, despite the strong disapproval of his socialist father. A Nazi-backed feature film of 1933, *Hitler Youth Quex*, presented a young boy in the Hitler Youth as a hero because he denounced his Communist father to the police.

**Fig. 7** *Children's book illustration promoting interest in* Der Stürmer

## Cross-reference

The social and cultural achievements of the Jews are discussed in Chapter 1, pages 13–19.

## Cross-reference

Alfred Rosenberg and Julius Streicher are profiled in Chapter 3, pages 42 and 47 respectively.

themes like Nationalism, anti-Communism and the god-like status of the Führer, youth organisations were fed a diet of anti-Semitic slogans. Members were taught how to identify Jews and were encouraged to verbally abuse and physically assault Jews and those who were 'too friendly' towards Jews.

Many youngsters disliked the regimentation of the uniformed youth groups, but it was not easy to stay out. Being given good grades at school, or getting an apprenticeship or a job, often depended on being in the Hitler Youth. Many anti-Nazi parents encouraged their children to join, simply to avoid trouble. In many families, propaganda was effective in brainwashing the young generation. Hitler Youth marches were part of the intimidation of potential opponents. The propaganda posters of idealised Aryan boys and girls reinforced the racial ideology.

### Media and culture

The mobilisation of mass culture was a key goal of Nazi propaganda. Culture was very important to Hitler, who thought of himself as an artist and who genuinely believed there was a powerful Jewish conspiracy controlling the arts and media. The 'rebirth' of traditional German values through purging culture of 'Jewish decadence' was a key ideological aim. Removing Jews from the media and the arts also fitted with Hitler's belief in the superiority of German art and culture.

In 1933, the regime set up the Reich Chamber of Culture (RKK), under Josef Göbbels, to coordinate the cultural life of Germany in areas such as cinema, literature and the theatre, the fine arts and music. Without having official approval through membership of one of the Reich Chambers, it was almost impossible to continue working. Göbbels used the RKK to mobilise media and culture, especially press, film and radio, as instruments of the propaganda machine. The coordination of culture and the arts was a key method of spreading anti-Semitism, both by purging 'Jewish decadence' and by promoting positive images of German values.

Many Jews found themselves under pressure from legal discrimination and hostile propaganda. Membership of the associations within the new RKK was not open to Jews. Thousands lost their posts and were forced into exile, such as the composer Arnold Schoenberg and the actress Elizabeth Bergner. Many ordinary Germans were receptive to the idea that Jews were over represented in these areas. There was relatively little protest against the cultural purge; there were also plenty of opportunists looking to gain from it.

Göbbels was charged with coordinating the indoctrination of German society, but he was never able to control all the different parts of the propaganda machine. The cinema industry, for example, was too big for Göbbels to dominate it completely; only a small proportion of films produced in the 1930s were propaganda films. Some aspects of Nazi propaganda were less successful than others. Göbbels, for example, was often furiously critical of the official Nazi newspaper, the *Völkischer Beobachter*, which was edited by his rival Alfred Rosenberg and was derided by Göbbels for being boring. Other forms of propaganda were openly and aggressively racist, such as *Der Stürmer*, the notorious paper edited by Julius Streicher. The method most favoured by Göbbels himself was to convey the propaganda messages indirectly, through culture and mass entertainment.

## The press

Starting with the 1933 Reich Press Law, Göbbels ensured that the content of newspapers was closely censored. Editors were briefed daily and were held responsible for any content in their papers that was unflattering towards the Nazis or contrary to their ideology. There was also extensive self-censorship. Many newspaper editors, both inside the Reich and abroad, tried to stay on the right side of the regime in order to keep their access to information, or to avoid harassment. Göbbels and his Number Two, Otto Dietrich, invested a huge amount of time and effort in influencing foreign journalists and providing them with material.

There were several official Nazi newspapers. The oldest and best-known, the *Völkischer Beobachter*, was controlled (and paid for) by Alfred Rosenberg from the early days of Nazism; after 1933, it gained massive government support and, in theory, had a large circulation. In reality, most Germans paid little attention to the paper, which they regarded as being so one-sided as to have little credibility. Göbbels prided himself that his own newspaper, *Der Angriff* (*The Attack*) was far superior, but most of its readers were already convinced Nazis. Julius Streicher's *Der Stürmer* was so violent and obscene that it turned off even many of those who already *were* convinced Nazis.

**Fig. 8** *Anti-Semitic cartoon from* Der Stürmer, *1934*

## A closer look

### Der Stürmer

The racist and often pornographic journal *Der Stürmer* was not an official Nazi publication, but the personal project of Julius Streicher, the 'Jew-baiter of Nuremberg', who founded it in the 1920s. Sales of *Der Stürmer* increased steeply in 1935, coinciding with the Nuremberg Laws. A contract with the National Labour Front ensured that copies were displayed in every workplace in Germany. Profits from the paper made Streicher extremely rich – and Hitler remained personally loyal to him, even though many Nazi leaders, including Göbbels, regarded Streicher as an embarrassment.

*Der Stürmer* was difficult to ignore, even though most people knew that its contents were exaggerated or false. The impact of such repetitive, hate-filled propaganda helped the process of dehumanising Jews. It intimidated even the people who despised it. Even those who were repelled by the nastiness of Streicher's propaganda could be indoctrinated. One idealistic Nazi youth leader, Melita Maschmann, described in her memoirs after the war how she and her friends found the content of *Der Stürmer* vulgar and unbelievable – but she remained a loyal supporter of Nazi race policies, convinced that 'the Jews are the enemies of the new Germany'.

The reactions of many other Germans were similar to Melita Maschmann's. They regarded the contents of *Der Stürmer* as unpleasant and uncivilised, but they shared many of the prejudices that were displayed there. There were, of course, many anti-Nazis who totally rejected *Der Stürmer* as proof that the Nazis were barbarians. *Der Stürmer* was not important in winning converts to

Nazism, but it revealed the intensity of the anti-Jewish hatred in Nazi ideology and it formed part of what has been called the 'stress' people were subjected to by Nazi propaganda.

## Radio

The Nazis were quick to see the propaganda potential of the new medium of radio. The cheap, mass-produced 'People's radio' sets produced in Germany had a deliberately limited range of reception. This meant that people were rarely able to tune in to foreign radio stations and allowed the Nazis to control the news and ideological messages that the German people heard. Radio was also an ideal means of bringing Hitler's speeches directly to a mass audience – by 1939, roughly 70 per cent of all German homes had a radio set.

Radio, like cinema, was an exciting new form of popular mass entertainment. Many Germans were receptive to the direct and indirect propaganda messages that were contained in the news, plays, comedy shows and, above all, music. There were regular broadcasts of classical music and live orchestral concerts. This promoted the idea of pure German culture – Jewish composers and performers, of course, were not heard. State censorship of the radio meant that the 'right' kind of safe and undemanding popular music dominated the airwaves – jazz, modernism and other kinds of non-Aryan music were ignored.

This attempt at cultural censorship was not entirely successful. There was a thriving 'black market' in gramophone records of jazz and swing music. On the one hand, many educated Germans were turned off by the Nazification of German culture. On the other hand, culture provided a 'distinguished camouflage' for the true nature of the Nazi regime and many people swallowed the subtle propaganda stereotypes contained in mass entertainment without really noticing the process of indoctrination. This was even more true of German cinema.

## Cinema

It is important to note that a media revolution was taking place at the time the Nazis came to power. Talking films were still an exciting new development in the early 1930s. Cinema presented the Nazi regime with a powerful tool for propaganda, through newsreels, documentaries and feature films for mass entertainment. Direct and obvious anti-Semitic propaganda was the style preferred by Hitler. Göbbels was more in favour of films that were entertaining and conveyed the propaganda message more subtly.

Göbbels was almost certainly right about the ineffectiveness of blatant propaganda. Only a small number of official propaganda feature films were released in the 1930s and none of them achieved much popularity. The deepest impact was made by films audiences enjoyed for their entertainment value, either as exciting drama, romance or feelgood comedy. The racist message was often most effective when it was not explicit. The blonde, beautiful and very popular actress Kristina Soderbaum represented the perfect Aryan racial image even when the film she appeared in, such as the historical epic *The Great King*, had no overt propaganda message. Such historical epics also encouraged audiences to associate the heroes and values of Germany's past with Hitler and Nazism.

Most Germans saw hundreds of newsreels and heard the same propaganda messages over and over again. Many were enthusiastic and convinced, but many others concentrated on the entertainment and rejected or ignored the ideological indoctrination, especially when it was obvious and heavy-handed. For a significant minority of people, the cinema was a place of escape, where they could sit safely in the dark and forget the world outside.

### ■ Cross-reference

The boycott of Jewish businesses in 1933 is covered in Chapter 6, pages 77–8.

**Fig. 9** Der Ewige Jude. *Poster for the Eternal Jew exhibition, 1937*

### ■ Cross-reference

The impact of Nazi propaganda films in artime is covered in Chapter 6, page 83.

Judging the success of propaganda is difficult, as it is almost impossible to know what the majority of Germans were really thinking at the time. Although much Nazi propaganda was skilful and effective, there was a huge amount of it that was crude, boring and counter-productive. Many people simply switched off. However, the anti-Semitic propaganda was transmitted in so many different forms, backed by censorship, terror and the law, that it had a significant impact. The constant negative stereotypes got into the subconsciousness of people. It may be that the most powerful effect of racist propaganda was to intimidate people into silence and acquiescence, rather than full-hearted conversion to Nazi doctrine.

The legislation and the propaganda of the Nazi regime often reinforced established beliefs rather than changing people's minds. The established Churches in Germany, for example, contained many leading figures and followers who held anti-Semitic beliefs. Many members of the Protestant churches were receptive to anti-Semitism. The Catholic Church leadership was willing to make a Concordat with Hitler in 1933 and many, though not all, Catholic bishops turned a blind eye to Nazi anti-Semitism.

In the late 1930s, as the Nazis became more certain of their hold over Germany, the intensity of anti-Semitic propaganda increased. The approach of war made it necessary to convince the people of Germany they were under threat from 'Jewish-Bolshevism'. This culminated in Hitler's sinister and prophetic speech to a roaring crowd of Nazi deputies in the Reichstag in January 1939 (Source 7).

> In the course of my life I have very often been a prophet, and have usually been ridiculed for it. During the time of my struggle for power, it was in the first instance the Jewish race that received my prophecies with laughter.
>
> I think that for some time now they have been laughing on the other side of their face. Today I will once more be a prophet. If the international Jewish financiers, inside and outside Europe, succeed in plunging the nations once more into a world war, then the result will not be the Bolshevisation of the earth, and thus the victory of Jewry, but the annihilation of the Jewish race in Europe!

**7** *Speech by Hitler to the Reichstag, January 1939. Taken from N. H. Baynes (ed), The Speeches of Adolf Hitler, I, 1942*

By the time Hitler made this speech in 1939, public opinion in Germany had been conditioned by years of legal discrimination and by anti-Semitic propaganda that saturated the audience with the endless variations on the same key ideological themes. Only a few years before, Germany had been seen as a comparatively good place for Jews to live. By the end of 1938, this situation had been utterly transformed. The organised violence of *Kristallnacht* marked a watershed in Nazi race policies. The restraints and compromises of the early years were thrown off and the way was opened for an intensification of Aryanisation, violence and terror.

## Summary question

How successful was Nazi anti-Semitism in the years 1933 to 1939 in winning the support of the German people?

**Cross-reference**

The impact of anti-Semitic propaganda films in the early years of the war is covered in Chapter 8, pages 110–11.

**Activity**

**Revision exercise**

Working in two groups, assemble a range of evidence to support the contention that Nazi propaganda:

- was highly effective in ensuring conformity
- was regarded by most Germans as boring and off-putting.

**Activity**

**Thinking point**

Study Figures 1, 8 and 9.

1 What do Figures 1 and 8 illustrate about the aims of Nazi anti-Semitic propaganda? Why do you think the propaganda was targeted like this?

2 How were the Nazis hoping the German people would react to Figure 8?

3 Describe the portrayal of Jews in Figures 1, 8 and 9. Explain why these portrayals might have been effective in spreading anti-Semitism.

4 Why might German people have reacted against the Nazi propaganda such as that portrayed in these pictures?

**Exploring the detail**

**The Catholics of Beuron**

In April 1938, the Catholic community at the monastery of Beuron voted in the referendum to approve Hitler's *Anschluss* with Austria. 432 voted 'yes'; 9 voted 'no'. The next day, the Abbott of Beuron called everyone together to express his disappointment and amazement that as many as nine people could have voted against the Führer.

# 6    Terror, Aryanisation and emigration

**Fig. 1** *SA men victimising a woman and her Jewish friend, Cuxhaven near Hamburg, July 1933*

One day in March 1933, my father, who was a lawyer, went to the police headquarters in order to lay a complaint on behalf of one of his Jewish clients who owned one of the big stores in Munich and who had been arrested. When he got there, somebody directed him to a room in the basement. It was full of Brownshirt thugs who proceeded to beat him up. They knocked his teeth in and burst his eardrums. The one thing my father was worried about was that they would damage his kidneys. So he held his arms against his back and of course that meant his head was unprotected. They then cut off his trouser legs and took off his shoes and socks and hung a placard around his neck with the notice, 'I'm a Jew and I will never complain to the Nazis again.' They led him around Munich like that.

> **1**      *Bea Green, a German Jewish schoolgirl, Munich. Taken from L. Smith, **Forgotten Voices of the Holocaust**, 2005*

The early days of the Nazi regime saw many violent actions against Jews, mostly by the SA. The violence included attacks on synagogues, the destruction of Jewish property and the beating up of individual Jews. In the years to 1938, however, Nazi violence was relatively restrained. The regime preferred to persecute Jews by legal methods and to avoid provoking outrage abroad. Some Jews gained a false sense of security, believing that the violence of the early days was a temporary aberration. On the night of 9/10 November 1938, their illusions were blown away by the storm of state-sponsored violence on *Kristallnacht* (The Night of Broken Glass).

Kristallnacht was followed by the intensification of other forms of discrimination and persecution. Jews in Germany suffered the expropriation of their businesses and property through Aryanisation. As war came closer in 1939, Nazi race policies became much more radical. Many Jews realised, too late, the true nature of the Nazi regime. Some Jews were able to escape by emigration, though the state extorted huge sums from them in the process. For many other Jews, emigration was no longer possible. The scene was set for the next stage in 'Hitler's war against the Jews'.

# Nazi terror, 1933–39

Between 1933–39, the use of terror and violence by the Nazi regime ebbed and flowed according to the political circumstances. There were times of relative calm and control when the regime preferred to keep violence on a leash. At other times, both on a local level and nationally, there were bursts of extreme violence.

Jews in Nazi Germany lived on a daily basis in an atmosphere of terror. They were always liable to random attacks in the street, and they knew that they could not look to the police to protect them. They also knew that opponents of the regime were likely to end up in a concentration camp. Perhaps, above all, Jews were oppressed by the all-pervasive Nazi propaganda machine and the fear and psychological stress it caused.

## The SS and the concentration camps

During 1933 and 1934, Nazi terror gradually became more systematic as the regime set up **concentration camps** and consolidated control over the police and security services. The rise of the SS was a key factor in this process.

### The SS (Schutzstaffel)

The SS had existed since 1925 but it was only after the Blood Purge of the SA leadership in the summer of 1934 that the SS became the main instrument of Nazi terror. After the purge, the SS took over the concentration camps. By 1937, the SS had taken complete control of all police and security services, including the regular police (*Ordnungspolizei*), as well as the Gestapo and the SD (*Sicherheitsdienst*, or Security Police). Under the leadership of the *Reichsführer SS*, Heinrich Himmler, the SS also played a leading role in ideology and race policy – Himmler was a racist fanatic who was determined to make the SS into a racial elite.

### Key terms

**Concentration camp:** (not to be confused with the death camps established during the Second World War) these were prison camps set up near major cities across Germany from 1933. The first was at Dachau near Munich. People such as socialists, pacifists, trade union officials and other 'unreliable elements' were held in the camps under hard conditions, though most were later released.

## Key chronology

**The rise of the SS**

| | |
|---|---|
| 1929 | Himmler appointed *Reichsführer SS* |
| 1931 August | Security Service (SD) created under Reinhard Heydrich |
| 1933 March | First concentration camp at Dachau |
| 1933 April | Himmler appointed 'Political Police Commander of Bavaria' |
| 1934 April | Control of the Gestapo given to Himmler |
| 1934 June | The SA leadership purged in the Night of the Long Knives |
| 1934 July | SS control of the concentration camps |
| 1936 June | Merger of SS and regular German police |
| 1936 autumn | The SD department of Jewish Affairs set up under Adolf Eichmann |

### Cross-reference

The Blood Purge of 1934 is outlined in Chapter 4, page 54.

Heinrich Himmler is profiled in Chapter 3, page 45.

The Gestapo is explained in Chapter 5, page 65.

The SS grew into a massive bureaucracy. The basis of SS power was methodical organisation and administrative efficiency. SS personnel were disciplined, physically fit and often extremely well educated. Himmler and other SS leaders such as Reinhard Heydrich, the head of the SD, Heinrich Müller, chief of the Gestapo, and Adolf Eichmann, head of the department of Jewish Affairs, were all very skilful in outmanouevring rivals and building up their 'empires' of power and responsibility. The expansion of the SS was a continuous process throughout the brief history of the Third Reich.

### Cross-reference

Reinhard Heydrich and Adolf Eichmann are profiled on page 86.

**Fig. 2** Reichsführer SS *Heinrich Himmler, with his daughter Gudrun, March 1938*

1 The SS is a band of German men of strictly Nordic origin selected according to certain principles.

2 In accordance with the National Socialist ideology and with the realisation that the future of our nation rests on the preservation of the race through selection and on the inheritance of good blood, I hereby institute from 1st January 1932 the 'Marriage Certificate' for all unmarried members of the SS.

3 The aim is to create a hereditary healthy clan of a strictly Nordic German type.

*SS Marriage Order, 31 December 1931. Taken from J. Noakes and G. Pridham, **A Documentary Reader: Nazism 1919–1945, Volume 2, State, Economy and Society 1933–1939**, 1984*

## Exploring the detail

### Himmler and 'racial purity'

Himmler was obsessed with 'racial purity'. SS personnel were to a large extent selected on the basis of their racial 'fitness'. He believed that the SS would become the spearhead of a new racial elite. Before entering the SS, recruits had to provide documentation tracing their ancestry back over many generations to ensure they were of 'pure Aryan blood'. Himmler also imposed strict regulations as to whom SS men could marry.

## Activity

### Thinking point

Using the evidence of Source 3 and your own knowledge, make a list of **three** reasons why Jews like John Silberman's father experienced the difficulties they did.

## Key terms

**'Asocials'**: term used to define 'social deviants' and 'un-German elements' imprisoned by the Nazi regime, including homosexuals, pacifists, Jehovah's Witnesses, jazz enthusiasts and others.

## Cross-reference

The Night of the Long Knives is outlined in Chapter 4, page 54.

However powerful and efficient the system of repression was under the Nazis, the regime depended upon cooperation from the public. Without a constant stream of information from informers, the security services could never have established the control they did. One example of this was the system of block wardens in order to provide the SS with eyes and ears on every street and in every apartment block. The block wardens were charged with spying on their neighbours and compiling reports on suspicious behaviour. The Jewish community was particularly vulnerable to being denounced by these block wardens after the Nuremberg Laws were passed. Fear led to Jews becoming isolated as non-Aryan friends and neighbours broke off contact with Jews.

My father's business simply died. Nobody would trade with Jews: you couldn't get supplies, customers, and you couldn't get staff to work for you. If you did you were at their mercy; they could do as they liked – they could steal, they could rob and there was no remedy. A Jew had no rights. I remember that my parents' Gentile friends did not stand by them.

3
*John Silberman, German Jewish schoolboy, Berlin. Taken from L. Smith, **Forgotten Voices of the Holocaust**, 2005*

### The concentration camps from 1933

Concentration camps were not a Nazi invention – as Göbbels frequently pointed out in his propaganda, they were first used by the British during the Boer War in South Africa (1899–1902). The first Nazi concentration camp was KZ Dachau near Munich, after which a network of camps was set up across Germany. The Nazis used the camps to hold political prisoners of all kinds, including socialists and Communists, Catholics, career criminals and what the Nazis called **'asocials'** or 'social deviants': homosexuals and members of the underclass. Prisoners were subjected to a harsh regime of hard labour and 're-education'. Jews were not sent to concentration camps in large numbers until after Kristallnacht in 1938.

The first commandant at Dachau was Theodor Eicke, who joined the Nazis in 1928 and gradually rose to high office in the SS. Eicke's brutal regime, with harsh rules and punishments, was admired by Himmler. Eicke played a key role in the Night of the Long Knives on which he was given responsibility for murdering the SA chief, Ernst Röhm. From this point, the SS took over control of the camps from the SA. Eicke then became chief inspector of concentration camps and the head of the 'Death's Head Units' – the military forces that guarded the camps.

The concentration camps were very different from the death camps established in the occupied territories during the Holocaust, but many of the administrative systems of the death camps were modelled on the regular camps. The future commandant of Auschwitz, Rudolf Höss, started his career in Dachau under the leadership of Theodor Eicke. Most Germans were aware of the existence of the camps without knowing much about what actually went on there – it was all part of the psychological intimidation.

> The carefully conceived regime at Dachau, inspired by Theodor Eicke, the first commandant of the camp, was not just brutal; it was designed to break the will of the inmate. Eicke channelled the violence and hatred the Nazis felt towards their enemies into systems and order. Dachau is infamous for the physical sadism practised there: whippings and other beatings were commonplace. Prisoners could be murdered and their death dismissed as 'killed whilst attempting an escape', and a significant minority of those sent to Dachau did die there. But the real power of the regime at Dachau lay less in physical abuse – terrible as it undoubtedly was – and more in mental torture.

**4**  L. Rees, *Auschwitz, The Nazis and the 'Final Solution'*, 2005

By 1937, the SS fully controlled the system of state security. Any expression of dissent was very difficult. Opponents of the regime were fragmented and the system of repression was so well established, with thousands of informers reporting to the Gestapo. One indication of the effectiveness of the repression was that numbers of prisoners held in the camps fell dramatically during the 1930s. In 1933, 100,000 Germans were arrested and held in camps (largely in SA-controlled 'wild camps'); this had fallen to only 4,761 prisoners by November 1936. There were even discussions in 1935 about closing the camps due to the low numbers of prisoners, but Himmler won Hitler's support to keep the camps open. Fear of the camps was more effective than actual imprisonment.

## The boycott of Jewish shops and businesses, 1933

The violence that erupted against Jews was sometimes due to spontaneous action by elements in the Nazi movement who were not completely under the control of the regime. On other occasions, it was initiated or authorised by the regime as a deliberate tactic. The two most notable examples of state-sponsored violence were the **boycott** of Jewish shops and businesses in 1933 and Kristallnacht, in 1938.

On 1 April 1933, the Nazi regime imposed a boycott of Jewish shops and businesses. Hitler claimed that this action was justified retaliation against Jewish interests in Germany and abroad who had called for a boycott of German goods. Göbbels organised an intensive propaganda campaign to maximise the impact of the boycott, which was carried out by gangs of brown-shirted SA men. The SA marked out which places of business were to be targeted and stood menacingly outside to intimidate would-be customers.

■ **Key terms**

**Boycott:** when a group of people purposely refuse to buy (and put pressure on others not to buy) goods and/or services in order to make a political protest.

**Fig. 3** *Anti-Jewish boycott of German shops and businesses, April 1933*

### ■ Cross-reference

Jewish commercial success in Weimar Germany is discussed in Chapter 1.

### ■ Exploring the detail

**Terror during the boycott**

There were some striking examples of terror and violence during this boycott; for example Jewish men had their beards shaved and at least one Jew in the industrial city of Chemnitz had his beard torn out from the roots. Other Jews were beaten up and threatened of worse if they told anyone about it. Other atrocities included forcing Jews to drink large bottles of castor oil, as happened to five Jews in Dresden.

### ■ Activity

**Talking point**

Working in two groups, assemble a range of evidence to support the view that:

■ organised violence against Jews strengthened the Nazi regime in 1933

■ uncontrolled violence against Jews in 1933 showed that Hitler was not in full control of the Nazi movement.

Shops were the main target of the boycott, but it also applied to Jewish professionals such as doctors and lawyers. Court proceedings involving Jewish lawyers and judges were disrupted in Berlin, Breslau and elsewhere. Many Jewish lawyers were attacked in the street and had their legal robes stripped from them. Jewish doctors, schoolteachers and university lecturers were also subject to similar rough treatment by the SA.

The boycott made a big public impact and featured prominently in news coverage both in Germany and in foreign countries, but it was not an unqualified success. It was unclear in many cases what was a 'Jewish' business and what wasn't – many were half-Jewish or half-German in ownership; many others were controlled by foreign creditors or German banks – and a number of German citizens defiantly used Jewish shops to show their disapproval of Nazi policies. The boycott was abandoned after only one day, even though the SA had hoped it would last indefinitely.

At the time, the boycott seemed to show the unleashing of Nazi violence by an aggressive new dictatorship flaunting its power just a week after the passing of the Enabling Law. The real situation was rather different. Hitler was not at all enthusiastic about a 'revolution from below' bringing chaos in Germany. He was anxious to keep the SA under control and he was genuinely concerned about adverse reactions from his conservative allies in Germany or from foreign public opinion.

Some historians believe that Hitler only ever intended the boycott to be a brief affair. In their view, Hitler allowed the boycott to go ahead only as a limited, grudging concession to the radical activists; his main aim was to avoid instability while he carried through his 'legal revolution'. However, Hitler was willing to allow a considerable degree of Nazi intimidation. It was useful to him as an expression of 'spontaneous public anger' that only his new government could satisfy. For Hitler, anti-Semitic violence was a two-edged sword. Just enough and the Nazis could claim that only they could maintain order in an unstable Germany; too much and Hitler's position might be threatened by the conservative elites on whom he still depended.

### Kristallnacht, November 1938

Between 1933 and 1938, Jews in Germany were subjected to increasing pressure of persecution, through anti-Semitic legislation, propaganda and the growing power of the police state. For many Jews, however, it was still possible to carry on some kind of normal existence. However, all this was changed on Kristallnacht (the Night of the Broken Glass) on 9/10 November. Jewish homes and businesses were looted and vandalised, synagogues were set ablaze and thousands of Jews were arrested, beaten up and killed.

The Kristallnacht pogrom can be viewed as an uncontrolled outpouring of anti-Semitic feeling amongst radical elements of the Nazi movement, partly supported by German public opinion. Certainly this was the view put out by Nazi propaganda, which announced that 'the National Soul has boiled over'. It is also true that some people in the Nazi hierarchy were concerned about the violence running out of control; in the days after the pogrom, Hitler gave Hermann Göring a coordinating role to 'sort things out'. From this point of view, it might appear that the situation in November 1938 was similar to that of April 1933, when the regime had to rein in the SA boycott.

**Fig. 4** *After Kristallnacht, 10 November 1938*

In reality, Kristallnacht was orchestrated by the Nazi leadership and the majority of those involved in the violence and vandalism were SA and SS men who had been instructed not to wear uniform. The Nazis seized the opportunity presented by the murder of Ernst vom Rath, a minor German official in Paris, who was killed by Herschel Grynszpan, a young Polish Jew angry at the treatment of his parents by the Nazi regime. The killing of vom Rath was much more an excuse for unleashing anti-Jewish terror than the real cause.

The chief instigator of the pogrom was Josef Göbbels. It was Göbbels who gave instructions to the Nazi officials in the regions to organise the violence and vandalism, but to be careful to make it appear that it was not orchestrated by the party. 9 November was the 15th anniversary of the 1923 Munich Putsch and Göbbels hoped to please Hitler by marking the anniversary with a spectacular event.

**Fig. 5** *Josef Göbbels opening the War Room at the House of German Art in Munich*

In the violence, 91 Jews were killed and thousands injured. There was looting of cash, silver, jewellery and works of art. Damage to shops and businesses amounted to millions of marks. Much of the vandalism was purely destructive, not for gain. Orders from the SS directed the police not to intervene against the demonstrators; they were ordered to place 20,000 to 30,000 Jews in 'preventive' detention. The fire brigades watched and did nothing as synagogues burned to the ground; their only concern was to stop the fires spreading to other buildings.

> The first known case of the killing of a Jew, a Polish citizen, was reported to Dr Göbbels on November 10th at about 2 o'clock and in this connexion the opinion was expressed that something would have to be done in order to prevent the whole thing from taking a dangerous turn. Dr Göbbels replied that the informant should not get excited about one dead Jew, and that in the next few days thousands of Jews would see the point. At that time most of the killings could still have been prevented by a supplementary order. Since this did not happen, it must be deduced from that fact as well as from the remark itself that the final result was intended or at least considered possible and desirable.

**5**  *Nazi Party Supreme Court secret report on the events of Kristallnacht. Taken from J. Noakes and G. Pridham,* **A Documentary Reader: Nazism 1919–1945, Volume 2, State, Economy and Society 1933–1939,** *1984*

### Did you know?

Göbbels was partly motivated by his desperate desire to get back into Hitler's good books. He had recently had a scandalous affair with a Czech film actress, Lida Baarova, and was in disgrace because Hitler took the side of Magda Göbbels.

The anti-Jewish violence of November 1938 was not received with universal approval in Germany. There were some ordinary citizens who joined in the violence and looting alongside SA thugs who were equipped with crowbars, hammers, axes and petrol bombs, but many German people were horrified by the destruction. In Leipzig, the American consul reported that silent crowds of local people were 'benumbed and aghast' at the sight of the burned-out synagogue and the looted shops the next morning. In Hamburg, a young mother, Christabel Bielenberg, witnessed similar crowds of pedestrians appalled by what they saw, murmuring quietly to each other: '*Schlimm. Schlimm* (It's terrible).' A British official in Berlin claimed 'he had not met a single German from any walk of life who does not disapprove to some degree of what has occurred.' All over Germany, the great majority of people understood that the violence was not spontaneous but organised by the state.

In Saarbrucken the Jews were made to dance and kneel outside the synagogue and sing religious songs; then most of them, wearing only pyjamas or nightshirts, were hosed down with water until they were drenched. In Essen, stormtroopers manhandled Jewish men and set their beards alight. In Meppen, Jewish men had to kiss the ground in front of SA headquarters while brownshirts kicked them and walked over them. In many places they were forced to wear placards round their necks with slogans such as 'We are the murderers of vom Rath'. In some places, whole classes were taken out of school to spit on the Jews as they were being led away.

**6**         *R. Evans, **The Third Reich in Power**, 2005*

The events of the night of 9/10 November 1938 were a watershed for Jews in Nazi Germany. Hermann Göring pronounced: 'Now the gloves are off.' In the aftermath of Kristallnacht, Göring moved quickly to prevent insurance companies from paying out compensation to Jewish victims. The 'Decree for the Restoration of the Street Scene' in relation to Jewish business premises meant that the Jews had to pick up the costs of repairs. The Jewish community was also made to make a 1 billion RM contribution in compensation for the disruption to the economy. The Decree Excluding Jews from German Economic Life was issued and the Aryanisation of Jewish businesses was accelerated.

## ■ The practice of racism in Nazi society

Nazi race policies were wide ranging, aimed at a total transformation of German society to bring about a 'racial state'. By 1939, the practice of racism in German society was becoming more radical than ever. This was demonstrated by the Aryanisation of the economy, deeper levels of discrimination against 'racial undesirables' and the introduction of policies of 'racial hygiene', such as sterilisation and the elimination of the disabled.

### Aryanisation

Aryanisation of the economy was part of a wider aim to enforce social conformity and racial purity. The Nazis aimed to remove the 'burden' of the Jewish population from the German economy, whilst also stripping the Jewish community of its wealth. The policy was also designed to force Jews to emigrate, leaving their wealth behind; Jewish property being firstly registered and then the ownership of Jewish businesses being transferred to Aryan owners. Jews were excluded from almost all economic activity and isolated from the rest of society.

Hitler attacked the right of Jews to own businesses in his speech at the Nuremberg Party Rally in 1937. This increased the pressure on Jewish businesses to sell 'voluntarily' to Aryan firms at a price well below market value. The economy had recovered since the depression of the early 1930s and German businesses were eager to expand and, at the same time, to eliminate Jewish competitors and secure their allocations of raw materials. In December 1937, Göring used his powers as head of the Four Year Plan to order a reduction in the foreign exchange and raw material quotas for Jewish firms. On top of this, on

**Fig. 6** *Reichsmarschall Hermann Göring on his 41st birthday, January 1934*

1 March 1938, Göring banned the granting of public contracts to Jewish businesses. In April 1938, the Decree for the Registration of Jewish Property over the value of 5,000 RM was introduced.

After the Anschluss, there was an 'orgy of confiscations' of Jewish business in Austria. This involved a disorderly grabbing of Jewish businesses by Austrian Nazis. This inspired Göring to increase the speed of Aryanisation in Germany, but also made him see the need to do it in a more orderly way.

■ A closer look

### Aryanisation of Jewish businesses in Germany

In April 1938, there were still 39,532 Jewish businesses in Germany. By April 1939, 14,803 had been closed down and 5,976 'dejewified'; 4,136 were in the process of being 'dejewified' and 7,127 were being investigated. From 1 January 1939, Jews could no longer run retail shops, mail order houses or work as independent traders. Jews could not sell items at markets or fairs. No Jew could manage a business, and businesses were required to dismiss all senior Jewish employees. No Jew could be a member of a cooperative society. Jewish-held patents were Aryanised.

Göring aimed to have a well-organised and planned process of Aryanisation of Jewish businesses, not the chaotic plunder that had happened in Austria. This was not, however, what happened. The party as an organisation and individuals were determined to take full advantage. As with much in the Nazi state with its ideology of struggle and the 'survival of the fittest', there was a free-for-all in which big business benefited most, not the small traders.

---

I have noticed in connexion with the Aryanization programme that legal regulations and decrees are undermined by a somewhat arbitrary interpretation not only on the part of organisations affiliated to the Party but also on the part of State authorities. Thus, in the process of drawing up the registry of Jewish business, one factory was declared Jewish simply because the Aryan owner was married to a Jew, although there was no regulation to support this.

**7**    *Extract from a report of 5 January 1939 to the Reich minister of economics from the City President of Berlin. Taken from J. Noakes and G. Pridham, **A Documentary Reader: Nazism 1919–1945, Volume 2, State, Economy and Society 1933–1939**, 1984*

Aryanisation was a terrible blow to the Jewish community in Germany. Losing family businesses was traumatic; so was the sense of humiliation felt by Jews who lost their right to work and the ability to support themselves and their families. The Nazis intended that Aryanisation would accelerate the process of separating Jews from mainstream society, encourage Jewish emigration and grab valuable assets at a time when the demands of the Four Year Plan meant a reduction in the amount of consumer goods available. All three aims were achieved.

■ Did you know?

The Nazi propaganda made a big issue of the Jews being 'unhygienic' and spreading disease. This may to some extent explain the banning of Jews from spas, swimming pools and restaurants. Later, during the war, this image was built on further as Jews were forced into cramped ghettos without basic amenities. This meant that Nazi propaganda could depict Jews as being unhealthy and 'unclean'.

■ Key terms

**Internal exile:** (sometimes called internal emigration) this was a mental process, not a physical one. People switched off from the Nazified outside world and retreated to a non-Nazi world inside their own homes or inside their own private thoughts.

■ Exploring the detail

**Eugenics**

The theory that a race or group of people could be genetically improved through selective breeding was first formulated by Sir Francis Galton (Charles Darwin's cousin) in 1883. In the decades before and after the First World War, these ideas gained support in America and Europe, especially in Scandinavia. Eugenicists suggested that 'interventions' were necessary to deal with 'handicapped' people such as the mentally ill, those with physical deformities, even homosexuals. Family planning, sterilisation (and in extreme circumstances even euthanasia) were proposed as a means of eliminating biological and social flaws. From 1899, 35 states in the USA permitted the eugenic sterilisation of mentally handicapped people.

■ Exploring the detail

**The asylums as propaganda**

The Nazis even encouraged guided tours of asylums to show the 'benefits' of its eugenic programme. Between 1933 and 1939, over 21,000 people visited Munich's Eglfing-Harr asylum. They were shown 'exhibits' aimed to arouse horror at the consequences of 'unfit' people being allowed to procreate.

## Discrimination

> On the same day (14.7.1935), there were anti-Jewish demonstrations in the swimming pool in Heigenbruken, Bezirksamt Aschaffenburg. Approximately 15–20 young bathers had demanded the removal of the Jews from the swimming bath by chanting in the park which adjoins the baths. The chant went: 'These are German baths, Jews are not allowed in, out with them' and such like. A considerable number of other bathers joined in the chanting so that probably the majority of visitors were demanding the removal of the Jews.

8  *Bavarian Political Police report from 1 August 1935. Taken from J. Noakes and G. Pridham,* **A Documentary Reader: Nazism 1919–1945, Volume 2, State, Economy and Society 1933–1939***, 1984*

Discrimination against Jews occurred all over Germany as a result of local interventions like that in Aschaffenburg described in Source 8. In this instance, local agitation resulted in the Lord Mayor issuing a ban on Jews using the swimming pool. It was a similar picture elsewhere. Pubs and other businesses put up signs saying that Jews were not welcome. Pro-Nazi activists took the lead in pushing for anti-Jewish measures in local schools, in village committees and almost all areas of public life.

Evidence suggests that these signs were often displayed to keep Nazi officials happy rather than to stop Jews from using the establishments. One Jewish customer was assured that a sign in his local pub was just there for show and he should ignore it. In other places, however, the discrimination against Jews was very real. Albert Herzfeld, a middle-class Jew who had served in the German army, was barred from his artists' club in 1935. Later, Herzfeld was barred from his favourite restaurants in Wiesbaden and from the spa.

Many Germans were embarrassed by overt discrimination. Such people were reluctant, for example, to break off from family doctors they had relied on for years, or were appalled to see literary classics purged from the local library. When Nazi activists in Leipzig demanded the removal of a statue to the great composer Felix Mendelssohn, even the local party boss drew the line and blocked the proposal. Open opposition to the discrimination was rare. Most people who were unhappy about the discrimination kept their heads down and retreated into '**internal exile**'.

Acts of localised social discrimination were occurring across Germany from 1933 onwards but, by 1938–39, they received more open government backing. Before this time, the actions of the Nazi government had been lagging behind the Nazi activists and supporters. With the regime secure at home and with increasing disregard for international opinion, the Nazis were ready for more radical implementation of their anti-Semitic ideology.

## Sterilisation

Nazi ideology was obsessed with the notion of selective breeding. This did not only relate to the prevention of 'Jewish blood' mixing with 'Aryan blood', but also in carrying out 'racial engineering' – purification of the gene pool by sterilising those who the Nazis believed would produce 'degenerate' offspring. This was rooted in the so-called science of eugenics.

Eugenic ideas were not new. In 1923, the state of Prussia drafted a law (though it was not actually enacted) providing for the compulsory sterilisation of those born blind or deaf, 'idiots', epileptics, mental patients, criminals, sex offenders and parents of more than two illegitimate children. There were other regional attempts to introduce eugenic voluntary sterilisation in 1924, 1928 and 1932. The Nazis built on these foundations.

In July 1933, the belief in eugenics led to the introduction of welfare benefits to encourage more births amongst the eugenically 'fit'. At the same time, a Sterilisation Law introduced compulsory sterilisation for certain categories of 'inferiors'. Two years later, the law was amended to permit abortions in cases where those deemed suitable for sterilisation were already pregnant. In 1936, X-ray sterilisation of women over 38 years was introduced (due to the greater risk of offspring with mental and physical handicaps). In the opposite direction, there was a ban on abortion and contraception for Aryan women and girls in an attempt to increase the birth rate.

### Propaganda and popular opinion

Hitler believed 'there is only one disgrace: despite one's own sickness and deficiencies, to bring children into the world, and only one highest honour: to renounce doing so'.

Nazi propaganda softened up public opinion with a barrage of publicity on the money 'wasted' on mentally ill and 'unproductive' people. Feature films shown in cinemas promoted eugenic theories. *Erbkrank* (1936) dramatised the supposed links between 'racial degeneracy' and criminality. *Victim of the Past* was shown in all 5,000 of Germany's cinemas to convince audiences that a disproportionate number of the 'mad' were Jewish. Graphic documentary films were broadcast to promote compulsory sterilisation in order to 'save the Volk from being overrun with congenital idiots'.

There was criticism, both on moral and religious grounds, of the Nazi idea of creating a master race. The playwright Samuel Beckett, who visited Germany in the 1930s, wrote mockingly about the Aryan racial characteristics of the Nazi leaders: 'They must be blond like Hitler, slim like Göring, handsome like Göbbels, virile like Röhm and be named Rosenberg.' Yet many people not otherwise supportive of the Nazis were receptive to eugenic ideas.

During the Third Reich, 400,000 people were sterilised. As early as July 1933, the Nazis introduced the Law for the Prevention of Hereditarily Diseased Progeny.

Decisions about sterilisation were made at Hereditary Health Courts. Most of the judges were strongly in favour of the policy of sterilisation. The process often took only 10 minutes. The operation took place, by force if necessary, within two weeks. Sixty per cent of those sterilised were 'feebleminded' – categorised as suffering from Idiocy (IQ of 0–19) or Imbecility (IQ of 20–49). The idea of 'moral insanity' was also used as a basis for sterilisation. This was often merely an excuse to prevent births among the 'criminal underclass' or 'anti-socials'.

The Nazi ideology of racial purity meant that it was only a short step from compulsory sterilisation to so-called mercy killings. Early in 1939, the SS began preparations for the secret euthanasia programme that later became known as *Aktion T4* – a policy of putting disabled children to death. It was a forerunner of worse things to come once Germany was at war.

## ■ Emigration

From the early days of the Nazi movement, Hitler had spoken of making Germany *Judenfrei*, or 'Jew free'. The culmination of this ideology was the mass killings of the Holocaust, but the first method of

### ■ Exploring the detail

**The Law for the Prevention of Hereditarily Diseased Progeny**

The Law for the Prevention of Hereditarily Diseased Progeny specified the 'hereditary diseases' that sterilisation was to be applied to: congenital feeblemindedness; schizophrenia; manic-depressive illness; epilepsy; chronic alcoholism; hereditary blindness and deafness; severe physical malformation (if proven to be hereditary). Later amendments permitted sterilisation of children over 10 years, and the use of force to carry it out after 14 years, with no right to legal representation.

### ■ Did you know?

There was a call to add debility (IQ of 50–70) to the list for sterilisation. This would have included nearly 1 million people, including 10 per cent of army recruits and many of the SA. Reich doctors stated that the low IQ of these groups was due to poor education, not racial matters.

### ■ Cross-reference

The T4 euthanasia programme is covered in Chapter 7, pages 95–9.

### ■ Key terms

*Judenfrei*: literally means 'Jew-free'. The Nazis promised to remove not only Jewish people from Germany, but also to purge all Jewish cultural influences.

**Fig. 7** *Luggage check for Jewish emigrants, 1938*

achieving it was through voluntary emigration. By 1938, a total of 150,000 Jews had chosen to leave Germany. As war approached and the Nazi regime moved to more radical policies, the focus moved to forced emigration. From late 1938 until as late as the autumn of 1941, emigration was seen as the 'solution to the Jewish problem' by the Nazi leadership.

■ **Activity**

**Statistical analysis**

Look at the figures for Jewish emigration in Figure 8.

**1** Which years saw the highest levels of emigres? Why?

**2** Are you surprised by the statistics for 1934 and 1935? Why?

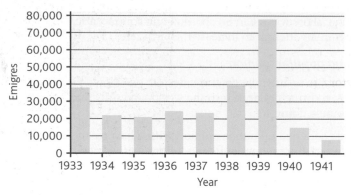

**Fig. 8** *Jewish emigration from Germany, 1933–41*

## Voluntary emigration

The Nazi regime allowed for Jewish emigration, but strictly controlled it. 37,000 Jews left Germany in 1933, including many leading scientists and cultural figures. Perhaps the most prominent was Albert Einstein, world-famous for his work on the theory of Relativity. Einstein described the German people as having a 'psychic illness of the masses'. Overall, 150,000 Jews left Germany in between March 1933 and November 1938. The question of whether to leave or stay was agonising and Jews frequently disagreed among themselves about the issue of emigration (Source 9).

> Lawyer Stern – 'He encouraged people to stay in Germany and warned against hasty emigration. In contrast to the words of the lawyer Stern, Superintendent Dr Kurt Singer from Berlin emphasized that the Nuremberg Laws were beyond discussion; the Jews, especially the young ones, must emigrate.'

*Report on a meeting of Jews in the Rhineland (January 1936). Taken from J. Noakes and G. Pridham, **A Documentary Reader: Nazism 1919–1945, Volume 2, State, Economy and Society 1933–1939**, 1984*

The situation was made even more confusing by the fact that the Nazis were both encouraging the Jews to emigrate and threatening to confiscate some of their assets. For those with skills that were easily transferable to other countries, the decision was easier – the same was true of those who had family members living in another country. The Nazis were willing to encourage Zionists to emigrate to Palestine, then under British rule. The majority of German Jews were not Zionists and did not choose this option.

Most German Jews, especially the older generation, felt thoroughly German and wanted to stay. Many Jews believed that the Nazi persecution was just one more example of the surges of anti-Semitism that had come and gone in the past. It was also the case that Jews who went abroad did not necessarily find a better life; a considerable number of Jews who left in 1933 had come back to Germany by 1937.

■ **Exploring the detail**

**Returning Jews**

During 1936–37, 75,000 of the Jews who had emigrated since 1933 returned to Germany. This was in part because they had faced anti-Semitism in the countries they had fled to, or had been unable to find work. Some believed that in the Nuremberg Laws the Nazis had completed the anti-Semitic programme and things would get no worse for Jews in Germany. This view was reinforced by the impact of the Berlin Olympics, when the Nazis had seemed to step back from extreme anti-Semitism.

Making the Reich 'Jew free' through emigration was not straightforward. It was difficult to find foreign countries willing to accept large numbers of Jews; many countries had begun to raise barriers to limit Jewish immigration. Even Palestine could only receive a limited number, partly because the British, who controlled Palestine, were worried about Arab hostility to mass Jewish immigration. Nazi policies were also contradictory, pressuring people to emigrate but, at the same time, making it harder for them to do so by stripping them of their wealth.

**Fig. 9** *Jewish children leaving Germany, 1939*

The situation became more urgent after Kristallnacht. Many Jews now desperately sought safe refuge from the obvious dangers they faced in Germany. Jewish parents were particularly keen to get their children out of Germany and to safe countries – 9,000 Jewish children were sent to Britain in 1938–39.

## The Reich Office for Jewish Emigration

**Fig. 10** *The expanding Reich: 'Greater Germany', 1938–39*

Controlling emigration was a key policy aim of the Nazi regime, not least because it enabled massive economic exploitation. After the Anschluss in March 1938, Reinhard Heydrich used Austria as a laboratory for developing SS policy. The Central Office For Jewish Emigration was set up – 45,000 of Austria's 180,000 Jews had been forced to emigrate. The illegal seizure of Jewish property was used to fund the emigration of poorer Jews.

### Did you know?

The *Kindertransport* (Children's Transport) was organised by voluntary organisations and private citizens in Britain, who persuaded the British government to give refuge to young people up to 17 years, separated from their parents and brought by train and ferry from cities like Berlin, Prague and Vienna. The first children arrived in December 1938; the last transport from Germany was in September 1939.

### Exploring the detail

#### Expulsion of Jews of Polish extraction from Germany

In October 1938, 17,000 German Jews of Polish origin were deported to the area near the town of Zbaszyn in the border region between Germany and Poland. These 'Eastern Jews' had been deprived of their German citizenship and were now stateless. Amongst the Polish Jews who lost their citizenship were the parents of Herschel Grynspan. It was in revenge for this that Herschel assassinated Ernst vom Rath in Paris in November 1938, and thus provided Göbbels with the excuse to launch *Kristallnacht* (described on pages 78–80).

### Cross-reference

The SD is explained earlier on page 75.

### Cross-reference

The deportation and 'resettlement' of Jews during the war is covered in Chapter 7, pages 89–91.

■ **Key profile**

### Reinhard Heydrich

Reinhard Heydrich (1904–42) was the most important senior commander in the SS after Himmler. He played a vital role in organising the RSHA. In 1941, he was given responsibility for coordinating the 'Final Solution' – the plans launched at the Wannsee Conference in January 1942 were codenamed 'Operation *Reinhard*'. In addition to his role in the 'Final Solution', Heydrich was also *Reichsprotector* of Bohemia and Moravia, governing the Czech territories incorporated into the Reich. In July 1942, Heydrich was assassinated by Jewish partisans trained in Britain.

In January 1939, Heydrich took charge of the Reich Office for Jewish Emigration, with the task of promoting the emigration of Jews 'by every possible means'. Göring's claims to have jurisdiction over Jewish affairs were bypassed. The SD set about amalgamating all Jewish organisations into a single 'Reich Association of the Jews in Germany'. The organisation was modelled on methods used in Austria by the SS emigration expert Adolf Eichmann in 1938. This system suited the Nazis because organisational difficulties had to be dealt with by the Jews themselves.

■ **Key profile**

### Adolf Eichmann

Eichmann (1899–1961) rose to prominence in the Race and Resettlement Unit of the SS. He was involved in planning for Jewish emigration to Palestine in the 1930s; but later became one of the architects of the 'Final Solution'. Eichmann had a key role in arranging the 1942 Wannsee Conference and was the main driving force behind the deportation and mass murder of Hungarian Jews in 1944. After the war, he escaped to South America. In 1961, Israeli secret agents kidnapped him in Argentina and brought him back to face trial as a war criminal; he was sentenced to death.

The situation changed with the outbreak of war in September 1939. The German conquest of Poland provided the regime with new territories in which Jews could be settled. The emphasis moved away from forced emigration to deportations and the 'resettlement' of Jews.

*Learning outcomes*

In this section you have looked at the anti-Semitic legislation brought in by the Nazi regime between 1933 and 1939, and seen how that legislation was influenced by the anti-Semitic ideology of the Nazis. You have looked at the impact of anti-Semitic policies on public opinion and have examined the role of propaganda in enabling the Nazi regime to intensify the persecution of Jews in Germany. You have also looked at terror and organised violence and seen how terror culminated in the state-sponsored violence of Kristallnacht in November 1938. The Aryanisation of the economy, the intensification of race policies and increased emigration have also been addressed in order to give you an overall understanding of the radicalisation of Nazi policies between 1933 and 1939, and how this laid the foundations for even more extreme policies once Germany was at war.

# AQA Examination-style questions

a) Explain why the Nazi regime used the cinema as a means of spreading anti-Semitic propaganda. *(12 marks)*

You should try to produce three (or more) developed reasons to explain why cinema was used. The key for higher levels is not the length of the answer, but the way the different reasons are handled and the answer is structured. To achieve top levels, you need to show links between the different factors, perhaps prioritising the factors in terms of their importance. The best answers will make a judgement about how the factors were connected, perhaps singling out and explaining the most significant.

b) How important was Nazi propaganda in gaining public support for anti-Semitic actions in the years 1933 to 1939? *(24 marks)*

The key to producing an effective answer to this question is first of all to consider what the 'anti-Semitic' actions that took place in Germany between 1933 and 1939 were and, secondly, in what ways propaganda was used to make them acceptable to the German public. You also need to think about ways in which propaganda was not important or failed to win over public support. The answer should compare the importance of propaganda to other factors – perhaps a readiness to look for scapegoats for past troubles, a concern for personal advancement and economic concerns. You might also mention actions where the public were noticeably lukewarm, most particularly the boycott of Jewish shops and Kristallnacht.

## 7 The impact of war on Nazi race policies, 1939–40

**Fig. 1** *Child's drawing of the main gate of the Kovno ghetto in Lithuania, 1941*

*In this chapter you will learn about:*

- the impact of the European War on Nazi policies from September 1939

- the fate of Polish Jews and the policy of 'ghettoisation'

- Nazi policies to deal with the 'problem' of the Jews in the occupied countries in 1940

- the euthanasia programme and schemes for 'racial hygiene'.

From September 1939, Nazi race policies were shaped by war. Nazi anti-Semitism had already become more blatant and extreme by 1938, but it was war that brought about the final radicalisation of race policies. War provided a national emergency that enabled the regime to act with more dictatorial power and in greater secrecy. War enabled the propaganda machine to whip up patriotism and hatred of Germany's enemies. War added new territories to the Reich under the expanding bureaucratic power of the SS. War opened the way for the Germanisation of the occupied territories in Poland. War prepared the way for a 'Jew-free' Nazi empire.

The Anschluss with Austria and the annexation of the Sudetenland in 1938, followed by the German occupation of Prague and the Czech lands of Bohemia-Moravia in March 1939, had expanded the territory of the Reich and brought new Jewish populations under Nazi control. These new territories also vastly increased the power of the SS, which had complete control there, without having to compete with other government authorities as they did within Germany. Reinhard Heydrich, for example, gained enormous political power as Reich Protector of Bohemia and Moravia.

The conquest of Poland in September 1939 brought even more extensive territories and even more millions of eastern Jews under Nazi rule. Nazi planners now dreamed of deporting mass Jewish populations to the East in order to 'Germanise' the lands 'liberated' by German expansion. This was not easy. The Nazi regime suddenly had to face urgent practical problems in dealing with the millions of Jews in Poland.

■ A closer look

### Germany's war in the East, 1939–45

The war in the East went through three distinct episodes: a short victorious war against Poland in 1939; the massive onslaught against the Soviet Union in June 1941; and finally the long and exhausting 'total war' that ended with the destruction of the Third Reich by May 1945.

*Act one: The war that Hitler won*

By September 1939, Hitler had already achieved several conquests without actually fighting a war. Austria and the Sudetenland were taken over in 1938; Prague and Bohemia-Moravia were seized from Czechoslovakia in March 1939. In August 1939, Hitler prepared the way for the conquest of Poland by agreeing the Nazi-Soviet Pact with Stalin. Invading Poland caused Britain and France to go to war, but this did not save Poland. In 1940, Hitler won a series of *Blitzkrieg* victories in the West, defeating France and leaving Britain isolated. France came under a Nazi puppet regime ruled from the town of Vichy. Hitler seemed to have a free hand to fulfil his aim of Lebensraum in the East.

*Act two: Operation Barbarossa*

The Nazi-Soviet Pact was only ever intended to be a temporary truce. Hitler started detailed planning for the conquest of the USSR in October 1940 – in June 1941, he launched Operation Barbarossa. German armies swept across the USSR, occupying vast territories in eastern Poland, the Baltic States (Lithuania, Latvia and Estonia), western Russia and Ukraine. Complete victory seemed almost certain. The way was open for the fulfilment of the dream of Lebensraum.

*Act three: Total war and total defeat*

The German invasion got close to Leningrad and Moscow, but then stalled because of stiffening resistance from Soviet forces and because of the onset of the terrible Russian winter. In December 1941, the Japanese attack on Pearl Harbour in the Pacific brought the United States into the war. The hope of another short victorious war was over. Nazi Germany now faced a world war against the Grand Alliance of the USSR, the USA and Britain. The enormous economic and military resources behind the Soviet and American war effort were far stronger than Germany's. Despite all efforts to mobilise the nation for 'total war', the tide turned decisively against Germany in 1942–43. By April 1945, the Reich was in ruins. Soviet and American forces linked up in the heart of defeated Germany, at Torgau-on-the-Elbe.

■ **Key chronology**

**The impact of war on Nazi race policies, 1939–40**

| | |
|---|---|
| **1939** | |
| September | German invasion of Poland<br>Ghettoisation of Jews in Poland |
| October | Euthanasia programme authorised by Hitler |
| November | Jews in occupied Poland made to wear Star of David |
| **1940** | |
| April | German invasion of Western Europe |
| June | Fall of France and establishment of Vichy regime<br>Madagascar Plan drawn up |
| November | Warsaw ghetto 'sealed' |

■ Cross-reference

To recap on the Nazi concept of *Lebensraum*, look back to Chapter 3, pages 48–9.

## ■ Polish Jews and the ghettos

The conquest of Poland enormously increased the number of Jews under Nazi control. According to the official census in Poland in 1931, there were 3,115,000 Jews in Poland of whom 1,901,000 (61 per cent) were in the

### ■ Did you know?

As part of the Nazi-Soviet Pact of August 1939, Stalin had agreed to allow ethnic Germans from the USSR and Baltic States of Lithuania, Latvia and Estonia to be resettled in the Third Reich once Poland had been conquered and carved up between Germany and the USSR. The ethnic Germans leaving the USSR to settle in German-controlled Poland would need homes, farms and businesses. To provide these, the SS had to clear out Poles and Jews from the parts of Poland that were to be incorporated into the Reich.

### ■ Cross-reference

The Nazi-Soviet Pact and the course of the war in the East is covered in A closer look on page 89.

The concept of *Lebensraum* is discussed in Chapter 3, pages 48–9.

### ■ Key terms

**General Government:** the area of Poland occupied by the Nazis in 1939 that was not incorporated into the German Reich but controlled as a semi-autonomous area under Governor Hans Frank. It became a dumping ground for Jews deported from the Reich. Most of the death camps that were built in 1941–2 were located within the General Government.

### ■ Cross-reference

Reinhard Heydrich and Adolf Eichmann are profiled in Chapter 6, page 86.

### ■ Cross-reference

The impact of the Nazi annexation of territories from Austria and Czechoslovakia in 1938–39 is covered in Chapter 6, pages 85–6.

**Fig. 2** *German occupied Poland, 1939–45*

territory occupied by Germany at the end of 1939. These 2 million Polish Jews were different from the assimilated Jews in Germany. They were in the main poor and more Orthodox – in their appearance they fitted the Nazi stereotype of racially inferior Slav *Untermenschen* (sub-humans). Their sheer numbers posed difficult strategic problems to the Nazi regime.

The conquest of Poland carved the country up into three separate areas. Eastern Poland was occupied by the USSR, in accordance with the Nazi-Soviet Pact of August 1939. The western parts of Poland, Upper Silesia, West Prussia and the Warthegau, were incorporated into the German Reich and placed under the rule of Nazi Gauleiters. The area in between was designated the '**General Government**' of Poland, under a Nazi Governor, Hans Frank. The Nazi master plan was to create Lebensraum for ethnic Germans by driving Poles and Jews out of West Prussia and the Warthegau so that the 'empty' lands could be completely 'Germanised'.

The Nazis intended to use the General Government district as a dumping ground for Poles and Jews displaced from the areas that were to be colonised by ethnic Germans. At the end of September, Hitler informed Alfred Rosenberg, his minister for the eastern occupied territories, that all Jews, including those from the Reich, were to be moved to the area between the river Vistula and the river Bug. On the same day, Heydrich reported that 'in the area between Warsaw and Lublin' a reservation, or 'Reich ghetto', was established to contain the deported Poles and Jews. The Nazis deliberately intended conditions in the reservation to be so bad that most of the people deported there would die.

In October 1939, the Gestapo chief, Heinrich Müller, instructed Adolf Eichmann, as head of Central Agency for Jewish Emigration based in Prague, to arrange the deportation of 70,000 to 80,000 Jews from the district of Katowice in Germanised Poland. Eichmann quickly expanded this to include Czech Jews from the Reich Protectorate of Bohemia-Moravia. On top of this, Hitler demanded the deportation of 300,000 Jews from Germany and the removal of all Jews from Vienna. Although these orders were given, it would prove to be impossible to implement them because the problems of dealing with Jews already in Poland were so pressing.

Between November 1939 and February 1940, the SS attempted to deport 1 million people eastwards – 550,000 were Jews. They were transported to the General Government where they faced terrible conditions. The fact that so many people were entering this area meant that the authorities there could not possibly cope with mass deportations of western Jews from Germany and Austria at the same time. Governor Hans Frank complained vigorously to his superiors in Berlin that the General Government could not take any more Jews.

## Ghettoisation

**Fig. 3** *Ghettos in Nazi-occupied Europe*

### Exploring the detail
#### Deportation problems

One example of the practical problems hindering the deportation of Jews was the fate of several trainloads of Jews, many of them elderly and infirm sent by Eichmann from Vienna to the area around Nisko in the General Government of Poland. Most of these Jews were forced into the countryside and left to fend for themselves. There was fierce criticism from the army and other government agencies and the transports had to be stopped after only a few days. The chaos of this operation convinced the Nazis that they had to find a better way to solve the 'Jewish problem'.

### Key terms

**Ghetto:** a controlled area of a town or city reserved for Jews. They had been a feature of life in Europe since medieval times and were especially numerous in Tsarist Russia before 1917. In the early stages of the conquest of the East, Nazi authorities herded Jews into overcrowded ghettos in cities such as Warsaw and Lodz.

The Nazi regime urgently needed a clear plan to deal with the huge Jewish populations that were displaced by military conquest and Germanisation. One solution they turned to was the creation of Jewish **ghettos**. In February 1940, the first ghetto was set up in Lodz, the second biggest city in Poland. About 320,000 Jews were living in the city. The Nazis considered their 'immediate evacuation' to be impossible. The majority of Jews were accommodated in a closed ghetto, set up in a single day by barricades – later the Jews had to build a surrounding wall. The remaining Jews were formed into labour gangs, accommodated in barrack blocks and kept under guard. The Jewish Council of Elders was given responsibility for food, health, finance, security, accommodation and registration.

**Fig. 4** 'Juden verboten.' *Jewish policeman and German soldier directing traffic in the Lodz ghetto*

Jews sent to the ghettos had their homes confiscated. Most Jews had to sell their valuables to survive. There was further economic exploitation in the form of forced labour. The Nazis massively restricted the amount of food, medical supplies and other goods that entered the overcrowded ghettos.

■ **Exploring the detail**

**The Jews as 'carriers of disease'**

According to Nazi ideology, Jews were the carriers of disease. This became a self-fulfilling prophecy as the overcrowded ghettos, with limited food and clean water as well as inadequate sewage systems, did become rife with disease. The Nazis then used this to further reinforce the negative stereotypes of Jews being the carriers of disease by putting footage of the ghettos into their propaganda.

■ **Exploring the detail**

**Deaths in the Warsaw ghetto, 1941**

| | |
|---|---|
| January: | 898 |
| February: | 1,023 |
| March: | 1,608 |
| April: | 2,061 |
| May: | 3,821 |
| June: | 4,290 |
| July: | 5,550 |
| August: | 5,560 |
| September: | 4,545 |
| October: | 4,716 |
| November: | 4,801 |
| December: | 4,239 |

Conditions in the ghetto were terrible. Six people shared an average room; 15 people lived in an average apartment. Few homes had running water. With no economic links to the outside world, basic necessities such as food and fuel were scarce. There were terrible lice infestations and diseases spread rapidly, including spotted fever, typhus and TB.

■ **A closer look**

**The Warsaw ghetto**

The largest ghetto established in Poland was in the capital city, Warsaw, where the Jews were forced to build a high wall around the Jewish Quarter – they also had to pay for its construction costs. Governor Hans Frank ordered the construction of the Warsaw ghetto in October 1940. In November, the ghetto was sealed off completely from the rest of the city. More than 400,000 Jews were concentrated there; over the following months many more Jews and gypsies were forced out of the countryside into the ghetto. Richer Jews were housed in the 'small ghetto'; the mass of ordinary people were squeezed into the so-called 'large ghetto' – which was not large at all and became desperately overcrowded.

Food rations in the large ghetto were at starvation levels. Germans in occupied Poland were consuming an average of 2,310 calories per day, close to the 2,500 calories a day for an adult man recommended by present-day nutritionists. In Warsaw in 1940, Poles received 634 calories per day. The figure for Jews was 300. Malnutrition and overcrowding inevitably led to outbreaks of killer diseases, above all typhus. More than 100,000 people died in the ghetto in 1940–41. Later, almost all the remainder died in the death camps after mass deportations to Auschwitz during Operation *Reinhard*, which began in 1942.

The Jewish authorities worked within the regulations laid down by the Nazis, but also tried to get around them where possible. There was a black market for food smuggled in from outside. Jewish leaders organised prayers and religious festivals, despite the fact they were strictly forbidden by the Nazis. The ghettos had illegal schools and even illegal printing presses. Most Jewish elders in positions of authority in the ghettos acted responsibly and did their best to relieve suffering. Others such as the chairman of the Jewish Council in the Lodz ghetto, Mordechai Chaim Rumkovski, were accused of corruption or collaboration with the Nazis.

■ **Key profile**

**Mordechai Chaim**

Mordechai Chaim (1877–1944) ruled the Lodz ghetto as a 'dictator', though obviously within the limits of what the Nazis allowed. He has been accused of using his power over deportations to get rid of people he disliked, of eating excessively well whilst his fellow Jews starved, and of giving extra perks to his cronies. Chaim was also accused of using his position to take advantage of young women, using the threat of deportation if they refused his advances. He is however credited by some with doing the best he could in appalling circumstances.

The Nazis never saw the ghettos as a long-term solution to the 'Jewish problem'. The conditions in the ghettos and work gangs did however give some insight into the fate that was intended for the Jews. The conditions of the ghettos were designed to ensure that Jews died in large numbers of starvation, cold and disease. Many were worked to death carrying out forced labour for the Nazis. In total, around 500,000 Jews died in the ghettos.

**Fig. 5** *Occupation. The victimisation of an elderly Polish Jew*

## ■ The 'problem' of the Jews in the occupied territories, 1939–40

The rush to carry through the Germanisation of the territories added to Greater Germany caused increasing chaos in the occupied territories and the Nazi regime struggled to gain control of the situation. In the General Government, the Governor Frank sent a stream of furious reports to Berlin, complaining about the excessive numbers of deportees sent into his area. Frank stated again and again that the General Government had neither the food nor the space to cope with the trainloads of deported Jews, Poles and gypsies that were arriving almost by the day. Frank gained support from Hermann Göring, who was concerned by the economic disruption. The deportations of Jews to the East were temporarily suspended while alternative solutions were considered. Source 1 gives some insight into the problems caused by uncoordinated deportations.

The Nazis moved swiftly to 'Germanise' the lands seized from Poland in 1939, claiming they were 'bringing back to the Reich' the territories taken away from Germany after the First World War. An extensive strip of territory along Germany's eastern borders was declared to be part of Greater Germany. These territories included Upper Silesia, Danzig, West Prussia and the region south of Danzig, known as Warthegau. The situation in the newly occupied territories quickly became violent and chaotic, so much so that the area became the 'Wild East'.

### ■ A closer look

#### The Wild East

The problems of the 'Wild East' were complicated by the rushed way in which the regime attempted to carry through its aim to make Greater Germany Jew-free. The SS urged the Nazi Gauleiters in West Prussia and the Warthegau to push ahead with Germanisation. This was done in a brutal and disorganised manner, especially by Arthur Greiser, the Nazi boss of the Warthegau.

### ■ Activity

**Research exercise**

Carry out some research to find first-hand accounts of life in the ghettos in Poland 1939–41. Use this information to produce either:

■ a PowerPoint presentation on conditions in the ghettos

or:

■ a survival guide booklet to show how some Jews coped with the horrors of the ghettos.

### ■ Cross-reference

A sample sources-based examination question focused on ghettoisation appears at the end of this section, page 113.

Attention must be drawn to the large number of evacuees from Posen and the Warthegau who are incapable of work. Further difficulties have been created by the uncoordinated direction of the trains. Thus, trainloads of Jews and townspeople were directed to rural districts, whereas transports with peasants arrived in the towns. Thus, transports of women and children were placed in overcrowded and unheated cattle trucks without even the minimum provisions necessary. As a result there were many deaths during the journeys and a large number of physical injuries and cases of frostbite.

**1** *Report (January 1940) from the SS chief of the Cracow district, Dr Karl Wachter. Taken from J. Noakes and G. Pridham,* **A Documentary Reader: Nazism 1919–1945, Volume 3, Foreign Policy, War and Racial Extermination,** *1998*

Greiser was a man in a hurry. He strongly supported the policy of deporting Poles and Jews to make room for ethnic Germans (*Volksdeutsche*) to settle in a Jew-free Warthegau. This meant the immediate 'ethnic cleansing' of his region, even though there were no efficient arrangements in place to carry out deportations in an orderly manner. His approach resulted in repeated conflicts with other Nazi leaders, such as Hans Frank, the Governor of the General Government, and Albert Forster, Gauleiter of Danzig.

Greiser and Forster had been bitter rivals in Danzig politics since the early 1930s. Now, in 1939–40, Albert Forster took a very different approach from Greiser – more patient and methodical, taking note of practical difficulties such as transport and food supplies. The rows between Greiser and Forster were typical of the confusion and disagreements in the Nazi regime and contributed to the chaos across occupied Poland, where thousands of Jews were dying of disease, starvation and being overworked in the forced labour camps and ghettos.

### ■ Key profile

#### Arthur Greiser

Greiser (1897–1946) was a fanatic racist from Danzig. He was a member of the *Freikorps* in 1919 and joined the SS in 1931. He was made Gauleiter of the newly-created Reichsgau Warthegau in 1939 when parts of western Poland were absorbed into Greater Germany. He later had a prominent role in implementing the 'Final Solution'. He was executed for war crimes in 1946.

1 All Jews and Jewesses resident in the General Government and more than ten years old must wear on the right sleeve of their clothes and outer garments a white strip at least 10cm wide with a Star of David upon it.

2 Jews and Jewesses must obtain this armlet themselves and provide it with the appropriate sign.

3 Infractions will be punished with imprisonment, or a fine up to an unlimited amount, or both.

**2**      *23 November 1939, degree concerning distinguishing marks for Jews in the General Government. Taken from J. Noakes and G. Pridham,* **A Documentary Reader: Nazism 1919–1945, Volume 3, Foreign Policy, War and Racial Extermination***, 1998*

Fig. 6 *'Jews Only.' Boarding a tram in Warsaw, 1941*

Another symbol of the radicalisation was the decree ordering all Jews in the General Government to wear the yellow Star of David to identify them in public (Source 2).

Away from the direct terror at the front, many Germans were involved in the implementation of Nazi policies, such as deportations and resettling

### ■ Activity

#### Thinking point

Using the evidence in Source 2 and in this chapter, suggest **three** reasons why the Nazis made Jews in Poland wear the Star of David.

ethnic Germans. They were not always comfortable with violence and suffering, but most of them remained committed Nazis with deeply ingrained anti-Semitic views.

## 'Racial hygiene' and the euthanasia programme

**Fig. 7** 'Aryan youth' on parade within the BdM (League of German Maidens)

The Nazi desire to create their 'master race' did not stop at sterilisation and banning sexual relationships between Aryans and Jews. By October 1939, the regime had authorised **euthanasia** for the mentally and physically disabled – regarded by the Nazis as an 'unproductive burden' on Germany's resources and as a threat to 'racial hygiene' and the 'biological strength of the *Volk*'.

The Social Darwinist nature of Nazism stressed the value to the national community of true 'national comrades' (*Volksgenossen*). Disabled people could not make the contribution of a *Volksgenosse*, but were merely a burden on society; thus they should be eliminated. Hitler's core ideology of struggle was also a factor – he famously championed strength and despised weakness.

A recurrent theme of Nazi propaganda was the idea that something had to be done about the 'burden' of the long-term ill and the disabled. The regime placed great emphasis on the idea that 'afflicted' children were taking money away from their healthy siblings and preventing their parents from having more children. The openly stated solution was to pass new legislation allowing mentally and physically disabled children to be mercifully put to death and so 'relieve the burden on the national community'. This idea was closely linked to the policy of sterilisation, which was a well-developed policy by 1939 and had attracted quite a lot of public support.

As a result of our modern sentimental humanitarianism we are trying to maintain the weak at the expense of the healthy. It goes so far that a sense of charity which calls itself socially responsible, is concerned to ensure that even cretins are able to procreate while more healthy people refrain from doing so, and all that is considered perfectly understandable. Criminals have opportunity of procreating, degenerates are raised artificially and with difficulty. And in this way we are gradually breeding the weak and killing off the strong.

| 3 | Hitler's speech at the party rally at Nuremberg, 5 August 1929. Taken from J. Noakes and G. Pridham, **A Documentary Reader: Nazism 1919–1945, Volume 3, Foreign Policy, War and Racial Extermination**, 1998 |
|---|---|

### Exploring the detail

**Melita Maschmann**

One example of this divided thinking was Melita Maschmann, an idealistic young woman working with other volunteers to help new German settlers in Poland. Maschmann's memoirs, *Account Settled*, reveal the tensions between her Nazi beliefs and her good-hearted better instincts. One of the striking admissions in her book explains how she managed to maintain her faith in the regime and its ideology even when she had misgivings about the brutality she heard about and sometimes witnessed.

### Key terms

**Euthanasia:** sometimes described as 'mercy killing' – the painless ending of a life to free victims of terminal illness or severe disability from their suffering. The Nazi euthanasia programme put to death mentally ill or physically-disabled people whose condition was not necessarily terminal and without the consent of patients or their family.

### Exploring the detail

The idea that the physically and mentally ill should be killed was not invented by the Nazis. In 1920 *Permission for the Destruction of Worthless Life, its Extent and Form*, written by Professor Karl Binding, promoted euthanasia as a solution to the problem of increased mental illness after the World War. Binding's views were also linked to the science of eugenics, which saw asocial or 'degenerate' behaviour (such as alcoholism, juvenile delinquency) as being in part congenital.

### Cross-reference

To refresh your knowledge of Social Darwinism, look back to Chapter 3, pages 46–7. To see how this became the basis of Nazi policies on sterilisation, see Chapter 6, pages 82–3.

The advent of the war enabled the regime to move forwards to more radical policies. The war accentuated the arguments about not 'wasting' valuable resources. The Nazis also calculated that public attention would be focused firmly on the war, so that the euthanasia programme was less likely to attract notice. Even as early as 1935, Hitler had predicted that:

> [...] in the event of a war he would take up the question of euthanasia and enforce it. He was of the opinion that such a problem could be more easily solved in wartime, since the opposition to be expected from the churches would not play so significant a role.

J. Noakes and G. Pridham, **A Documentary Reader: Nazism 1919–1945, Volume 3, Foreign Policy, War and Racial Extermination**, 1998

### Activity

**Thinking point**

Design a poster to support a campaign of opposition against the idea of 'mercy killings' in Germany in 1941. Highlight the main arguments used in favour of euthanasia and explain why they should be rejected.

## The euthanasia programme

### Children

The first euthanasia programme for disabled children originated from one specific case of a badly disabled child early in 1939. The child's father wrote a personal letter to Hitler asking for his child, 'this creature' as he called him, to be put to sleep. Dr Philipp Bouhler, chief of the Führer's party office, made sure the letter was brought to Hitler's attention. The baby had been born blind, appeared to be mentally handicapped and was lacking one leg and part of one arm. Hitler sent a senior SS doctor, Karl Brandt, to examine the baby; Brandt's report advised euthanasia for the child. Hitler approved the

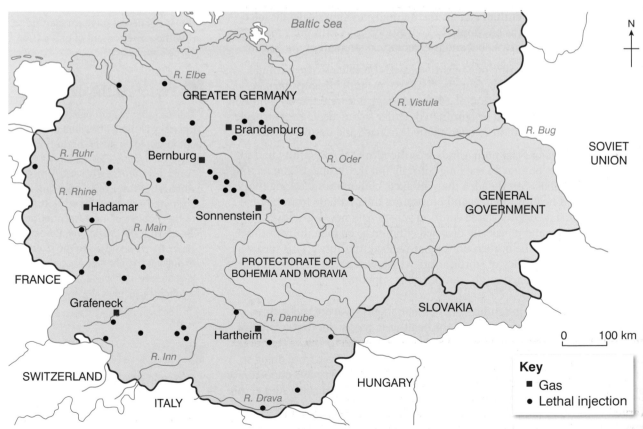

**Fig. 8** *Asylums where euthanasia was carried out*

report and issued a directive announcing he would personally protect from prosecution the doctors who carried out 'mercy killings'.

This one case was the catalyst for the whole euthanasia programme. Hitler gave Philipp Bouhler authority to deal with similar cases in the future. All petitions were to go through the 'Chancellery of the Führer', Bouhler's area of responsibility. Hitler also made it clear that any such actions were to be secret. There was an obvious element of manipulation on Bouhler's part – he exploited his responsibility for Hitler's correspondence to guide the Führer to the conclusion that Bouhler wanted, giving him more power and promoting a policy he believed in.

■ Key profile

### Philipp Bouhler

Bouhler (1899–1945) served in the First World War and worked for the Nazi Party newspaper, the *Völkischer Beobachter*, in the 1920s. He became Reich secretary of the NSDAP in 1925. In 1933, he was appointed head of Hitler's party office, handling internal correspondence. He used his control over letters to Hitler to influence the decision to introduce the euthanasia programme, later known as *Aktion T4*, in 1939. Together with an SS doctor, Karl Brandt, Bouhler was one of the chief architects of the programme of killings. He committed suicide in 1945 to avoid arrest by American forces.

Bouhler's close ally in originating the euthanasia programme was Karl Brandt, who already had a key role in implementing the existing policy of sterilisation under the Law for the Protection of Hereditary Health. In August 1939, Bouhler and Brandt set up a Reich Committee for the Registration of Hereditary Diseases. This committee organised research into the practicalities of selecting children for euthanasia.

■ Key profile

### Dr Karl Brandt

Brandt (1904–48) was a senior SS doctor who was a member of Hitler's inner circle. He was frequently invited to the Führer's private retreat at Berchtesgaden and was a friend of top Nazi leaders such as Albert Speer. Together with Philipp Bouhler, he founded the Nazi euthanasia programme in 1939. Brandt rose to the rank of SS Major General and was appointed Reich Commissioner for Health and Sanitation. He was guilty of supervising medical experiments during the war. He was arrested in 1945 and executed for war crimes in 1948.

Medical staff in hospitals and asylums had to report on children suffering from mental illnesses, or physical 'deformities' such as spina bifida. On the basis of these reports, children were sent to special hospitals to be starved to death or given lethal injections. Parents were assured their child had died in spite of receiving the very best treatment. The technical and administrative methods used to kill more than 5,000 innocent children deemed by the Nazis to be 'incurable' and worthless to society would be applied later to the Jews of occupied Europe.

### Adults

Philipp Bouhler and Karl Brandt used their authority to extend euthanasia to adults. The legal basis for this was a brief handwritten note from Hitler in October 1939, giving Bouhler and Brandt the powers they required for a full-scale adult euthanasia programme. Hitler's scribbled note was backdated to 1 September, the first day of the war in Poland. From October 1939, the programme was rapidly expanded and later moved to new, larger headquarters in Berlin, Tiergarten No. 4. It was from this address that the name by which the euthanasia programme is best known, *Aktion T4*, originated.

**Fig. 9** Aktion T4. *Disabled patients at the Schoenbrunn asylum*

The basis of T4 was bureaucracy and paperwork. Forms about patients were to be filled in at clinics and asylums and passed on to assessors, who were paid on a piecework basis to encourage them to process as many patients as possible. Those who made judgements of life and death did so without having to look the patients in the eyes, but rather simply looked at forms. Some doctors took part because they were careerists. Several doctors and nurses complained about the programme, but their objections were ignored.

In the many psychiatric hospitals in the Reich, there are endless numbers of incurable patients of all kinds who are of no use to humanity. They take food away from other healthy people and often require two or three times as much care. The rest of the public must be protected from them. Since urgent measures are already needed to look after healthy people, it is all the more necessary to eliminate these creatures. The space thus made available is needed for all sorts of war-essential things. Moreover, it will greatly relieve the pressure on municipalities, since for every individual case the future costs of accommodation and care would not have to be paid.

**4**     *Viktor Brack, Second-in-Command to Philipp Bouhler, speaking to the Conference of Mayors, April 1940. Taken from G. Aly, 'Final Solution': Nazi Population Policy and the Murder of the European Jews, 1999*

### ■ Exploring the detail

#### 'Cost savings' of the euthanasia programme

The Nazis were typically thorough in calculating the costs that would be saved by eliminating 'unproductive lives' (Source 5). On an average daily cost [per patient] of 3.50 RM, there would be a daily saving of 245,955 RM; a yearly saving of 88.5m RM; over a life expectancy of 10 years, 885m RM.

There cannot be a subjective view of unrestricted individual human rights. Five thousand idiots cared for at an annual cost of 2,000 Reichsmarks each equals a total cost of 10 million Reichsmarks per year. At 5 per cent interest this would take 200 million marks of government capital.

**5**     *A memorandum by Hitler's personal doctor, Theo Morell, July 1939. Taken from G. Aly, 'Final Solution': Nazi Population Policy and the Murder of the European Jews, 1999*

Bouhler and Brandt instituted 'scientific' research to calculate the numbers of 'incurables' who would need to be dealt with (they estimated approximately 70,000) and to investigate the most efficient methods of killing. In Poland, SS units carried out several 'experimental' mass killings by carbon monoxide gas poisoning carried out in specially adapted vans. These mobile gas chambers represented a clear link between the euthanasia programme and the 'Final Solution'.

The regime tried to keep the policy secret but, despite an elaborate cover up, the news started to get out. Administrative mistakes led to errors in communicating the news of deaths to families. Some conscience-stricken doctors and nurses leaked information to their priests. Some patients in the asylums started to become aware of what was happening. This led to panic and resistance against the asylums and word of what was happening there spread to the families and beyond.

By 1941, rumours about the policy of euthanasia were spreading widely and aroused opposition. One public official, Dr Lothar Kreyssig of Brandenburg, filed an official complaint with the Reich Justice Ministry and also filed an accusation of murder against Philipp Bouhler. These proceedings got nowhere, but they worried the regime. From July 1940, there was also a groundswell of protests from the Churches. Protestant Pastor Braune wrote a long memorandum on July 1940, protesting about the T4 programme. On 12 August, Braune was arrested by the Gestapo. The Roman Catholic Church hierarchy made official protests behind the scenes. This led to intervention on behalf of the Pope; an official statement from Rome on 2 December 1940 pronounced that the direct killing of people with mental or physical defects was against 'the natural and positive law of God'.

On 3 August 1941, Count August von Galen, the Cardinal Archbishop of Munster, preached a sermon making an emotive attack on euthanasia, backed by specific evidence provided by members of local congregations. Galen's sermon was deliberately designed to mobilise mass protest on behalf of the strongly Catholic population of Munster and the whole province of Rhineland-Westphalia. Thousands of copies of Galen's sermon were printed and widely distributed. As intended, this sparked further protests and public demonstrations. The Nazi regime was alarmed by the hostile public reactions. On 24 August 1941, Hitler halted the programme.

However, this was an isolated success for public protest against Nazi race policies – Count Galen never took a public stance on behalf of the victims of Jewish persecution. The halting of the T4 programme in August 1941 did not mean the end of the drive to implement Nazi racial ideology; it was only a tactical pause. In many respects, the euthanasia programme provided the techniques, the trained personnel and the administrative experience for the coming 'Final Solution'.

### Cross-reference

The 'Final Solution' is the subject of Chapter 9.

### Activity

**Thinking point**

Imagine you have just learned of the euthanasia programme. Write an article for a German newspaper explaining your objections.

### Exploring the detail

**Count Galen's campaign**

The effectiveness of Count Galen's campaign might seem surprising, but the Nazis were always very concerned about the public mood. An official in the propaganda ministry talked wildly about hanging Count von Galen. Göbbels snarled at him: 'Yes, and if we do that we might as well write off any hope of having public support anywhere in Rhineland-Westphalia for the rest of the war!'

### Summary questions

1. Explain why Hitler halted the euthanasia programme in 1941.

2. In the years 1939 to 1941, how successful was the Nazi propaganda machine in gaining the support of public opinion inside Germany for radical anti-Semitism?

# The impact of war on Nazi race policies, 1940–42

*In this chapter you will learn about:*

- the Madagascar Plan, the ideological goals of *Lebensraum* and links between anti-Semitism and foreign policy

- Operation *Barbarossa* and its impact on Nazi race policies

- the activities of the *Einsatzgruppen* on the Eastern Front

- attitudes to Jews in Germany and the occupied territories by January 1942.

**Fig. 1** *Heinrich Himmler and senior SS officers on the Northern Front near Minsk, 1941*

In September 1939, Britain and France declared war against Germany but did little or nothing to fight. Hitler had a free hand in Poland while Britain and France waited for his next move. In April 1940, Germany launched the invasion of Western Europe, overrunning Denmark, Norway, Holland and Belgium before completing the conquest of France in a matter of weeks. Hitler's stunning victories in the West in 1940 opened up new possibilities for Nazi race policies. After the defeat of France, serious consideration was given to the Madagascar Plan, using France's former colony in the Indian Ocean as a faraway reservation to hold Europe's Jews.

Hitler's obsession, however, was always the war in the East: first the war in Poland and then the war Hitler had always desired and predicted – the 'fight to the death against Jewish-Bolshevism' that began in June 1941. This was to be a war of racial annihilation, fought with a savagery and ideological intensity on a completely different scale than the relatively civilised struggle against the western allies. It is no accident that the so-called Nazi '**Final Solution**' took place during Germany's war on the Eastern Front between late 1941 and 1945. That war enabled the conquest of huge territories in the East, populated by millions of European Jews. Total War against the Soviet Union provided the circumstances and the stimulus for Total War against Germany's 'racial enemies'.

## Links between anti-Semitism and Nazi foreign policy: the Madagascar Plan, *Lebensraum* and Operation *Barbarossa*

Anti-Semitism fitted closely with all the ideological aims of Nazi foreign policy. Hitler's territorial gains in 1938, his war against Poland in 1939, the Madagascar Plan of 1940 and the war against the USSR in 1941 were all influenced by the Nazi vision of racial superiority, a Jew-free Europe and Lebensraum for the German *Volk*. Even Hitler's confident belief that Germany would defeat the USSR, in spite of all its massive resources, was based on the conviction that the 'Jewishness' of the USSR made it weak and incapable of withstanding all-out war.

### The Madagascar Plan

The idea of removing Europe's Jews to the island of Madagascar was first promoted by French anti-Semites in the late 1930s. At that time, it was merely a wild idea with little or no prospect of becoming a reality. The rapid conquest of France by German armies during May to June 1940 changed the situation. The foreign ministry's department for Internal German Affairs proposed that the island of Madagascar should be taken away from France to become German mandate. Vichy France would be responsible for resettling the French population of approximately 25,000 so as to make Madagascar available for a 'solution' to the 'Jewish question'.

The Nazis planned to send 4 million Jews to Madagascar. In the first phase, farmers, construction workers and artisans up to the age of 45 would be sent out to get the island ready to receive the mass influx of Jews. The sale of remaining Jewish property in Europe would finance the initial costs. As with the ghettos being established in Poland at this time, the living conditions on Madagascar were intended to be harsh, leading in the long term to the elimination of the Jews by 'natural wastage'.

Since 1936, SS experts at the **RSHA** (Reich Security Head Office) led by Adolf Eichmann had been working on schemes for mass emigration of Jews to Palestine. (This actually involved a remarkable cooperation between SS racists and the leaders of the Zionist community in Germany.) However, there were huge practical problems about Palestine, which was a small territory under British rule and not so far from Europe. Madagascar was far away, offered infinitely more space and there were no serious political problems to get around.

There were other considerations. The Jews would remain under German control and could be used as hostages to influence American public opinion if it seemed the United States might become involved in the war. The scheme could even be skilfully presented by Nazi propaganda as a

### Key terms

**'Final Solution'**: this 'solution' to the 'Jewish question' was a Nazi euphemism for the extermination of European Jews. It is also known as the Holocaust.

**RSHA**: *Reichssicherheithauptamt* or Reich Security Head Office was formed on 22 September 1939 when the SD (Security Service) and Sipo (Security Police) merged. Between 1939 and 1941, it grew enormously under the control of Reinhard Heydrich and contained departments including the Gestapo and Criminal Police (Kripo). It played a major role in anti-Semitic policy in Germany and the Holocaust.

### Cross-reference

To recap on Nazi ideology, including the concept of *Lebensraum*, look back to Chapter 3, pages 48–9.

### Did you know?

Madagascar, a large island off the eastern coast of Africa, was a French colony. The rapid conquest of France in the summer of 1940 suddenly raised the possibility of deporting large numbers of European Jews to a vast 'empty' territory in an easily controlled location far away from Germany.

**Fig. 2** *Adolf Eichmann*

demonstration of Germany's 'generosity' towards the Jews. The plan also gained approval from Hitler and Himmler. The RSHA under Eichmann began working out how to implement the project.

There was only a short period of time, however, in the late summer and early autumn of 1940, when the Madagascar Plan seemed viable. Germany's failure to end the war with Britain, either by military victory or a peace agreement, meant that the Royal Navy would be able to disrupt the mass transportation of Jews by sea to Madagascar. Attention turned back to the East. By October 1940, Hitler was already planning for Operation *Barbarossa*. The Madagascar Plan was shelved in favour of the plan to send Europe's Jews deep into Siberia, 'East of the Urals', once the forthcoming conquest of the USSR was complete.

What the Madagascar Plan reveals about Nazi intentions towards the 'Jewish question' in 1940 is open to debate. On the one hand, it is plausible that it proves the decision to exterminate all Jews had not been made at this point, that all kinds of different plans were under consideration and that the 'Final Solution' was still not inevitable. On the other hand, the driving force behind the Madagascar Plan was the determination to remove the Jews from Europe to some reservation where they would slowly die off through harsh conditions. The Plan could be regarded as proof that the long-term goal sending the Jews to die somewhere far away was fixed, even if the exact location was not.

### Lebensraum

*Lebensraum* (living space) was a key element in Nazi ideology from the beginnings of the Nazi movement. It is possible to argue that the concepts of 'race and space' were all-important in shaping Hitler's foreign policy. To win living space, it was essential for Germany to expand eastwards. This meant the conquest of Poland and the incorporation of the territories on Germany's eastern borders into the Reich; but there were wider ambitions beyond that. For example, Hitler's aims also included control over the resources of Ukraine, which he saw as essential in order to avoid Germany being blockaded into economic collapse, as had happened in 1914–18. These territorial aims meant, sooner or later, a war against the Soviet Union.

In 1939, Nazi Germany was not ready for such a war. Indeed, Hitler and Göbbels hoped that Germany would be allowed to take over Poland without having to fight a European war. Hitler had got away with carving up Czechoslovakia without a war in 1938 and he hoped he could get away with it again in Poland. To gain what he wanted in Poland, Hitler needed to be reassured that the USSR would not intervene militarily. This is why he was willing to go against his own ideology and make a deal with his arch-enemy, Stalin.

The Nazi-Soviet Pact caused amazement at the time, especially among committed Nazis. Hitler seemed to be betraying his own ideological goals regarding 'Jewish-Bolshevism'. It was a tactical move Hitler had to make in order for the invasion of Poland to be launched a week later. At the time, Hitler seemed to have made big concessions and it was Stalin who seemed to have gained what he wanted; but all Stalin's plans came unstuck with the sudden collapse of France in 1940.

Stalin had banked on another long war in the West, an exhausting struggle that would drain the resources of Germany and of Britain and France, just as in 1914–18. Hitler's stunning victory left the USSR in a very vulnerable position, as Stalin well understood. By October 1940, Hitler

### Cross-reference

The 'Final Solution' is the subject of Chapter 9.

### Cross-reference

The ideology of Lebensraum is covered in depth in Chapter 3, pages 48–9.

### Exploring the detail

#### The Nazi-Soviet Pact

The Nazi-Soviet Pact was signed by the foreign ministers, Ribbentrop and Molotov, in August 1939. This non-aggression pact supposedly guaranteed 10 years of peace, though Hitler undoubtedly expected war sooner than that. The pact enabled Germany to go ahead with the invasion of Poland. Its secret clauses also carved up Poland and Eastern Europe between German and Soviet domination. The Pact caused amazement because it went against everything Nazi ideology stood for – but Hitler had no intention of sticking to it in the long run.

and his generals were planning for the invasion of Russia. The all-out war on the Eastern Front that was launched in June 1941 was a war of racial ideology as well as a struggle for power. It was a war to prove German racial superiority over Slavs and Jews and a war to win living space for Hitler's dream of a future empire of 250,000 racially-pure Germans.

The Nazis envisaged a German 'Master Race' ruling over inferior Slav *Untermenschen* (sub-humans). The Slavs would be educated to a basic primary level of education in mathematics and technical subjects, but not in literacy. The aims associated with Lebensraum were already being pushed forward in occupied Poland in 1940, for example in the Nazi administration of the General Government and in the rush to settle ethnic Germans from the Baltic States in Warthegau, but the overcrowding in the ghettos and other problems indicated that far more living space would be required. That could only be gained through war against the USSR.

A key figure in the development of plans for the implementation of Lebensraum in the lands that would be won in the coming war in the East was Alfred Rosenberg, appointed by Hitler to be minister for the eastern occupied territories. Rosenberg had been one of the founders of Nazi ideology in the formative years of the movement; now it was Rosenberg who mapped out German administration of the lands that would be conquered:

- Ostland – the Baltic States, eastern Poland (seized by the USSR since 1939) and Belarus.
- Moskau – the Moscow region and European Russia.
- Kaukasus – southern USSR and the Caucasus region.
- Ukraine – Ukraine and the Crimea.

Living space for Germans, of course, meant the removal of Jews. In Poland in 1940, whilst some districts were Germanised, some Poles were allowed to remain where they lived. However, Jews were ghettoised or deported to the General Government. As the expectations of total victory over the USSR grew in 1941, plans were drawn up to remove the millions of **Soviet Jews** east of the Ural mountains into the vast spaces of Siberia. Anti-Semitism was as central to Lebensraum as smashing the USSR.

## Operation *Barbarossa*

The German invasion deep into the western parts of the USSR in 1941 was a key turning point in the Nazi treatment of Jews. It immediately brought more than 3 million Soviet Jews under German rule. The war was especially brutal. Before the invasion, codenamed Operation *Barbarossa*, had even been launched, Hitler issued the instruction to 'eliminate' the 'Bolshevik-Jewish intelligentsia'. The Nazis made it clear in numerous directives that the war was to be one of 'extermination' of Germany's racial enemies.

### Cross-reference

For details on the ghettos, Warthegau and the General Government in Poland in 1940–1, look back at Chapter 7, pages 89–93.

### Cross-reference

Alfred Rosenberg is profiled in Chapter 3, page 42.

### Key terms

**Soviet Jews:** those living within the borders of the USSR before June 1941. 'Polish Jews' were those living in Poland before the 1939 war; 'German Jews' were those living in Greater Germany. None of these terms is very precise (some of the Jews living in Germany and in parts of the USSR were actually of Polish origin), but it is important to understand the different general categories.

**Operation *Barbarossa*** launched the invasion of the Soviet Union, without any declaration of war, on 22 June 1941. Three German battle groups made amazingly rapid advances. They overran eastern Poland and the Baltic States in the north and penetrated deep into Ukraine, capturing more than a million prisoners. By the end of September 1941 the complete defeat of the USSR appeared imminent. Then came stiffening Soviet resistance and the onset of winter; the German advance was halted short of Moscow.

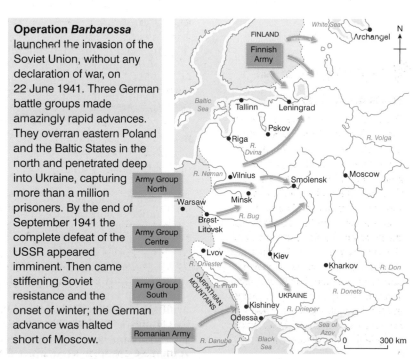

**Fig. 3** *Operation* Barbarossa: *the German invasion of the Soviet Union, 1941*

Given the instructions to the army before the campaign began, it is hardly surprising that uncontrolled atrocities by ordinary soldiers began immediately. 'I have observed that senseless shootings of both prisoners of war and civilians have taken place', commented one troop commander only three days after the attack had started. Five days later, he had to repeat his order to desist from 'irresponsible, senseless and criminal' shootings, which he bluntly described as 'murder'. He nevertheless reasserted the need to uphold 'the Fuhrer's calls for ruthless actions against Bolshevism (political commissars) and any kind of partisan'[...]

**1**

*I. Kershaw, **Fateful Choices: Ten Decisions that Changed the World 1940–41**, 2008*

**Cross-reference**

Hermann Göring's role in the Nazi regime is covered in Chapter 3, page 45.

There was no explicit Hitler order in June 1941 to kill all the Jews of the Soviet Union. There was, however, an atmosphere in which troops saw killing as part of the overall mission. In July 1941, Hermann Göring issued a general order to kill Communist commissars (party officials assigned to the Red Army) and Jewish sympathisers. Göring's 'Commissar Order' was a key step in Nazi policy towards racial extermination. Many soldiers interpreted it very loosely, as justification for almost indiscriminate shootings. Nazi propaganda had always aimed to convince the German people that Jews and Communists were linked in the same 'Jewish-Bolshevik conspiracy'; this is also part of the explanation why German soldiers frequently shot Soviet Jews on the spot.

*Barbarossa* was a catalyst for the escalation of Nazi anti-Semitic policy. Race policy was linked to the aims of launching the invasion in the first place. Race policy was linked to the apparently unstoppable progress of the invasion, raising hopes that the Nazis could do anything they liked after a swift victory. Race policy was also linked to the disappointments of November to December 1941, when the invasion stalled and winter set in, blocking any idea that the Nazis might soon send Jews east of the Urals. This link leads to the heart of the historical debate about the origins of the 'Final Solution'. There are three fundamentally different points of view:

1 The Nazi regime had a deliberate, long-term plan for the extermination of the Jews. War against the Soviet Union was a logical part of this plan. Tactical decisions changed according to the ebb and flow of events, but the overall intention was utterly consistent.

2 There was no long-term plan, only a general ideological goal. The speed and success of *Barbarossa* suddenly opened up new possibilities for a drastic solution to the 'Jewish problem'. The 'Final Solution' was launched in the 'euphoria of victory' in the summer of 1941.

3 There was no coherent policy concerning the Jews. The Nazis tried a range of contradictory policies, from Palestine to Madagascar to Poland and Russia. The 'Final Solution' was thrown together hurriedly when the war turned against Germany in the autumn of 1941.

**Cross-reference**

The 'Final Solution' is the subject of Chapter 9.

There is no simple or certain way to decide which of these interpretations is the 'right' one. There is convincing circumstantial evidence in favour of all three views. What *is* certain is that the war against the Soviet Union was closely linked to the fate of the Jews and the Holocaust could never have happened without the fog of war on the Eastern Front. It was in the context of the slowing progress of Operation *Barbarossa* that the first mass gassings of Jews took place at Chelmno in December 1941, and that invitations were sent out for the top-secret conference that eventually took place at Wannsee in January 1942. Long before then, it was in the context of *Barbarossa* being so successful so quickly that the *Einsatzgruppen* death squads carried out mass killings behind the lines as the frontline troops advanced through western Russia.

**Fig. 4** *Children from the Lodz ghetto being deported to the Chelmno extermination camp*

## The Einsatzgruppen

As German forces overran the western territories of the USSR in June and July 1941, Special Groups, the **Einsatzgruppen**, were sent in to eliminate Communist officials, **Red Army commissars**, partisans and the 'Jewish-Bolshevist intelligentsia'. The activities of the Einsatzgruppen went far beyond their original remit. They carried out numerous mass killings of Soviet Jews in the second half of 1941. Possibly half a million Soviet Jews were killed by the Einsatzgruppen in June and July. The total number of Soviet Jews and other victims killed between 1941 and 1943 was 1.3 million.

The Einsatzgruppen were temporary units made up of police and regular troops commanded by men from the Gestapo, the SD and the Criminal Police under the overall direction of the SS. Einsatzgruppen had been in operation before 1941. Reinhard Heydrich and the RSHA had organised Special Groups in 1938 and 1939 to secure government buildings and to seize official files at the time of the Anschluss with Austria and when Germany occupied Prague. Special Groups were used extensively in support of military operations in the invasion of Poland in 1939, when they were involved in '**special actions**' against Jews and many Poles, especially Communists and the 'intelligentsia'. Local volunteers were often recruited to assist them.

The Einsatzgruppen played an important role in the 'ethnic cleansing' of the territories in western Poland that were incorporated into Greater Germany. One of these 'task forces', under the command of SS Obergruppenführer Woyrsch, carried out mass shooting of Jews in Upper Silesia. In Warthegau, the Gauleiter, Arthur Greiser, took a particularly brutal approach to clearing his territory of Jews and Poles and the Einsatzgruppen were very active there. One key responsibility of the Einsatzgruppen was to force Jews into ghettos in the cities. It is estimated that 7,000 Jews were killed in Poland in 1939 and, in total, it is believed that the Einsatzgruppen in Poland killed 15,000 people including Jews and members of the 'intelligentsia'.

The Einsatzgruppen operations on the Eastern Front in 1941 were far more systematic and on a far larger scale than in Poland in 1939–40. Göring's 'Commissar Order' of July 1941 did not call for the wholesale killing of the Jewish population, but it did allow the local population to 'purge' the 'Jewish elements' of society. Local volunteers from the native population were to be 'secretly encouraged' to organise pogroms.

Four Einsatzgruppen, of between 600 and 1,000 men, followed behind the first wave of the German army as it swept into the Soviet Union. 'Special Group A' led the way, followed by a 'second sweep' by Special Groups B, C and D as more areas deeper into the USSR were overrun.

### Cross-reference

For more on the Wannsee Conference, including the timing of the decision, look ahead to Chapter 9, pages 115–17.

The SD is explained in Chapter 6 on page 75.

### Key terms

**Einsatzgruppen**: these were 'special forces' of police and regular troops operating under SS commanders behind the frontline as German armies advanced through Poland and Soviet-controlled territories. According to their records, *Einsatzgruppen* killed 1.3 million Jews.

**Red Army commissars**: these were put in place alongside army officers to ensure political obedience to the Communist regime.

**'Special actions'**: this was a Nazi euphemism for mass killings, almost always carried out by shooting at close range on the grisly principle 'one bullet, one Jew'.

### Cross-reference

Arthur Greiser is profiled in Chapter 7, page 94.

## Exploring the detail

### Bialystok

In the massacre at Bialystok, approximately 2,000 Jews were shot, including a high proportion of women and children. The remaining Jews were driven into the wooden synagogue (the largest in Eastern Europe at the time) and the synagogue was set on fire; around 800 Jews burnt to death in the synagogue.

The Einsatzgruppen were supported by police reserve units. Police Battalion 309 carried out a massacre in Bialystok in eastern Poland on 27 June 1941. The police battalions included many 'ordinary men' conscripted into the police instead of the regular army. The total number of men involved in the mass killing of Jews and Communist party officials (especially Red Army commissars) now rose to 40,000 men. Jewish men were routinely being shot; with the extra manpower, Jewish women and children too were now to be shot. The Einsatzgruppen were also supported by auxiliary groups that they recruited from the local populations in areas such as Ukraine and Latvia. There were many eager volunteers.

**Einsatzgruppe A**
for Baltic States led by Dr Walther Stahlecker.

**Einsatzgruppe B**
for White Russia (Belarus) led by Artur Nebe.

**Einsatzgruppe C**
for North and Central Ukraine led by Dr Otto Rasch.

**Einsatzgruppe D**
for Bessarabia and Black Sea Russia led by Otto Ohlendorf.

**Fig. 5** *The Einsatzgruppen and their area of operations, 1941–42*

**Fig. 6** *'Special action.' A mass killing by Einsatzgruppe D, Vinnitsa in Ukraine*

In August 1941, Himmler personally visited the Einsatzgruppen and witnessed a 'special action' near Minsk in Belarus. During this visit, Himmler is said to have given a verbal order extending the shootings to women and children. There is no concrete proof of this, however, and the escalation of the killings may have been on the initiative of the Einsatzgruppen themselves rather than from orders above. This view is supported by the fact that there was considerable disparity between the actions of the different Einsatzgruppen. Some groups restricted their killing of Jews to the 'intelligentsia' and **partisans**. In other areas, the Einsatzgruppen and local volunteers set about killing as many Jews as possible. In the Baltic States, Special Group A under Stahlecker shot 250,000 Jews in 1941. In the same period, Special Group B under Artur Nebe shot 45,000.

## Key terms

**Partisans:** bands of irregular forces fighting a guerrilla war against the Germans behind the front.

At times, the Einsatzgruppen were frustrated by the intervention of the Wehrmacht (the German Army). Many regular army officers hated the SS and disapproved of the terrible actions of the Special Groups – though some top-level commanders actually supported them. In mid-October 1941, the Wehrmacht was being given orders to assist in the killing of Jews, all of whom were to be viewed as partisans. There were also, however, complaints from both the Wehrmacht and civilian authorities over the killing of Jews who were useful workers.

## Activity

### Revision exercise

Write a brief report from a senior officer in the Wehrmacht protesting to his superiors about the activities of the Einsatzgruppen in his area.

# Attitudes to Jews in Germany and occupied Europe to 1942

The intensification of Nazi terror during the war had an impact on attitudes, both within Germany and in the Nazi-occupied Europe. These attitudes included German soldiers and officials serving in the occupied territories, the governments and peoples of countries under Nazi control and public opinion inside Germany itself.

Nazi persecution of the Jews was not confined to Greater Germany and Poland. By June 1941, on the eve of the German invasion of the Soviet Union, Nazi Germany had established dominance over a range of 'satellite states'. In the West, Denmark, Norway, the Netherlands and Belgium were under occupation; France was ruled from Vichy by a pro-Nazi regime headed by Marshal Petain and Pierre Laval. In the East, Slovakia, Hungary and Romania were ruled by regimes sympathetic to or completely controlled by the Third Reich. Yugoslavia was invaded and overrun by German armies in June 1941.

## Attitudes to Jews in the occupied territories June 1941 to January 1942

### Western Europe

In France, the authoritarian Vichy regime headed by Marshal Petain was strongly influenced by anti-Semitism. French Jews were subjected to discrimination and anti-Semitic legislation similar to those in the Third Reich. At first, the Vichy regime was allowed the illusion of self-rule, but in 1942 the Germans put most of northern France under direct occupation. Many Jews were rounded up and sent to the Drancy internment camp near Paris and from there to the death camps in the east. This had tragic consequences for many Jews who had escaped from Germany to France before 1940, but who were no longer safe.

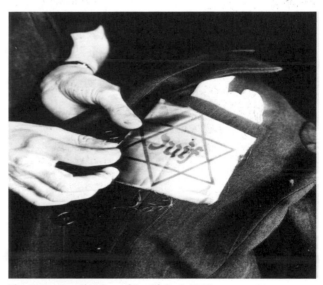

**Fig. 7** *Sewing on a Star of David, Paris 1942*

In Denmark, Norway, Holland and Belgium, pro-Nazi elements influenced or directly controlled the government. Jews suffered various levels of discrimination. The fate of the Frank family, Jews of German extraction living in Amsterdam in Holland, became famous after the war because of the publication of the diaries of the teenager Anne Frank, but the persecution the family suffered was typical of thousands of others all over Western Europe. Many were excluded from the economy and the professions. As in the case of France, there were no large-scale deportations until 1942 because the Nazis were so focused on the problems in the eastern occupied territories. The Jews of Western Europe and Germany within the pre-1937 borders had to wait.

**Fig. 8** *Anti-Semitic poster in Brussels, 1942*

### Did you know?

After the German conquest in 1940, France was seen as a possible destination for Jews removed from Germany. Twenty thousand Jews from western parts of Germany and from the recently annexed territories of Alsace and Lorraine were deported to France from July 1940. The Vichy government objected to France being used as a 'dumping ground' for German Jews and the policy was abandoned.

### Cross-reference

Anne Frank is profiled in Chapter 9, page 127.

## Activity

### Research exercise

Working in two groups, research the life of Jews living in occupied Western and Eastern Europe. One interesting angle could be comparing the diaries of Anne Frank with the diary of Rutka Laskier (a Polish girl of similar age).

## Activity

### Thinking point

What can you learn from the case study of Slovak Jews (see A closer look)?

## Cross-reference

The fate of the Slovak and Hungarian Jews is examined in Chapter 9, page 124.

### Eastern Europe

The rulers of Slovakia, Romania, Hungary and Bulgaria all introduced anti-Semitic measures, partly to please Hitler and partly to fall in line with anti-Semitic feelings within their countries. After June 1941, Croatia's pro-Nazi leaders introduced anti-Semitic legislation; later, thousands of Jews died in Croatian concentration camps. The Romanian dictator Ion Antonescu encouraged violence against Jews without directly ordering it. At first, Hungary was seen as a safe refuge for Jews from Germany, Austria, Poland and Czechoslovakia to flee to. The Jewish population of Hungary swelled from 400,000 in 1939 to almost 700,000 by 1944.

In the long term, they did not escape. Nearly 500,000 Jews were deported from Hungary to the death camps in 1944. Apart from the territories conquered by war and terror, the German authorities could rely on willing help from countries that had established 'friendly relations' with the Third Reich. Nazi policies were implemented by the governments of Germany's allies such as Italy, Hungary and Romania, or by sympathetic puppet regimes like those of France, Norway and Slovakia. One example of the extent to which governments in areas under German control were ready to assist Nazi race policies was Father Tiso, leader of the pro-Nazi regime in Slovakia from 1939.

## A closer look

### Slovak Jews

Slovakia was part of Czechoslovakia from 1919 until it became a separate, supposedly independent state in March 1939, when Hitler occupied the Czech lands, Bohemia-Moravia. In fact, Slovakia was a Nazi puppet state. The president, a Catholic priest, Father Josef Tiso, willingly signed the Treaty of Protection, giving Germany control over Slovakian foreign policy.

Tiso also followed the Nazi line in race policy. He was leader of the nationalistic and anti-Semitic Hlinka party. There were also particularly strong prejudices in Slovakia against gypsies. Tiso's government adopted harsh anti-Semitic policies against Slovakia's 90,000 Jews. Jewish businesses were confiscated and Jews were excluded from public life and forced to wear the yellow star. The government encouraged Jewish emigration and excluded Jewish children from schools.

Testimony from Slovak Jews reveals how quickly attitudes changed. Children they had played with all their lives turned on them. Tiso's militia, the Hlinka Guard, acted much like the SA in Germany in the 1930s, beating up Jews and attacking their businesses. Shops put up signs saying 'No Jews' and anti-Semitic posters were posted around Slovakian towns.

As elsewhere in Europe, the public attitudes in response to this were mixed, but there were many people who were motivated by long-standing anti-Semitic feelings and also many seizures of Jewish property. In 1942, Tiso agreed to hand Slovakia's Jews to the Germans for deportation to the death camps. Tiso's government paid Nazis 500 RM for every Jew they deported from Slovakia – on the express condition that they never came back.

The ferocious nature of the war on the Eastern Front and the Nazi rule of terror there had a significant effect on the Germans who were involved, not least the ordinary men in the Einsatzgruppen death squads. A true picture of the beliefs and feelings of regular soldiers and the Einsatzgruppen is difficult to draw because so many men died in the fighting on the Eastern Front, or were imprisoned in the USSR or returned to civilian life after the war and didn't speak of their experiences.

Many letters home from German soldiers at the front seem to suggest they had been brainwashed by the Nazi propaganda and believed they were doing the right thing. They had been taught that Soviet Jews were sub-humans and treated them as such. Other evidence indicates a deep psychological impact. There was often heavy drinking before and after the mass shootings by the Einsatzgruppen. Men were not always punished for refusing to participate; SS commanders, including Himmler himself, realised that many of the men were undergoing serious stress. When Himmler witnessed the 'special action' near Minsk in August 1941, he was personally shaken by what he saw and heard of the psychological impact on the men carrying out the mass shootings.

**Cross-reference**

The activities of the Einsatzgruppen are described on pages 105–6.

> Reichsführer, those were only a hundred. Look at the eyes of the men in this Kommando, how deeply shaken they are! These men are finished for the rest of their lives. What kind of followers are we training here? Either neurotics or savages!

**2**     *Comments by a senior SS officer to Himmler at a 'special action' near Minsk, August 1941. Taken from L. Rees, **Auschwitz: The Nazis and the 'Final Solution'**, 2005*

Not all the men, however, reacted in this way. One German-Austrian member of an *Einsatzkommando*, Felix Landau, wrote a diary. The entry for 3 July gives an insight into the psychology of mass killings (Source 3).

The Nazi occupation of Europe also brought out into the open deep anti-Semitic feelings among local people. There had always been a lot of virulent anti-Semitism in Eastern Europe and many local people shared the Nazi ideology. Another powerful motive was the desire for revenge against Bolshevik rule. In the Baltic States, the Soviet authorities had deported thousands of people to Siberia in 1940. In Ukraine, people had bitter memories of the man-made famine of 1933 when millions died due to Stalin's forced collectivisation of the countryside.

Among the local populations of Eastern Europe, few people were willing to defend the Jews against discrimination when they came under Nazi occupation. At worst, the local populations carried out pogroms and men volunteered to join the mass murder of Jews. This pattern was repeated all over Nazi-occupied Europe.

> I have little inclination to shoot defenceless people – even if they are only Jews. I would far rather fight in good honest open combat. Isn't it strange, you love battle and then you have to shoot defenceless people. Twenty-three had to be shot. The death candidates are organised into three shifts, because there are not enough shovels. Strange, I'm completely unmoved. No pity, nothing. That's the way it is and then it's all over.

**3**     *Comments by an SS officer. Taken from L. Rees, **The Nazis: A Warning From History**, 2005*

> I had expected people to tell me how much they hated the Communists; that seemed ludicrous, especially since there were hardly any Jews in the places I was visiting – Hitler and the Nazis had seen to that. Yet the old man in the Baltic States who had helped the Nazis shoot Jews in 1941 still thought he had done the right thing 60 years ago. And even some of those who fought against the Nazis held wild anti-Semitic beliefs.

**4**     *Account of an interview with a man who had volunteered to work with the Einsatzgruppen shooting Jews in the Baltic States. Taken from L. Rees, **Auschwitz: The Nazis and the 'Final Solution'**, 2005*

## Attitudes towards Jews in Germany

The war against the Soviet Union had top priority in 1941. The main focus of Nazi race policies was on the urgent problems in the eastern territories. The question of what to do about Reich Jews was pushed aside. Hitler's paranoia about the Jews, however, grew. From 1939, the impact of war had radicalised Nazi policies to a considerable extent. The *Aktion T4* euthanasia programme revealed the willingness of the regime to take extreme measures. The war with Soviet Russia intensified the pressure Hitler felt to deal with the 'Jewish question'.

A series of measures had further isolated Jews from German society by late 1941. Radio sets were confiscated from Jews; in November 1939, Jews were banned from buying radios. A month later, Jews were banned from buying chocolate. In 1940, Jews were excluded from the wartime rationing allowances for clothing and shoes. In July, an order limited them to entering shops at restricted times – in Berlin it was from 4pm to 5pm only. In 1941, regulations were tightened up to require Jews to have a police permit to travel. An order of December 1941 compelled Jews in Germany to wear the yellow Star of David, as was already the case with Jews in the occupied territories.

Nazi propaganda also became harder edged in presenting race issues. Three propaganda films of 1940 demonstrated this tendency towards a more openly anti-Semitic approach in the context of the war. The first, *The Eternal Jew*, was direct propaganda, in an outwardly factual documentary style. The presentation of Jews in the film was ugly and extreme. This seems to have had a negative effect on audiences. Blatant anti-Semitism may have reinforced the views of those who were already confirmed anti-Semites, or those from rural areas who had not come into contact with Jews in real life, but for other people it was often a turn-off. More subtle propaganda films with subliminal messages, leaving the audience to draw its own conclusions, were far more effective.

Another racist film released in 1940 was *Die Rothschilds: Aktien in Waterloo (The Rothschilds: Shares in Waterloo)*. This film depicted the rise of the Rothschild banking empire in the early 19th century – it was as much anti-British as anti-Jewish propaganda, though the danger from the Jewish world conspiracy was a key theme. Göbbels was closely involved with the production of *Die Rothschilds*, but he was disappointed by the audience reactions. He pulled the film from distribution and had it re-edited to strengthen its anti-Semitic messages before it was re-released in 1941. By then, however, Britain was no longer Germany's main enemy – and a new propaganda film was monopolising all the attention.

The third big anti-Semitic propaganda film of 1940 was the historical epic *Jud Süss*, a film that used the novel by Lion Feuchtwanger, ironically a Jewish author, about events in Württemberg in 1738. It showed the events leading to the execution of the Jewish merchant Süss for the rape of the beautiful Dorothea – an idealised German woman, played by the beautiful (and blonde) actress Kristina Söderbaum. The film was directed by one of Göbbels' favourite directors, Veit Harlan, director of two other impressive historical films with a powerful propaganda impact: *The Great King* in 1942 and *Kolberg* in 1945. *Jud Süss* used an entertaining period drama as a vehicle for a propaganda message that was intended to rouse Germans to take revenge against Jews.

Opinion research indicated that people responded better to propaganda sugar-coated as drama. The educated middle classes in particular found the extreme propaganda of films like *The Eternal Jew* crude and unappealing. They found the message of *Die Rothschilds* a bit confusing. Even *Jud Süss* received a very mixed reaction.

### ■ Cross-reference

The T4 euthanasia programme is discussed in Chapter 7, pages 95–9.

### ■ Activity

**Thinking point**

What effect do you think these different measures had on:

a Jews

b ordinary Germans?

### ■ Exploring the detail

*The Eternal Jew*

*The Eternal Jew* was a blatantly racist propaganda film that presented a corrupting influence associated with violent and sexual crimes, and with anarchism and Communism. In the film's most notorious sequence, images of largely eastern Orthodox Jews were interwoven with images of a plague of rats. The film was released in 1940, following the presentation of a series of large exhibitions of the same name. A poster from the film can be found in the section on Nazi propaganda, Chapter 5, page 72.

### ■ Cross-reference

The Rothschilds banking empire is profiled in Chapter 1, page 14.

## A closer look

### The impact of propaganda on racial attitudes: the case of *Jud Süss*

**Film: *Jud Süss***

| Credits: | Cast: |
|---|---|
| Story: From the novel by Lion Feuchtwanger | Dorothea: Kristina Söderbaum |
| Director: Veit Harlan | Süss Oppenheimer: Ferdinand Marian |
| Photography: Bruno Mondi | The Rabbi: Werner Krauss |
| Censor approval: August 1940 | The Duke of Württemberg: Heinrich George |
| Premiere: Venice, August 1940 | |

**Synopsis:**

The Jewish merchant, Süss Oppenheimer, arrives at Stuttgart in Württemberg from Frankfurt in the 1730s. He ingratiates himself with the Duke and gains great wealth and political power. Süss uses his power to kidnap the fiancé of the beautiful Dorothea – he uses the torture of the young man as a means of forcing Dorothea to have sex with him. She escapes and drowns herself in the lake. Süss is tried and condemned to death. Locked in an iron cage, he is hoisted up to be hanged; during the execution, pure white snow covers the scene. The Jews of Württemberg are driven out of the city. As they leave, a bystander shouts a warning: 'May the citizens of all other German states never forget this lesson'.

**Fig. 9** *French poster for the film* Jud Süss, *1940*

It is quite clear how Germans in 1940 were supposed to respond to this story set in 1738. Veit Harlan said of his film: 'I show age-old Judaism, as it was then and as it remains today. The film shows Süss the elegant court adviser, the treacherous schemer – in short, the disguised Jew'. Göbbels regarded the film as an artistic and propaganda triumph. It got a huge ovation at the Berlin premiere in October 1940.

The SS showed special interest in assessing reactions to the film. Many police reports indicated a negative response. There were comments like 'it makes you want to go and wash your hands' and many parents and teachers were heard to say that the film would have 'very harmful effects' if shown to children. On the other hand, the police reports noted with satisfaction that during a scene when the Jews enter Stuttgart, the cinema audience in Berlin shouted: 'Kick the last Jews out of Germany! Every last one of them!'

*Jud Süss* made a lasting impression. Himmler made it compulsory for SS personnel to see the film. The actor who played Süss Oppenheimer, Ferdinand Marian, was so appalled by the obvious links between the film and the Holocaust that he never got over his sense of guilt at being involved. Marian committed suicide by driving his car into a tree in 1950.

The pressure from social restrictions and the propaganda further isolated Jews in Germany, to the point where they became almost invisible to the wider community. Jews were increasingly viewed as the 'enemy within', but there is evidence that, despite all the anti-Semitic propaganda, there were still people in Germany who sympathised with the plight of the Jews.

Some German Jews received occasional acts of kindness or words of sympathy, even though open expressions of sympathy towards Jews

## Activity

**Thinking and analysis**

Produce a summary diagram to show the different techniques used in Nazi propaganda films.

There were numerous indications of distaste and disapproval for the introduction of the Yellow Star, along with sympathy for the victims. According to the diary entry of one woman in Berlin, 'the mass of the people is not pleased at this new decree. Almost all who come across us are ashamed as we are'. The Jewish intellectual Victor Klemperer, fearful at venturing out of doors once the Star of David singled him out, encountered indirect words of comfort from a tram-driver.

**5** *I. Kershaw, **Hitler: Nemesis 1936–1945**, 2001*

**Fig. 10** *Deportation of Jews from Germany, 1943*

could be a dangerous act. However, the more usual attitudes were open hostility or embarrassed silence. By the end of 1941, the position of Jews in Germany was desperate. Living any sort of normal life was becoming impossible. There was no longer any hope of escape by emigration. Public opinion was either in support of Nazi anti-Semitic policies or keeping silent.

The deteriorating situation of the war in the East and the potential entry of America into the war made matters even worse for Jews in Germany. Once the United States entered the war, there was no longer any need for Hitler to hold back. By the start of 1942, both within Germany and in Nazi-occupied Europe, everything was in place for the final phase of the deportation and extermination of Germany's remaining Jews.

■ **Activity**

**Revision exercise**

Working in pairs, make a chronological list of the key events in the practice of racism by the Nazi regime between September 1939 and December 1941. Compare your list with others and discuss which events were the most important and why.

*Learning outcomes*

In this section you have examined the development of anti-Semitic policies and actions by the Nazi regime in Germany and in the occupied territories between September 1939 and January 1942. You have gained an understanding of various strategies devised by the Nazis in order to deal with the 'Jewish question'. You have seen how the course of the Second World War influenced Nazi race policy – in Poland, in Western Europe and in the great war in the East against the USSR. You have examined the experiences of millions of Jews under the Nazi policies of Germanisation and ghettoisation, the implementation of the euthanasia programme and the mass killings by the Einsatzgruppen, and have considered how these policies prepared the way for the Holocaust to come.

AQA Examination-style questions

Study the following source material and answer the questions that follow.

In November 1938, when discussing how to deal with the housing issue when German Jews were evicted from their houses, Reinhard Heydrich of the SS said: 'As for the question of ghettos, I would like to make my position clear right away. From the point of view of the police, I don't think we could control a ghetto where Jews congregate amid the whole Jewish people. It would remain a hideout for criminals and also for epidemics and the like.'

**A**

*L. Rees, **Auschwitz: The Nazis and the 'Final Solution'**, 2005*

The deportation of the Jews to the General Government has been approved by the Führer. However, the whole process is to take place over a period of one year. The Jews are to be brought together in ghettos in the cities in order to ensure a better chance of controlling them and later of removing them. The most pressing matter is for the Jews to disappear from the countryside as small traders. This action must have been completed within the next three to four weeks. In so far as the Jews are traders in the countryside, it must be sorted out with the Wehrmacht how far these traders are needed to secure provisioning of the troops.

*Reinhard Heydrich's order to create ghettos: 21 September 1941. Taken from J. Noakes and G. Pridham (eds), **A Documentary Reader: Nazism 1919–1945, Volume 3, Foreign Policy, War and Racial Extermination**, 1998*

The ghetto system was a temporary phenomenon – it existed longer than had been expected initially but was always destined to be finished off at some point in the future – and thus ranked low in any claim on priorities. The inhabitants of the ghettos were at the very bottom of the Nazi racial hierarchy. Even the surrounding Polish population (which on Hitler's explicit orders was kept to a bare subsistence standard of living) had a greater right to scarce wartime resources than Jews. Nonetheless, the Polish ghettos should not be seen as some covert scheme cynically perpetrated by local German authorities to carry out gradual extermination, even though Jews in the ghettos understandably drew such conclusions. The Germans had every incentive to maximise ghetto productivity and they knew that starving Jews did not make the most productive workers.

*C. Browning, **The Origins of the Final Solution 1939–1942**, 2004*

(a) Study Sources A and B and use your own knowledge. Explain how far the views in Source B differ from those in Source A in relation to the policy of 'ghettoisation'.

*(12 marks)*

**AQA** Examiner's tip  Before writing your answer, you need to read both sources carefully and make a note of the main points on which the views of the sources differ. You should also make a note of at least one similarity. Once you have decided how you will argue, begin to write, looking at differences and similarites and providing an overall conclusion which answers 'how far'.

(b) Use Sources A, B and C and your own knowledge. How successful was 'ghettoisation' as a method of dealing with 'the Jewish question'?

*(24 marks)*

**AQA** Examiner's tip  It is important to remember that this type of question requires evaluation. You need to consider the ways in which ghettoisation was successful and the ways in which it was not. Remember there is also a focus on 'the Jewish question' and you will need to assess whether ghettoisation furthered a specific Nazi policy or was essentially a haphazard and inadequate response to circumstance. Whatever your argument, ensure that you provide some precise detail in support and reach a clear conclusion.

# 5 The Holocaust, 1941–45

## 9 The extermination of the Jews

*In this chapter you will learn about:*

■ the controversy surrounding the decision to begin the so-called 'Final Solution'

■ developments in 1941 and the Wannsee Conference in 1942

■ the gassings and deaths of Jews and other 'non-desirables'

■ the activities within the camps, including Auschwitz, and economic considerations

■ the situation in 1945, including the liberation of the camps.

**Fig. 1** Arbeit Macht Frei *(Work Sets You Free). The main entrance of Auschwitz I*

### Key chronology

**The 'Final Solution', 1942–45**

| 1942 | |
|---|---|
| January | Wannsee Conference |
| July | Round up of Jews from Vichy France |
| **1943** | |
| May | Concentration of all killings at Auschwitz |
| June | Start of deportations of Reich Jews from Germany |
| **1944** | |
| June | Mass deportation of Hungarian Jews to Auschwitz |
| November | Destruction and evacuation of Auschwitz |
| **1945** | |
| January | Liberation of Auschwitz |
| April | Liberation of Belsen and KZ Mauthausen Hitler's suicide |
| May | Germany's surrender |

From the beginning of 1942 to January 1945, the Nazi regime implemented its so-called 'Final Solution' to the 'Jewish question'. What had been rather confused and uncontrolled actions in 1940 and 1941, mixing mass killings with ghettoisation and deportations, were coordinated into a bureaucratic killing machine. Between 5 and 6 million people were systematically murdered. Most were Jews: from the Soviet Union after it was overrun by German forces; from the countries that were under Nazi occupation, such as Poland, France and Hungary; and from Germany itself. Countless other victims died in the same way – Soviet prisoners of war, gypsies, the disabled, and the dissidents regarded by the Nazis as 'asocial elements', or 'social undesirables'.

Even when the Third Reich faced inevitable defeat, the killings were accelerated, coming to an end only when invading allied armies liberated the camps in 1945. Soviet forces reached Auschwitz in January 1945. American and British forces liberated camps such as Dachau, Mauthausen, Buchenwald and Belsen in the spring of 1945. In those chaotic months, thousands of camp prisoners were driven on long forced marches. Many died along the way. Many more died even after the war was over, victims of malnutrition and disease.

This chapter records the where, the when and the how of the programme of systematic murder known as the **Holocaust**. The deaths of millions in the Holocaust amounted to an appalling historical crime, but it was one made up of millions of individual tragedies. The wider questions: *why* it happened, and *who* was responsible for it, are addressed in Chapter 10.

# The decision to begin the 'Final Solution'

The origins of the 'Final Solution' were complex and had deep roots. Hitler's ideological goals were fixed before 1933; if the Nazis ever came to power, it was certain that the Jewish people faced harmful consequences. Kristallnacht in November 1938 opened the way for increasingly violent persecution. For the Holocaust to take place, however, the Second World War was an essential precondition. Hitler himself explicitly linked the war in Europe with the fate of the Jews. When the decision was taken, late in 1940, to turn the war eastwards against the Soviet Union, it was clear that this would be a war of racial annihilation.

## Developments in 1941

By the time Operation *Barbarossa* was unleashed in June 1941, many aspects of the Holocaust were already in place. Under the T4 euthanasia programme, carried out against disabled children from 1939 to August 1941, the technical issues of using gas chambers to dispose of victims had already been developed. On the eastern front in the autumn of 1941, the so-called 'special actions' of the Einsatzgruppen had killed many thousands of Communist commissars and 'racial enemies of the Reich'.

Until late in 1941, however, the situation in the East was still confused by the war and by the chaotic nature of the Nazi regime. Many Nazi officials still believed that the aim was to make Germany 'Jew-free' by emigration, deportations and resettlement. Only a handful of well-informed senior Nazis knew Hitler's real intentions. The killings in the East had not yet been coordinated into systematic murder.

By the end of 1941, the Nazi regime had to face the fact that the complete conquest of the Soviet Union had not been achieved; and that final victory would have to wait until the summer of 1942 at the earliest. Some of the previous plans to send millions of deported Jews to be resettled on the island of Madagascar, or east of the Ural mountains into Siberia, had to be abandoned. It was clear by then, too, that the vast numbers of Jews already deported to the General Government area of Poland were too much for the authorities there to cope with. It was the urgency of the problems facing the Nazi regime late in 1941 that led to radical new policies being devised.

The key moment in the implementation of systematic murder was the Wannsee Conference, on 20 January 1942. It is important not to confuse Wannsee with the decision to kill Europe's Jews – that decision had been taken many weeks earlier. Wannsee was a meeting of senior bureaucrats to begin the implementation of policies already decided upon. The meeting was originally scheduled to take place in December 1941 – invitations went out in November. The timetable had to be pushed back due to the military crisis caused by the Soviet counter-offensive in front of Moscow in the first week of December, followed by Pearl Harbour and the entry into the war of Japan and the United States. New invitations went out on 6 January for the meeting to be held two weeks later.

This fact provides historians with a chronological framework for the launch of the 'Final Solution'.

- Wannsee was all about implementation, not decision taking.
- Invitations for the Wannsee meeting first went out in late November.
- Therefore, the decision itself had already been taken, at the latest, by November 1941.

## Key terms

**Holocaust:** term derived from the Greek word for 'burnt offering', used to define the mass murders of the Third Reich. Some historians claim it should refer exclusively to the Jews; in this book it refers to all the victims of Nazi racial extermination.

## Cross-reference

For Hitler's early ideology see Chapter 3, pages 45–9.

For *Kristallnacht*, see Chapter 6, pages 78–80.

For links between Nazi foreign policy and the fate of the Jews, see Chapter 8, pages 101–5.

For Operation *Barbarossa*, see Chapter 8, pages 103–5.

For the T4 euthanasia programme see Chapter 7, pages 95–9.

For the actions of the *Einsatzgruppen*, see Chapter 8, pages 105–6.

## Cross-reference

Emigrations, deportations and resettlement are covered in Chapter 7, pages 89–93.

The Madagascar Plan is the subject of Chapter 8, pages 101–2.

## Exploring the detail

The best short account of the decision-making process that produced the 'Final Solution' in 1941 is by Ian Kershaw in Chapter 10 of *Fateful Choices: Ten Decisions That Changed The World 1940–1941* (2007).

## Cross-reference

The origins of the decision to implement the 'Final Solution' are covered in Chapter 8, pages 104 and 112.

## The Wannsee Conference, 20 January 1942

**Fig. 2** *The Villa by the Lake. The scene of the Wannsee meeting, January 1942*

The importance of the Wannsee Conference is frequently misrepresented as the occasion when the final decision was taken to exterminate European Jewry. In reality, Wannsee was a meeting to inform high-level bureaucrats of their roles in implementing a decision that had already been taken – most historians now agree that the decision came fairly soon after the invasion of the Soviet Union on 22 June. Exactly what that decision *was*, however, is still a matter of controversy and debate. Was it the signal for a new policy of all-out **genocide**? Or a decision to widen the existing programme of deportations to 'reservations' somewhere in the East? Or was it a sudden emergency decision, forced by the fact that the German conquest of the Soviet Union has unexpectedly stalled?

Fifteen high Nazi officials were in the villa at Wannsee on 20 January for the top-secret meeting. The chairman was Reinhard Heydrich, the most powerful man in the SS after Heinrich Himmler. Heydrich had received orders from Hermann Göring, empowering him to organise the preparations for the 'Final Solution' to the 'Jewish question'. Some historians believe that the driving force was an unwritten order from Hitler; others have speculated that Heydrich was involved in 'empire building' – acting on his own initiative to enhance his power and authority.

The officials invited to Wannsee represented important bureaucratic organisations:

- Gauleiter Meyer and Dr Leibbrandt from the ministry of the eastern occupied territories.
- Dr Stuckart of the Reich ministry of the interior.
- Secretary Neumann, from the Office of the Four Year Plan.
- Dr Freisler, from the Reich ministry of justice; Secretary Buhler, from the General Government Poland.
- Dr Luther, from the foreign office.
- SS Oberführer Klopfer, from the party chancellery.
- Director Kritzinger, from the Reich chancellery.
- SS Gruppenführer Hofmann, RSHA (Reich Security Head Office).
- SS Gruppenführer Müller of the Gestapo.
- SS Sturmbannführer Lange, Security Police Latvia and Ostland.
- SS Oberführer Schongarth, Security Police General Government Poland.
- SS Obersturmbannführer Eichmann, RSHA (in charge of administrative arrangements for the meeting).

Some of these men, like Kritzinger, were old-style bureaucrats, present to receive instructions; others, like Buhler, were rabid anti-Semites. Some, like Luther, were opportunists, keen to advance their careers. Some, like

### ■ Key terms

**Genocide:** the deliberate attempt to destroy an entire race or people. This term can be very controversial – for example, many people have insisted that it should be applied to the Jewish Holocaust and nobody else; others have used the term for the mass killings of Armenians by Turks in 1915–16, or the massacres in Rwanda in 1994.

### ■ Exploring the detail

The best factual account of the Wannsee Conference is by Mark Roseman, *The Villa, The Lake, The Meeting* (2002). There is also an excellent dramatised reconstruction in the film *Conspiracy*, starring Kenneth Branagh as Heydrich.

### ■ Cross-reference

Reinhard Heydrich and Adolf Eichmann are profiled in Chapter 6, page 86.

Müller and Eichmann, were high-level operatives at the heart of the SS police state and its killing operations.

According to the one surviving copy of the official minutes, Heydrich began proceedings with a review of the previous policy of emigration between 1939 and October 1941, when Himmler banned all further emigration. Heydrich then announced that the 11 million European Jews were to be 'evacuated' to the East.

> In the course of the Final Solution, and under appropriate leadership, the Jews should be put to work in the east. Doubtless, the large majority will die of natural causes. Any final remnant that survives will doubtless consist of the most recalcitrant elements. They will have to be dealt with appropriately because otherwise, by natural selection, they would form the germ cell of a new Jewish revival. Europe will be combed through from west to east. Germany proper, including Bohemia and Moravia, will have to be dealt with first, due to the housing problem and other social necessities.

 *Reinhard Heydrich speaking at the Wannsee Conference, 20 January 1942*

**Fig. 3** *Reinhard Heydrich*

The discussions that followed considered how *Mischlinge* (people of 'mixed race') were to be categorised, what to do about transportation bottlenecks and other administrative issues. It was agreed that there would still be exemptions for 'irreplaceable' Jews working in vital war industries. There was also discussion of the legal position under the 1935 Nuremberg Laws.

### Aftermath of the Wannsee Conference

What happened after Wannsee seemed to prove that the purpose of the meeting was to clarify the previously confused situation concerning deportations to the East. Heydrich considered the meeting a great success. The civilian authorities had all shown to be willing to follow the lead of the RSHA and not to make objections. The deportations of Jews became much more organised – no longer sent to vague destinations somewhere in Poland, but sent to specific areas where there was an organised camp system.

The way was open to coordinate and accelerate mass killings. It was from February 1942 to February 1943 that more than half of all Jews to die in the Holocaust were exterminated. However, it is not certain that the acceleration of mass killings from early 1942 was entirely due to the effect of the Wannsee Conference. In *Hitler's Unwritten Order*, the historian Peter Longerich argues that Heinrich Himmler (who was not involved at Wannsee) played a key role in intensifying the 'Final Solution' and that there must have been further high-level decisions taken after Wannsee.

> Wannsee itself was not the key moment of decision. Nobody at Wannsee, not even Heydrich was senior enough to decide on such matters. The fate of the *Mischlinge* revealed that, if the right arguments were passed up to Hitler, agreements secured at Wannsee could be undone. It is also true that, if Hitler's approval was assured, Himmler would undoubtedly have proceeded as he did even without the agreements Heydrich secured at Wannsee. The Wannsee meeting was rather a signpost indicating that genocide had become official policy.

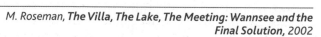 *M. Roseman, **The Villa, The Lake, The Meeting: Wannsee and the Final Solution**, 2002*

## Activity

### Thinking point

As a class, watch part of the TV film *Conspiracy*. Working in two groups, set out a range of arguments to support the view that:

**a** the film gives a convincing representation of historical truth

**b** the film does not give a convincing representation of historical truth.

## ■ Mass killings of Jews and other 'racial undesirables'

In his 1997 book, Henry Friedländer wrote:

> Racial ideology prepared the way. There was no substantive difference between the handicapped, the gypsies and the Jews. The Nazi obsession with 'eugenics' and racial purity dictated the complete elimination of all 'racial undesirables'.

*H. Friedländer, The Origins of Nazi Genocide: From Euthansia to the Final Solution, 1997*

From early 1942, this became a war aim in itself, as important as winning military victory over the Soviet Union and its allies. By 1942, ideology and propaganda had already prepared the way for the 'Final Solution'. The bureaucratic machinery of the SS was fully functioning. The system of camps in the eastern occupied territories was in place, ready to be expanded as needed. The Nazi regime was nearly at the end of the 'twisted road to Auschwitz'.

### ■ A closer look

#### The role of the SS

The SS was a dynamic, ever-expanding organisation. In 1925, it was a small personal bodyguard, completely overshadowed by the huge sprawling militia of the SA. In the early 1930s, the SS took a leading role in developing Nazi racial ideology, through the Race and Resettlement Unit set up under R. W. Darré in 1931. After the Night of the Long Knives in 1934, Himmler was established as one of the most powerful Nazi barons and the SS steadily began to absorb all security powers in the Third Reich. By 1937, the SS controlled all regular police as well as the secret security police. In 1938 and 1939, the annexation of territories from Czechoslovakia enabled the SS police empire to expand into areas where there were no bureaucratic rivals to the SS. During the war, the SS expanded its role in guarding the camps to set up a powerful independent army, the Waffen SS.

### ■ Cross-reference

To recap on the Night of the Long Knives, look back to Chapter 4, page 54.

Himmler is profiled in Chapter 3, page 45.

### ■ Key profile

#### R. W. Darré

Darré (1895–1953) was born in Argentina and educated in England. He was a specialist in agriculture and the land, a passionate believer in the ideology of 'Blood and Soil' (*Blut und Boden*) and selective breeding (he was at one time a pig farmer) whose ideas had a lot of influence over Heinrich Himmler in the late 1920s and early 1930s. In 1931, Darré was placed at the head of the new SS Race and Resettlement Unit, but was an ineffective organiser and did not have much power within the SS. From 1933, he was in charge of the Reich Food Estate, the Nazi organisation set up to help small farmers.

The SS was above all things a bureaucracy, built on administrative efficiency. Its power was based on 'terror by typewriter' – tightly organised systems, controlled from the centre. Heinrich Himmler and Reinhard Heydrich were the ultimate examples of bureaucratic power, with the ability to exploit little pieces of authority granted by Hitler and then to widen them out through a network of offices and departments. As *Reichsführer SS*, Himmler was the closest to Hitler at the top. Heydrich had a power base in the RSHA (Reich Security Head Office) and was also Protector of Bohemia and Moravia, the Czech lands annexed in 1938–39. Below Himmler and Heydrich, a mass of SS leaders controlled the various organisations. The Wannsee Conference was part of this expansion of SS power, strengthening the SS grip on ideology, race policy and the camps system.

## The camps system

It is important not to confuse the death camps in operation from 1942 to 1945 with the wider system of concentration camps for political prisoners that had existed from the earliest stages of the Third Reich, commencing with **KZ** Dachau, near Munich, in 1933. There were 'ordinary' concentration camps near almost every main population centre in Germany: Dachau, KZ Sachsenhausen near Berlin, Bergen-Belsen near Hannover, Buchenwald near Weimar, and so on. After the Anschluss, KZ Mauthausen was built near Linz in Upper Austria.

Such camps were brutal places, but they were not designed as centres of extermination. They housed political prisoners of all kinds, from Catholics to homosexuals, from socialists to petty criminals. Most Germans knew at least a little about the concentration camps. Some approved of their existence, satisfied with the punishment of 'social deviants'. Most people feared them, intimidated into silence and compliance by the threat they posed to anyone who provoked the regime.

**Fig. 4** *Concentration camps and death camps in Nazi-occupied Europe*

The system of camps in the eastern occupied territories that came into operation from the end of 1941 was on an enormous scale and fulfilled many different functions. At the heart of the system was the machinery of extermination – death camps built for the specific purpose of killing Jews and other 'racial undesirables'. The railway entrance to Auschwitz-Birkenau has become the ultimate emotive symbol of this process, the place where trainloads of new arrivals were unloaded and those deemed 'unproductive' were selected for immediate transfer to the gas chambers. But Auschwitz took time to build up its factory of death. Only about one-fifth of the victims of the Holocaust died there. Other death camps also had a key role in the system:

■ Chelmno (Kulmhof), about 40 miles from Lodz, was the first killing centre to be established, in December 1941. At Chelmno, killings were first carried out by mobile gas vans using carbon monoxide – the use of **Zyklon B** was developed later. About 145,000 died there. Chelmno was situated in a part of Poland designated for 'Germanisation' – other death camps were built further east, outside the German Reich.

■ Majdanek, near Lublin, was built late in 1940 as an ordinary concentration camp. From late 1941 it became a death camp. About 200,000 people died there, 60 per cent of them Jews, the others Soviet POWs or Polish political prisoners.

■ **Key terms**

**KZ:** stands for *Konzentrationslager* (concentration camp).

**Zyklon B:** the poison gas that was used in the gas chambers of the death camps. Zyklon B was a form of cyanide, originally developed by a Jewish scientist as a weapon for use in the First World War. The role of the chief manufacturer, I. G. Farben, led to controversy after the war.

■ Belzec, near Lvov, was originally a labour camp but was used as a death camp from March 1942 until the spring of 1943, when the camp was closed down. More than half a million Jews were killed there, together with several thousand gypsies.

■ Sobibor was built near Lublin as part of the construction programme agreed upon at the Wannsee Conference. Its SS commandant, Franz Stangl, later commanded the camp at Treblinka. About 250,000 victims died there, mostly Jews and Soviet POWs. In October 1943 a Jewish revolt led to the escape of 800 prisoners. The camp was closed down on Himmler's orders soon afterwards.

■ Treblinka, about 75 miles from Warsaw, was constructed for the purpose of mass killing. From July 1942 until operations ceased in September 1943, almost 1 million people were murdered there, first about 300,000 Jews from Warsaw and later Jews from all over central Europe.

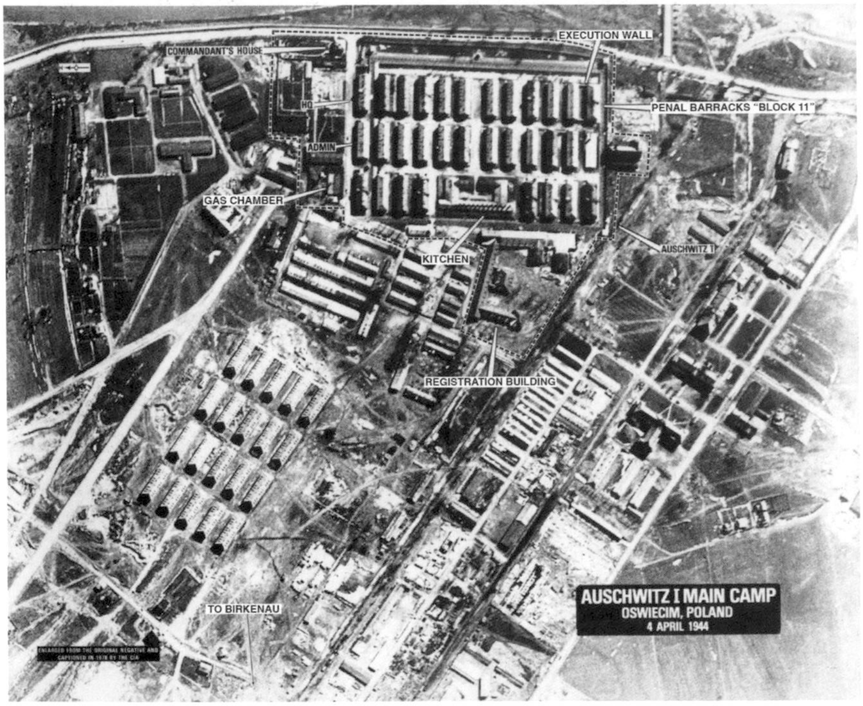

Apart from Chelmno, the death camps were built deep in the occupied territories away from the incorporated German Reich. This was partly opportunistic (the camps were built near the centres of population that had been overrun by advancing German forces), but also because their locations would supposedly be out of sight from mainstream Germany. Not even the Nazis wished to boast publicly what 'resettlement' actually meant in practice. In fact, it was impossible to maintain complete secrecy. Polish farmers living near the camps could all too easily see and smell what was happening there; many Germans, such as railway workers, witnessed the trainloads of deportees rolling eastwards out of Germany. By late 1943, the first camps had all finished operating – from then on, killing operations were concentrated at Auschwitz-Birkenau.

### Auschwitz

In 1943 and 1944, Auschwitz (Oswiecim in Poland), a few miles west of Crakow, became the hub of the vast killing machine established by the Nazis. The development of Auschwitz took a considerable time; until mid-1943, the main killing centres were at camps such as Sobibor, Belzec and Treblinka. Most of these camps were closed down after the Jewish populations in their vicinity had been killed.

**Fig. 5** *Plan of Auschwitz*

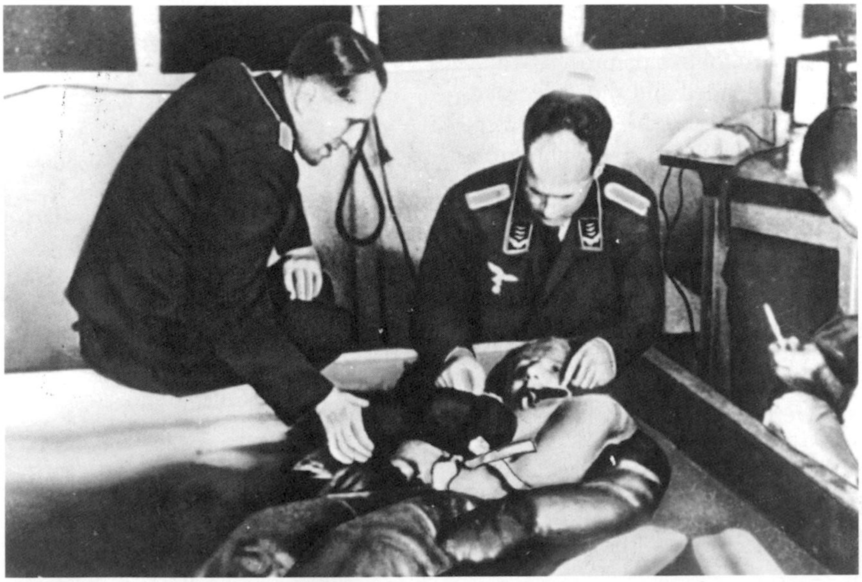

**Fig. 6** *The cold water treatment. SS 'medical' experiments at KZ Dachau*

Auschwitz was more than a death camp. It was a huge sprawling complex of buildings with many different functions. Auschwitz I, in the old Habsburg army barracks, remained active, but was overshadowed by Auschwitz II, the huge camp at Birkenau, the arrival centre for transports from the West and the place where the main gas chambers and crematoria were situated. Auschwitz III, on the other side of the railway tracks at Monowitz, was a huge industrial complex, producing munitions and other essential goods for the war effort. In outlying districts, a chain of smaller satellite camps contained industrial enterprises run by the SS and were dependent upon forced labour provided from Auschwitz.

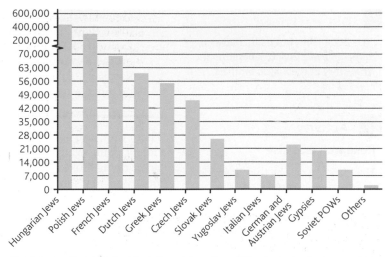

Note: Estimates of the total deaths at Auschwitz vary between 1.1m and 1.8m.

**Fig. 7** *Murders at Auschwitz, 1942–45*

## Key profile

### Josef Mengele

Mengele (1911–79) was the notorious camp physician in Auschwitz from 1943. Known as the 'Angel of Death', Mengele supervised **selections** when transports arrived at Auschwitz and conducted appalling medical experiments on inmates. He was obsessed with 'research' on identical twins. He left Auschwitz just before it was liberated in January 1945 and carried on his work at Gross-Rosen in Silesia and then in Bohemia. He was captured by the Americans, but managed to assume a false identity and was not charged as a war criminal. He worked as a farm labourer in Bavaria until 1949, when he escaped to South America.

## Key terms

**Selections:** the process of selecting which people would be sent to the gas chambers immediately on arrival at a death camp, as opposed to those who might have skills that would be useful for forced labour.

## A closer look

### Jewish resistance

One of the persistent myths about the Holocaust is the theme of victimhood and Jewish passivity – the idea that the victims of the Nazis invariably accepted their fate with docility and resignation. In reality, there was extensive Jewish resistance. The Nazi authorities went to great lengths to prevent this, both by intimidation and by concealing what was actually happening until the last possible moment. This had only partial success and there were many instances of resistance and protest. The fact that resistance could only ever be small in scale and had no chance at all of lasting success should not obscure the fact that it was there.

Across Eastern Europe, groups of partisan fighters established base camps deep in the forests and carried out acts of sabotage against the German occupiers. Many of these groups were nationalist or Communist, but there were also numerous Jewish groups. About 10,000 Jewish partisans were active in Lithuania in early 1942. In the General Government of Poland, the Nazi governor,

■ Activity

**Research exercise**

The question of why the allies did not do more in response to the reports they received about the Holocaust from 1942 remains controversial. There have been persistent accusations ever since that allied inaction was due to insufficient caring for the Jews – even anti-Semitism. Most historians place more emphasis on the practical problems, such as the difficulty of saving lives by the use of heavy bombers.

Do some research on the reports of the 'Final Solution' that were reaching allied governments from 1942; and on the reasons why these reports did not lead to more decisive action.

Hans Frank, had to commit large security forces to try to deal with more than 20 different Jewish partisan groups. In Belarus, from autumn 1941 onwards, a Jewish resistance group led by the Bielski brothers eventually became a permanent community of 1,200 partisans. In addition to acts of sabotage, the Bielski group also provided a refuge for Jews escaping from the ghettos.

There were also sporadic revolts in the ghettos and the camps. One violent rising against the Nazis took place in the ghetto of Bialystok. A larger rising broke out in the Warsaw ghetto in January 1943. This rising took the SS by surprise; 80 per cent of the Jews in Warsaw had already been sent to the death camp at Treblinka. The first attempts to crush the rising failed. It was only in May 1943 that the last resistance in the Warsaw ghetto was finally crushed by 2,000 German troops, using heavy weapons and supported by air strikes.

There were organised revolts in the Sobibor and Treblinka death camps in 1943. At Auschwitz-Birkenau in 1944, Jewish prisoners blew up Crematorium 4. A network of Jewish organisations smuggled detailed evidence to inform the western allies about the Nazi extermination programme. Messages were passed successfully to western embassies, but had little impact, partly because western governments found it difficult to take in the full horror of what was happening, partly because it was so difficult to take any practical action to stop it.

Deportations became more frequent. Jews were made to leave their homes. Children were separated from their mothers. Forced labour on slave wages was common. Reports were received from time to time of torture and murder, of Jews being exterminated for no other reason than that they were Jews. Finally, in the middle of the year 1942, when many people thought such horrors had reached a climax, evidence was forthcoming of a plan of extermination that goes beyond anything in history. That destruction is proceeding, by shootings and by lethal gas. And it is not confined to one country but is continent-wide. The number of Jewish victims who have 'perished' in Axis-controlled Europe now approaches two million; five million are in danger of extermination.

3 *'The Persecution of the Jews', a report by the Inter-Allied Information Committeee, London (December 1942). Published by HMSO*

**Fig. 8** *The crematorium at Terezin (Theresienstadt) north of Prague*

## The intensification of Nazi policies in 'Total War'

When the war turned against Germany in 1942–43, it might have been expected that the Nazi regime would slacken its attempts to exterminate the Jews; what actually happened was that the mass killings were accelerated and were given higher priority than military needs. Nazi propaganda became even more hate-filled than before.

A rising river of anti-Semitic hatred in the period from June 1941 to late 1942 had accompanied Nazi military success and expansion, the murders by the *Einsatzgruppen* and *Ordungspolizei* units, and the start of full operations in the death camps. In 1943 the combined and coordinated efforts of Dietrich, Goebbels, and their staffs turned that river into a raging flood. The flood of radical anti-Semitic propaganda began in late winter 1943. The torrent continued in two intense bursts, in April through July, and in October and November. Between January 1939 and April 1945, eighty-four anti-Semitic lead stories appeared in the *Der Völkische Beobachter*.

**4**        *J. Herf, **The Jewish Enemy: Nazi Propaganda During World War II and The Holocaust**, 2006*

## ■ Key profile

### Otto Dietrich

It is a mistake to think of Dr Göbbels as a one-man band, personally responsible for Nazi propaganda. There was a huge range of organisations and agencies pumping out the propaganda message – one key player was Dr Otto Dietrich (1897–1952), head of the Reich Press Office. Dietrich was press officer of the Nazi Party from 1931 to 1945; from 1937 he was secretary to Göbbels. He was sentenced to a long prison term at the Nuremberg War Crimes Tribunal, but was released in 1950.

---

The intensification of the Nazi propaganda war against the Jews ran in parallel to the periods of crisis in Germany's war effort. The weeks and months after the German surrender at Stalingrad in February 1943, for example, witnessed the epic 'Total War' speech by Göbbels in the Berlin Sportspalast in mid-February, followed by a massive propaganda drive in the Nazi press. There was another similar surge of anti-Jewish propaganda in the autumn of 1943, at a time when Mussolini had been overthrown in Italy, Germany was suffering from mass bombing raids and the Red Army was beginning to push back German forces in the East. There was another surge in the summer of 1944 at the time of the allied landings in France.

Numerous articles and speeches by Göbbels and other Nazi leaders emphasised the idea that the war would result in the destruction of the Jews. The Nazi regime did not spell out what was actually taking place in the 'Final Solution', but the general threat of destruction was hammered out again and again (Source 5).

We are moving ahead. The fulfilment of the Führer's prophecy about which world Jewry laughed when he made it in 1939 stands at the end of our course of action. Even in Germany the Jews laughed when we stood up for the first time against them. Among them laughter is now a thing of the past. They chose to make war against us. But Jewry now understands that the war has become a war against them. When Jewry conceived of the plan for the total extermination of the German people, it wrote its own death sentence.

**5**        *Josef Göbbels, radio speech, 9 May 1943. Taken from J. Herf, **The Jewish Enemy: Nazi Propaganda During World War II and The Holocaust**, 2006*

■ **Exploring the detail**

**The murder of Hungarian Jews, 1944**

The largest single example of the urgency to push through the 'Final Solution' was the mass murder of Hungarian Jews between April and June 1944. Organised by Adolf Eichmann, 454,000 Jews were transported from Budapest by 147 trains. Most were sent to the gas chambers immediately on arrival.

The radical propaganda was reflected in the urgency of Nazi actions. Mass killings were accelerated. The Jewish populations of states such as France, Italy, Greece and Slovakia were rounded up for deportation. A fifth crematorium was built at Auschwitz. The Jewish ghettos at Minsk and Vilnius were destroyed. In February 1944, the remaining Jews of Amsterdam were deported to Auschwitz.

By the summer of 1944, it was clear that Germany faced inevitable defeat in the war, but this realisation did not cause the 'Final Solution' to be abandoned – it had the reverse effect. Only in November 1944, when the Soviet armies had advanced deep into Poland, did the Nazis move to close down the killing machine and try to conceal what they had been up to. The crematoria at Auschwitz were blown up and hastily covered over. The surviving prisoners were pressed into forced marches westwards, away from the approaching Red Army. These efforts at concealment were half-hearted and futile. The sheer size of the complex at Auschwitz-Birkenau made total destruction impossible. Even today, more than 60 years after the war, it is all too easy to walk around the ruins of the camp and recognise ways in which it operated.

**Fig. 9** *Slave labour. Polish women working at a mine in Silesia c.1941*

## Forced labour and economic considerations

Auschwitz was a massive complex that included factories and a wide range of SS economic enterprises. One profitable industry was recycling the valuables seized from victims. Camp labour was utilised in the big synthetic rubber factory at Monowitz (Auschwitz III). Jewish prisoners with special skills were employed on individual projects such as Operation *Bernhard*.

■ **A closer look**

### Operation *Bernhard*

Operation *Bernhard* was an example of the way forced labour was exploited by the Nazis through the camps system. SS planners believed that it might be possible to destabilise the British economy by printing vast quantities of forged £5 notes that would then be circulated throughout Europe. From 1942, high-quality forgeries were produced by Jewish prisoners, hand-picked for their special skills, as printers or as experienced criminals. Secrecy would be guaranteed by keeping production in Auschwitz-Birkenau. One of the peculiar features of the plan was that the notes were to be 'laundered' through *Salon Kitty*, the large SS-run brothel in Berlin.

The SS cunning plan did not actually achieve any significant success. The Jewish craftsmen were capable of producing almost perfect forgeries, but this took time – not least because the craftsmen realised that they would certainly be exterminated once their work was finished. They contrived to delay the project by inventing all sorts of technical hitches. Even if the forged £5 notes had gone into mass production, it was unrealistic to hope that this would ever have had more than a nuisance effect on Britain's war economy by that stage of the war. The project was abandoned in 1944. The money was hidden in the mountains of the southern Alps. American troops arriving in the area early in 1945 were puzzled to discover a large number of metal cases containing enormous amounts of £5 notes.

■ **Exploring the detail**

The story of the SS forgery plan is told by Anthony Pirie in his entertaining book, *Operation Bernhard* (1961).

The economic importance of Auschwitz extended far beyond the camp itself. Many smaller SS camps were situated within easy reach of Auschwitz. In the surrounding area, there were also more than 100 private industrial enterprises that depended upon labour provided by prisoners who were leased out by the camps, often marched out and back on a daily basis. According to some estimates, nearly 30 per cent of the Nazi war economy depended upon the use of forced labour. The SS became an economic empire as well as a police and security empire. Forced labour did not only apply to the Jews. Other categories, such as Soviet POWs, were also exploited for their labour, though this merely postponed their fate for as long as they were useful.

Camp Dora was one significant example of the importance of forced labour to the SS. In 1943, near Nordhausen in the Harz mountains, Nazi engineers employed a mass army of forced labourers to build top-secret factory installations deep underground, safe from allied bombing raids, for the V2 and V3 rocket missile programme. Conditions in the caves were appalling and the death rate was extremely high.

**Fig. 10** *Sub-camps around Auschwitz*

Camp Dora seemed to symbolise the irrationality of Nazi policies. On the one hand, the work being carried out there was vital to the Nazi war effort; keeping the workers alive and fit to work was in the Nazi interest. On the other hand, the logic of the SS operations was racist and destructive, designed to bring about the deaths of 'racially inferior beings' in the end. As a result, a valuable source of labour, often selected because they had vital skills, was wasted by being literally worked to death.

Many senior officials knew this. One high-level SS administrator, Otto Bräutigam, made persistent protests to his bosses about the waste of human resources. The munitions minister, Albert Speer, the man with overall responsibility for war production, claimed in his memoirs that he had made frequent complaints to Himmler. The protests had little or no effect. The slave labourers continued to die. What happened at Camp Dora and other installations exploiting forced labour appeared to show that racial extermination was an even more important aim than winning the war. By no means were all the workers at Nordhausen Jewish, but the twisted ideology of the SS saw them all as 'sub-humans' – not merely expendable but racial enemies of the true German *Volk*.

■ Key profile

### Albert Speer

Speer (1905–81) became munitions minister in early 1942, when Hitler unexpectedly chose him to replace Fritz Todt, who had been killed in a plane crash. This was precisely at the time when the German economy had to be geared up for 'Total War'. Speer was brilliantly successful in reorganising the war economy. His 'production miracle' boosted war production by 400 per cent. In doing so, Speer relied extensively on forced labour. Speer always claimed that he knew next to nothing about the terrible conditions in the camps (run by the SS) but, after the war, he was sentenced to 20 years' imprisonment for war crimes.

### Activity

**Talking point**

Working in two groups, make a list of the reasons why the SS kept Jews alive for use as forced labour, but did not feed and house them well enough to enable them to be productive.

## ■ The situation in 1945

The implementation of the 'Final Solution' was never completed. By the end of 1944, Auschwitz had to be closed down. In January 1945, Soviet forces advancing westwards through Poland liberated Auschwitz. In the months that followed, allied armies drove deeper into the Reich. In the West, American forces liberated Dachau and Mauthausen. In the North, British forces liberated Bergen-Belsen and Buchenwald. By May 1945, Hitler was dead, Germany had surrendered and the full horror of the camps was finally becoming apparent.

### Evacuations and forced marches

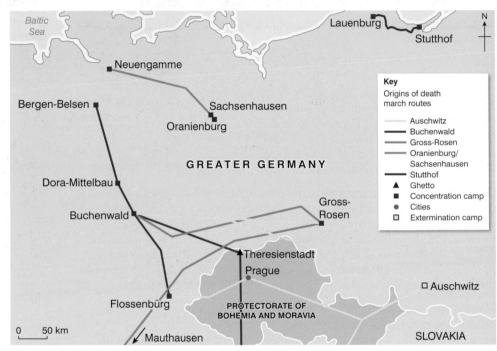

**Fig. 11** *Major death marches and evacuations, 1944–45*

The military defeat of the Third Reich did not bring a neat and tidy end to the death and suffering of the victims of the Holocaust. From autumn 1944, as German forces pulled back, the Nazi regime carried out a frantic programme of evacuations and forced marches. Camps were hurriedly closed down and the inmates sent on long marches westwards, away from the advancing Red Army.

These '**death marches**' caused terrible suffering and loss of life. Often in freezing winter weather, people who were already malnourished and had inadequate shoes and clothing were forced to march. Many died of illness and exhaustion; hundreds were shot by their guards for failing to keep up the required pace. Even if they survived their first forced march from one camp to a new one, many prisoners had to repeat the awful experience all over again as that new camp was evacuated when enemy forces approached.

It is difficult to know exactly how many victims died on the death marches; estimates range from 250,000 to 400,000. Many of them were women. The death marches continued right up to the end of the war. One well-known victim among the many thousands who died during the mass movement of prisoners to the west was 15-year-old Anne Frank, the Jewish Dutch girl who was made world famous by the publication of her diary after the war.

### ■ Key terms

**Death marches:** the forced marches of 1945, when thousands of prisoners in the camps were moved westwards as Soviet armies liberated the eastern territories of the Reich. Conditions were appalling and many died.

## Key profile

### Anne Frank

Anne Frank's (1929–45) family was sheltered by non-Jewish neighbours who hid them in a secret annexe to their home in Amsterdam. After nearly two years in hiding, the Franks were arrested and sent to Auschwitz. Late in 1944, the Nazis evacuated the camp and forced the prisoners to march west to Germany. Anne, now 15, died of exhaustion and despair during the deportations to the west in March 1945. Her mother and her sister also died during the forced march. Anne's father survived, because he was too sick to be moved, and remained at Auschwitz until the liberation.

## Key chronology

**The liberation of the camps in 1945**

| | |
|---|---|
| January | Liberation of Auschwitz by Soviet forces |
| April | Liberation of Dachau by American forces |
| | Liberation of Belsen by British forces |
| | Death of Adolf Hitler |
| May | Liberation of KZ Mauthausen by American forces |
| | Surrender of Germany |
| | Capture and suicide of Heinrich Himmler |

At KZ Mauthausen near Linz in 1989, Sarah, an A Level student from Chorley, stood alone in the Garden of Remembrance. She translated for herself the German text of the inscription on a memorial plaque commemorating the 2,500 women, mostly Jews, who had been marched hundreds of miles west from Auschwitz to Mauthausen and who had all died there in a typhus epidemic in May 1945, just after the camp had been liberated by the Americans. Through the tears she said aloud: 'It wasn't fair.' It was as good an epitaph as any.

## The liberation of the camps

On 27 January 1945, advance units of the First Ukrainian Army Group reached the massive complex of camps at Auschwitz-Birkenau. By then, most of the camp prisoners had been evacuated and sent on forced marches to the west. The Soviet liberators found mostly children and those adults who had been too sick to be evacuated. As they fought their way westwards, Soviet forces encountered more and more former camps; they finally liberated KZ Sachsenhausen, at Oranienburg, north of Berlin, in May 1945.

## Exploring the detail

Striking accounts of the liberation of the camps are provided by the live radio report by Richard Dimbleby for the BBC; in the 'Nemesis' episode of *World At War* and the colour film coverage of the recently-liberated camp at Dachau in *D-Day to Berlin* by George Stevens.

The liberation of the camps was often a traumatic experience for the liberators. The organisation of the camps had collapsed, leaving sick and starving prisoners to fend for themselves. Many thousands died after the liberation because malnutrition and diseases such as typhus had gone too far. It was frequently necessary to use bulldozers to push bodies into emergency mass graves because of the danger of an epidemic.

Reports of atrocities had circulated in allied countries during the war years, but the reality of the camps was far worse than anyone had been able to imagine. Some camp guards were summarily executed by allied soldiers; some were beaten to death in revenge attacks by prisoners.

**Fig. 12** *The liberation of Auschwitz, 27 January 1945*

## Summary question

Explain why Auschwitz became the main Nazi death camp in 1942.

# 10 Responsibility for the Holocaust

In the last resort, the reason why my parents died in Auschwitz was down to one man – Adolf Hitler.

> **1** George Clare, author of **Last Waltz in Vienna**. Live TV comment in **Seduction of a Nation**, ITV, 1989. George Clare and his family emigrated in 1938, when he was 15 years old. He settled in England and became a British citizen. His parents hated living in Ireland and chose to go back to France. They were deported to Auschwitz in 1943

The most important force behind the escalating persecution of the Jews was Heinrich Himmler, whose ambition made him determined to outbid other Nazi officials seeking a role in Jewish policy and whose organisation, the SS, gave him the means to carry out mass murder.

> **2** H. Mommsen, **From Weimar to Auschwitz**, 1991

During World War II anyone in Nazi Germany who regularly read a newspaper, listened to the radio, or walked past the Nazi political posters between 1941 and 1943 knew of the threats and boasts of the Nazi regime about intentions to exterminate European Jews, followed by public assertions that it was implementing that policy. Claims of ignorance regarding the murderous intentions and assertions of making good on such threats defy the evidence, logic, and common sense. With confidence we can say that millions of Germans were told on many occasions that the Jews had begun a war to exterminate the Germans, but that the Nazi regime was exterminating the Jews instead.

> **3** J. Herf, **The Jewish Enemy: Nazi Propaganda During World War II and the Holocaust**, 2006

Hitler's responsibility for the Holocaust is often thought of in simplistic terms:

- ■ He was motivated from the start by fanatical anti-Semitism.
- ■ He dominated all aspects of power and propaganda in Germany.
- ■ All Germans either supported his ideas or were incapable of opposing him because of terror and intimidation by Hitler's regime.

Therefore, the Holocaust was 'Hitler's War Against the Jews'; without Hitler it could never have happened.

There is a lot of truth in this, but the 'Final Solution' involved much more than one man. Industrialised murder on such a huge scale required actions and decisions by many Nazi leaders and by thousands of lesser officials. Millions of ordinary people were involved in acts of persecution, deportations or mass killings.

Apportioning the responsibility for the Holocaust, therefore, raises difficult questions. How far did Hitler and leading Nazis carry though the 'Final Solution' by force, terror and secrecy? Did Hitler provide the German people with a convenient alibi for a dreadful crime that they were actually responsible for, but could be excused as the action of a minority of 'evil Nazis', as opposed to the majority of 'good Germans'?

## Who was responsible?

**Fig. 1** *Hitler during the war*

At one extreme, it can be argued that the Holocaust was entirely the responsibility of Adolf Hitler. The trouble with this argument is that it is based on simplistic assumptions about the Nazi dictatorship – that Hitler was an all-powerful dictator and that any kind of opposition to Nazi policies could be crushed with ease. Historians are agreed that the Nazi regime was not like that at all. In many ways, the Nazi regime depended on a mixture of 'chaos and consent'. However central Hitler's role, the responsibility could not have been *only* Hitler's.

The Nazi regime had many overlapping centres of power and many rival Nazi 'barons' competing for Hitler's approval. Men like Himmler, Heydrich, Eichmann, at the head of the enormous bureaucratic machinery of the SS, were key architects of mass murder. Other leading Nazis were responsible, too, including Hermann Göring, Martin Bormann, the propaganda ministry under Josef Göbbels, and Albert Speer as the overlord of Germany's war industries and the use of forced labour. In the middle and lower levels of the Nazi regime, thousands of lesser officials carried out the orders that meant persecution, deportation and death for the victims of the Holocaust. All shared at least some of the responsibility.

At the opposite extreme, it can be argued that the German people as a whole were responsible for genocide. This view suggests that there was some kind of national defect in the Germans that made them vote for Hitler and then become his 'willing executioners'. It can be argued that the 'German people' was not one indoctrinated mass, but consisted of countless diverse elements, many of them opponents of everything the Nazis stood for, and that many well-intentioned Germans found themselves compelled against their will to compromise or to keep silent. Even so, large numbers of ordinary Germans shared in the responsibility for Nazi crimes.

An evaluation of the various levels of responsibility for the Holocaust, therefore, requires judgements to be made about the nature of power in the Third Reich and about the attitudes of millions of individual Germans under the stress of living in a dictatorship. The first place to search for answers is the personal role of Adolf Hitler.

### Cross-reference

The origins and the timing of the decision to launch the 'Final Solution' are covered in Chapter 8, pages 104 and 112.

### Exploring the detail

The controversial right-wing historian David Irving (see Conclusion, page 142) used to provoke his critics by waving a cheque for £10,000 above his head, promising to give it to the first person who produced a written document with Hitler's signature on it authorising the mass murder of the Jews. He knew there was little or no chance he would ever have to pay up.

## The responsibility of Adolf Hitler

Hitler's precise role in the 'Final Solution' may never be known. No written order signed by Hitler has ever been discovered and it is highly unlikely that one will ever be found in the future.

Hitler rarely issued written orders. Even when he did, such 'Führer Orders' were often merely his signed approval for a ready-made policy presented to him by a subordinate. Hitler's lifestyle was not suited to efficiency nor attention to bureaucratic details. He was frequently absent from Berlin, either because he preferred to relax at his mountain hideaway at Berchtesgaden in the Bavarian mountains, or because he was fully occupied with matters at military headquarters during the war.

Especially during the war years, Hitler relied heavily on his secretary, Martin Bormann, who handled the mass of paperwork and virtually controlled access to Hitler. Even the most powerful Nazi leaders such as Josef Göbbels were often frustrated by their inability to get to see Hitler in person. In February 1943, Göbbels called a secret meeting with Albert Speer and two other leading Nazis to discuss the problem of access to Hitler (Source 4).

'Things cannot go on this way', Göbbels began. 'Here we are, sitting in Berlin. Hitler does not hear what we have to say about the situation. I cannot influence him politically, cannot even report the most urgent measures necessary in my area. Everything goes through Bormann. Hitler must be persuaded to come to Berlin more often.'

**4**
*A. Speer, **Inside the Third Reich,** The Memoirs of Albert Speer, 1970*

### Key profile

#### Martin Bormann

Bormann (1900–45) is often described as 'mysterious', partly because of the rumours that he escaped to South America after the war (he didn't, he was killed in Berlin in May 1945), but mostly because he kept a very low public profile. Bormann was deputy to Rudolf Hess until Hess flew to Britain on his peace mission in 1941; he then became very powerful behind the scenes as Hitler's secretary. In fact, Bormann had already been a powerful influence for years, but nobody noticed him. Bormann controlled access to Hitler. He was also a rabid anti-Semite, fully committed to Nazi race ideology.

Hitler's very personal approach to government often led to confusion and delay as various leaders and officials competed to gain his attention. Decision making often seemed unpredictable and inefficient, but many historians believe that this outwardly chaotic system actually made Hitler even more powerful. He was almost never bogged down in the time-consuming business of reading reports, attending meetings and spelling out orders in detail. He remained 'institutionally unattached', keeping his hands free to intervene as and when he chose.

By standing 'alone and above', Hitler also benefited from the eagerness with which subordinates tried to 'outbid' each other in competing for his approval – what was known as 'working towards the Führer'.

### 'Working towards the Führer'

Hitler spent surprisingly little time on the actual business of government. He rarely read detailed reports and briefing papers – often leaving the details to subordinates and then intervening at the last minute to impose a decision. The munitions minister, Albert Speer, noted in his memoirs how 'complicated technical issues that had been discussed by me and my men for weeks would be decided by Hitler in a fraction of a minute'. Because of this, Hitler is sometimes described as the 'final court of appeal' – the man who always had the last word.

Hitler's informal and unstructured approach has led to some historians describing Hitler as a 'weak dictator' because there was so much infighting and duplication of responsibilities as various rival Nazi officials competed for his approval. Other historians take a different view – that Hitler was actually much *more* powerful because he was not weighed down by a mass of administrative details. He always had a free hand.

As a result, Hitler rarely needed to issue direct orders telling people what to do; he preferred to let subordinates try to 'outbid' their rivals by coming up with plans that would gain his approval. In this way, leading Nazis were constantly trying to work out what Hitler would most want to happen and then present proposals or take actions to bring it about. This process has been called 'working towards the Führer'.

---

Hitler's role in the Nazi 'Final Solution' was typical of his political style. He played no part in the Wannsee Conference, for example, which was organised by Reinhard Heydrich, taking advantage of powers given to him by Himmler and Göring. Hitler never visited any of the death camps and it is plausible that he knew little about what went on there. Hitler was similarly uninvolved in planning or carrying out the violence of *Kristallnacht* in 1938 – it was only after the event that he ordered Göring to 'sort it out'.

Responsibility for the Holocaust, however, goes much deeper than giving orders or supervising the actions of officials. Hitler, more than anyone, shaped Nazi ideology and gave it a special direction towards anti-Semitism. Hitler, more than anyone, built the Nazi Party into a national mass movement. Hitler, more than anyone, created the cult of personality that enabled him to dominate Germany in the 1930s. Hitler, more than anyone, pushed Nazi Germany towards a particular kind of Lebensraum and a war of racial annihilation in the East. Whether Hitler was a 'weak dictator' or not, it is difficult to argue against the sweeping claim 'No Hitler, No Holocaust'.

## The responsibility of Nazi leaders and the SS

It is undeniable that Hitler played a dominant role in the ideology and politics of Nazi Germany. Even so, there are many conflicting interpretations of the

**Fig. 2** *Heinrich Himmler (centre) and senior SS leaders. From the left: Josef Huber, Artur Nebe, Reinhard Heydrich and Heinrich 'Gestapo' Müller*

**Polycratic regime:** this is a regime in which there are many different centres of authority, with competition between rival power bases. In the Nazi regime, there was constant infighting between the various Nazi 'barons', such as Hermann Göring, Josef Göbbels, Ernst Röhm, Heinrich Himmler, Reinhard Heydrich, Albert Speer and Martin Bormann.

■ Activity

**Talking point**

Working in two groups, assemble the evidence for and against the view that Hitler's role in the Nazi 'Final Solution' showed him to be a weak dictator.

extent of his control over the state. By 1941, the population of the Third Reich was 65 million, with ever-expanding occupied territories gained by military conquest. Ruling over this huge state depended on several huge bureaucracies: various government ministries, Nazi organisations, the armed forces and the rival 'private empires' of powerful Nazi leaders. Political power constantly shifted from one place to another according to circumstances and personal rivalries. This complex, multi-centred political system has frequently been described as a '**polycratic regime**'.

> In 1939, the Nazi policy of child euthanasia originated not just out of racist ideology, but from the chaotic manner in which decisions were taken in the Third Reich. A chance letter to the Führer on a subject dear to his heart resulted in the deaths of more than five thousand children. In a typical example of how policies could spiral out of control, staff selected independently the children they wanted to kill. The chaotic radicalism inherent in the Nazi system meant that any idea, given a leader who spoke in visions and enthusiastic supporters anxious to please, could grow radically to an extreme almost in an instant.

**5**  L. Rees, *The Nazis: A Warning From History*, 2005

In this complex political system, it is difficult to assess precisely how far the Nazi leaders were responsible for initiating and implementing Nazi race policies, but they *were* indeed responsible. Hermann Göring played a key role in the Aryanisation of Jewish shops and businesses after Kristallnacht – and it was Göring's order of 16 July 1941 that encouraged the mass shootings after the invasion of the USSR in 1941. Albert Speer made extensive use of forced labour from concentration camp prisoners during the war and (at least partially) admitted his own sense of guilt for Nazi war crimes at the Nuremberg trials after the war.

Many other Nazi leaders such as Hitler's secretary, Martin Bormann, and Robert Ley, the head of the DAF (National Labour Front), were aggressively racist and relentlessly promoted anti-Semitism. The chief Nazi propagandists, Alfred Rosenberg, Otto Dietrich and, above all, Josef Göbbels made a major contribution to the Holocaust. The 'Nazi brainwash' saturated all aspects of education, culture and public life in Germany with the anti-Semitic ideology, reinforcing the prejudices of those who supported the regime and intimidating those who did not. The constant pressure of Nazi propaganda was essential in preparing the way for the Holocaust.

More than anyone, it was the top SS leaders, Himmler, Heydrich and Eichmann, who controlled the bureaucratic machinery that implemented Nazi race policies. They did so without relying on a stream of direct orders from above, often acting on their own initiative, as Reinhard Heydrich did when organising the Wannsee Conference in January 1942. In both ideology and action, the 'Final Solution' was an SS operation.

From the early 1930s, SS ideologists in the Race and Resettlement Office developed the theories that led towards genocide. By 1937, the SS had taken control of all aspects of internal security and repression. From 1938, the SS ruled over the new territories taken over by the Third Reich: first Austria, then the Czech lands in Bohemia and Moravia, then the territories conquered in Poland and further east. SS commandants like Rudolf Höss ran the death camps. SS doctors like Josef Mengele carried out the euthanasia programme, the appalling medical experiments on camp prisoners and the selections for the gas chambers.

### Rudolf Höss

Höss (1900–47) became notorious as the SS commandant at Auschwitz. He won the Iron Cross as a teenage soldier in the First World War and was in the Rossbach *Freikorps* from 1919, along with Martin Bormann. He was jailed for murder in 1924, but released in 1928. He joined the SS in 1934 and worked his way through the camps system from Dachau to Sachsenhausen to Auschwitz by 1940. It was Höss who pioneered the use of Zyklon B gas in the gas chambers. He was captured after the war and executed, at Auschwitz, in 1947.

The fact that Hitler had very little personal involvement, beyond setting overall objectives and giving Himmler the necessary authority, has persuaded some historians that the origins of the 'Final Solution' were more from the bottom up than from the top down – that there was a process of 'cumulative radicalisation' as officials on the spot reacted to the circumstances they faced with a series of ad-hoc measures. Most historians now reject the idea that Hitler was a 'weak dictator', but it is clear that responsibility for the Holocaust spread far beyond the Führer, not only to other top Nazi leaders but also to thousands of lesser officials.

Yet, it can be argued that it was Hitler who chose all these Nazi leaders and that they all depended on Hitler for their power and authority. Even the most senior Nazi 'barons' were overawed by Hitler and were almost slavishly loyal to him. Göbbels' diaries are full of expressions of admiration for the Führer and belief in his special powers. As *Reichsführer SS*, Himmler was

**Fig. 3** *Supervisors of death. From the left: Josef Mengele, Rudolf Höss and Josef Kramer*

massively powerful, but he knew his power came from Hitler. After the war, somebody suggested to Heinrich Himmler's elder brother, Gephardt, that the 'Final Solution' had been independently organised by Heinrich, without reference to Hitler. 'Rubbish!' said Gephardt. 'Heini was such a little worm. He would never have dared do anything that big all on his own.'

## The responsibility of ordinary Germans

Students of history need to remind themselves that the way people remember terrible events afterwards is not always an accurate reflection of what happened and how they felt about it. Events often seem different afterwards than they did at the time. Nobody who has never experienced it can really know what they would have done in circumstances of extreme fear and oppression. 'Ordinary Germans' experienced the Holocaust in countless different ways. After the war, they frequently had a strong desire to forget all about it, or to construct a moral justification to lessen any sense of guilt.

This deliberate forgetting or 'collective amnesia' encouraged the idea that ordinary German people had little or no knowledge about the Holocaust. The death camps were secret and far away. The Nazi regime employed a powerful system of censorship and repression, so it was difficult to find out the truth. If people did know the truth, the dictatorship was strong enough to silence any dissent or opposition. Hitler was to blame. The top Nazi leaders were to blame. And by the end of the war or soon afterwards they were all conveniently dead.

Oskar Schindler was immortalised by Thomas Keneally's book, *Schindler's Ark*, later filmed by Steven Spielberg as *Schindler's List*. Schindler was an ambivalent hero. He was a failed businessman who eagerly collaborated with the Nazis after the invasion of Poland and originally employed Jewish workers in his Crakow factory because it was very profitable to do so. Later, he spent all his profits on elaborate schemes to save more than 1,000 'Schindler Jews' from deportation and death. The state of Israel declared him a Righteous Gentile in 1963.

The reality, of course, was very different. Many ordinary Germans witnessed or participated in mass murder, as soldiers or policemen. Many civil servants took part in rounding up Jews for deportation. Many railway workers had a role in the transport system that brought the trains to the death camps. Many ordinary Germans knew, from what they saw or from letters home from loved ones at the front, at least something about the fate of the Jews.

Many ordinary Germans had enthusiastically supported Hitler and all he stood for. Nearly half of them voted Nazi in 1933. Many Germans had applauded acts of discrimination against Jews. Many had been happy to profit from it, by acquiring new homes or valuable works of art at knockdown prices. Many ordinary Germans had seen anti-Jewish violence such as Kristallnacht in 1938. Many had served in the armed forces on the Eastern Front. In pubs, queues outside shops and in private homes, there had been many whispered conversations passing on horrific rumours about the fate of the Jews.

Equally, many ordinary Germans had *not* participated in or known about the Holocaust – or, if they had heard stories about atrocities, simply could not believe they were true. A very patriotic and religious army officer, Axel von dem Bussche, who later risked his own life in a plot to assassinate Hitler, was told in 1939 about whole classes of Polish schoolchildren being machine-gunned to death in Warsaw. In an interview in 1989, Bussche explained his reaction at the time: 'I didn't believe it. I'm sorry but I simply could not believe it. Knowing what I know now, there is no alternative but to accept it happened.'

Some people living in remote rural areas had little awareness of the world outside their farm or village. In the spring of 1945, American troops advancing through Bavaria took over a farmhouse. They listened to a radio news bulletin about a heavy bombing raid on the city of Würzburg. The German family got out an old atlas to find where Würzburg was – as if it were a faraway place in a foreign country.

Many people, however, remained in ignorance about what was happening because they were careful not to find out. They knew something awful was going on, but avoided finding out what it was. There were places you did not go, things you did not look at, questions you knew not to ask. This awareness that some terrible things might be happening was very different from having full knowledge about the horrors of the death camps. The vast majority of ordinary Germans were totally shocked when the truth was exposed.

Another issue for ordinary Germans was whether they could have done anything to prevent the Holocaust if they had known the truth earlier. The secret police, the Gestapo, never numbered more than 30,000 – a large and efficient organisation, but far too few men to spy on every individual in a population of 65 million. To keep effective control, the Gestapo relied on a constant stream of information from informers ready to denounce their neighbours. Many ordinary Germans who were responsible for committing terrible acts while serving in the armed forces or in Einsatzgruppen claimed that they did so only because refusing to obey orders would have meant almost certain death. This was not really the case. The regime was almost as frightened of popular discontent from ordinary people as they were afraid of the regime. Many ordinary Germans carried out their terrible actions without any protest, often with apparent enthusiasm.

The extent of the evidence showing how many ordinary Germans supported or were willing to collaborate with the Nazi regime has persuaded many historians to accuse large sections of the German people of having been responsible for the crimes of the Third Reich. The most extreme example of this view is the 'Goldhagen Thesis'.

## Exploring the detail

### Reserve Police Battalion 101

In his 1991 book *Ordinary Men*, the historian Christopher Browning analyses the actions of Reserve Police Battalion 101, who carried out a series of mass killings in the eastern territories over several months in 1941. These men were not trained SS killers, but reservists called up from civilian life. The point of Browning's book is to show how these 'ordinary' men became accustomed to their awful work. There were few cases of refusing to obey orders – the vast majority either willingly accepted the mass murder of eastern Jews or else went along with it in silent acquiescence.

## A closer look

### The Goldhagen Thesis

In 1996, the American-Jewish political scientist, Daniel Jonah Goldhagen, caused a storm of controversy by the publication of *Hitler's Willing Executioners: Ordinary Germans and the Holocaust*. In 2002, Goldhagen published another book, *A Moral Reckoning: The Role of the Catholic Church in the Holocaust and its Unfulfilled Duty of Repair*. Both books were written with a similar tone of aggressive denunciation. Both have led to intense debate among historians.

The title of *Hitler's Willing Executioners* is unequivocal. Goldhagen dismissed all claims that the German people 'did not know', or 'were incapable of opposing' Hitler's crimes. According to Goldhagen, the German people knew about and enthusiastically supported Nazi race policies. In his view, the entire German people were motivated by a 'murderous eliminatory anti-Semitism'. Other historians have put forward similar views, though not with such sweeping condemnation of the German people as a whole.

In *Ordinary Men*, Christopher Browning showed how the men of Reserve Police Battalion 101 carried out mass killings in Poland in 1941, often without any signs of remorse or psychological strain. Claude Lanzmann's monumental documentary film *Shoah* contains many oral testimonies revealing how much of the Holocaust was witnessed by ordinary people. In *All Or Nothing: The Axis Powers and the Holocaust*, Jonathan Steinberg contrasted the reluctance of Italian troops to take part in acts of violence against the unquestioning obedience of German troops.

Such works have proved that many Germans were aware of terrible things taking place; but they do not accuse the German people as a whole of supporting genocide. Goldhagen's thesis has come under attack from many angles. Norman Finkelstein, like Goldhagen the son of Holocaust survivors, wrote a devastating article *Goldhagen's Crazy Thesis* in 1999. Later, in *Nation on Trial*, Finkelstein and the German historian Ruth Bettina Birn attempted a stage-by-stage demolition of Goldhagen's claims, as did Donald Niewyk in the new edition of his book *The Jews In Weimar Germany*.

Goldhagen's book raised important issues, but his central thesis has failed to gain acceptance from most serious historians. For a more balanced and differentiated view of the responsibility of ordinary Germans, see the key works by Christopher Browning, Richard Evans and Ian Kershaw.

---

In April 1945, British forces liberated the concentration camp at Bergen-Belsen. What they found there was truly horrific. Belsen had always been a place of terror, but in the final months of the war the organisation of the camp completely fell apart. Many SS guards left to try to escape their fate as war criminals. Food supplies ran out. Thousands of new prisoners arrived after terrible forced marches from the east. Belsen was filled with emaciated victims of starvation and disease.

The British army commander on the spot was so angry that he compelled the entire adult population of the nearby town of Celle, including any hospital patients who could walk, to tour the camp to see the horrors first-hand. News film taken at the time showed ordinary Germans from

### Exploring the detail

Vivid colour film of the terrible conditions in Dachau after its liberation can be found in *D-Day to Berlin*, a compilation of material shot by a film crew under the Hollywood director George Stevens.

**Fig. 4** *The liberation of Camp Dora at Nordhausen, mid-April 1945*

Celle crying, being sick, holding handkerchiefs to their faces because of the smells, running away from the scene. Afterwards, the mayor of Celle and his wife went straight home and hanged themselves.

The shocked and disgusted reactions of the townspeople of Celle showed that they had had no real conception of what the Nazi regime had really been up to. Many of them, no doubt, had known or suspected something about the fate of the Jews, the gypsies or disabled children. They had heard rumours, had anxious conversations in the privacy of their homes, heard of Jewish neighbours being arrested. But it is clear that scarcely anyone really *knew* the awful truth.

Reaching conclusions about the extent to which ordinary Germans were responsible for the Holocaust remains difficult and controversial. There was no homogenous 'German people' living under Nazi rule, but a complex mixture of different classes, regions, generations and social attitudes. Nor do people always think and behave in the same way – huge numbers of those ordinary Germans who welcomed Hitler's rise to power in 1933 later changed their minds as they realised what the actual effects of Nazi rule were.

## ■ Exploring the detail

Even within one German city there were wide differences in people's response to the Nazi regime and its race policies. One Englishwoman, Christabel Bielenberg, lived through the 12 years of the Third Reich in Hamburg as a young wife and mother. Her vivid memoirs written after the war described the wide variety of attitudes towards Nazi rule among people in Hamburg.

## ■ Key profile

### Christabel Bielenberg

Christabel Bielenberg was the adventurous daughter of an English aristocrat who married a wealthy German lawyer and lived in Hamburg from 1934 to 1944. The first volume of her memoirs *The Past Is Myself* provides a vivid picture of life for her and her two young sons. In 1944, her husband, Peter Bielenberg, was involved on the edges of the bomb plot to kill Hitler; he narrowly escaped being executed, partly because of Christabel's connections to English high society. After the war, the Bielenbergs lived in Ireland.

## ■ A closer look

### Sixteen case studies: 'Ordinary Germans'

- The SA men parading through the Brandenburg Gate on 30 January 1933, shouting '*Juda Verrecke*'.
- The liberal journalist who saw the SA parade on 30 January 1933, went home and drew the curtains.
- The retired civil servant in Württemberg ('a sociable man who liked his beer') who stopped going to the pub on Sundays 'in case I let rip and end up in Dachau'.
- The rebellious schoolgirl who took a gramophone to her school and played records of music by the Jewish composer, Kurt Weill.

- The passers-by who shouted abuse at Jews being forced to clean the streets of Vienna with toothbrushes after the 1938 Anschluss.
- The owner of a bakery who had a lucrative contract delivering bread each day to KZ Mauthausen in Austria.
- The hairdresser in Hamburg who apologised to a teenage Jewish boy as she was cutting his hair the day after Kristallnacht.
- The hatshop assistant who apologised to his mother the same day, saying: 'We never wanted this.'
- Resi Kraus, a young woman in Augsburg who denounced her Jewish neighbour to the Gestapo because she wanted to take over her nice apartment.
- Hannelore, the wife of a minor Nazi official, who gave bread to starving Jewish workers on a building site near her home. (Her husband pleaded with her not to do it again because it could get them into terrible trouble; Hannelore promised she 'would be good', but 10 days later she again baked extra bread for the Jewish labourers.)
- The cinema audiences in Leipzig who cheered at the scenes of anti-Jewish persecution in the film *Jud Süss* when it was first shown in 1940.
- The civilian reservists who carried out mass killings while serving with reserve police battalions in 1941.
- The students at Munich University, led by Sophie Scholl and her brother, who distributed anti-Nazi leaflets and were executed in 1943.
- The career soldier, Axel von dem Bussche, who was told about the students at a Jewish school in Poland being machine-gunned to death one class at a time – but simply could not believe it was true.
- The concentration camp guard who showed a recently-arrived colleague how to push Zyklon B gas canisters into the gas chamber at Auschwitz. When his friend was sick, he said: 'Yes, it's terrible; but you can get used to anything in the end.'
- The mayor of Celle and his wife who went home and hanged themselves after they had been forced to tour the concentration camp at Belsen in 1945.

## Activity

### Thinking point

Making generalisations about the 'German people' is almost impossible. Working in groups and using the evidence of this chapter, make a list of five different categories of 'ordinary Germans'. Place the **five** categories in order of importance according to the number of people who were 'typical' of those groups.

## The importance of war and the degree to which the 'Final Solution' was planned

There is an obvious link between war and the 'Final Solution'. Hitler did not unleash all-out persecution against Jews until 1938, by which time he was ready to use war and the threat of war to force through the Anschluss with Austria and the annexation of the Sudetenland from Czechoslovakia. The conquest of Poland following the outbreak of war in Europe opened the way for 'Germanising' parts of the occupied territories and deporting millions of eastern Jews. The invasion of the USSR in June 1941 led to further conquests and to the radical policies aimed at racial annihilation. When Germany failed to achieve a quick victory in the East, and the Third Reich faced 'Total War', propaganda and race policies became even more radical and extreme.

It is difficult to conceive of the Holocaust outside the context of war. Nazi anti-Semitism was always framed in the language of war and struggle. The vast majority of the victims of the Holocaust came from the territories in Eastern Europe overrun by German armies in 1939–41. The death camps were situated in these eastern occupied territories. War gave Hitler the opportunity to pursue much more radical and brutal policies than would

**Fig. 5** *War Crimes Tribunal, Nuremberg. Front row from left: Hermann Göring, Rudolf Hess, Joachim von Ribbentrop, General Keitel, Alfred Rosenberg, Hans Frank, Wilhelm Frick, Julius Streicher, Wilhelm Funk and Dr Hjalmar Schacht*

have been possible in peacetime. War also enabled a greater degree of secrecy and censorship, as well as the excuse for even more intense propaganda. In 1944, impending defeat drove the Nazi regime to speed up the 'Final Solution'; the Holocaust only came to an end when allied armies drove German forces back to Berlin.

It is more difficult to assess the exact relationship between war and Nazi race policies. Was there a long-term plan to achieve Lebensraum through wars of conquest, thus opening the way for Hitler to implement his plans for racial extermination? Or was the 'Final Solution' a policy the Nazis made up as they went along, reacting to the shifting circumstances of unexpectedly rapid victories, followed by unexpected defeats?

Most historians agree that Hitler's ideological aims were remarkably consistent. Just before he committed suicide in the ruins of Berlin in 1945, Hitler summoned a young typist, Traudl Humps, to take down his political testament. Long after the war, Traudl Humps described her excited feelings at the time. With her 'heart bumping' she thought she would find out the real reasons why there had had to be a great war and so many lives lost. She was disappointed: 'But there was nothing new, just the same old accusations against the Jews.' The ideas of 'a war against international Jewry' in Hitler's testament were very similar to those in his Reichstag speech of September 1939, which in turn were similar to speeches he had made in the 1920s.

This ideological consistency has convinced many historians that 'Hitler's war against the Jews' was the core aim of Nazism. Certainly, everyone knew that if Hitler ever came to power there would be harmful consequences for the Jews of Germany and Europe. Other historians have seen a similar consistency in Hitler's foreign policy – a *Stufenplan* (step-by-step plan) first to tear up the Treaty of Versailles and win back the territories and peoples lost in 1919 (which he did in 1938 and 1939), then to destroy Germany's enemies in Western Europe (which he did in 1939 and 1940) and finally to carry out a war in the East to achieve Lebensraum and wipe out Germany's 'racial enemies' (which he set out to do in 1941 and 1942).

Most historians also agree that the Nazi regime was in many ways confused and chaotic, with many internal rivalries. There were changes of direction in policy to adjust to events as they happened; even high Nazi officials were often uncertain about what Hitler's real intentions were. There are good reasons to suppose that war with the western powers in 1939 was 'the Wrong War', a war Hitler did not want at all, caused by diplomatic miscalculation. A lot of convincing evidence suggests that the decision to launch the 'Final Solution' was hurried and unplanned, driven by the deteriorating situation in the occupied territories when the invasion of Russia stalled in the autumn of 1941.

There are no easy answers to these questions. Building up your own interpretation requires clear thinking about the issues and then *choosing* between alternative opinions before selecting appropriate supporting evidence. Sitting on the fence is not an option!

■ **Cross-reference**

Various interpretations of the origins of the 'Final Solution' are covered in Chapters 7–9.

## Activity

### Thinking point

Working in two groups, use the table below and evidence from previous chapters in this book to select a range of **six** arguments to support the view that the 'Final Solution' resulted from:

**a** a deliberate long-term plan

**b** a confused response to short-term emergency conditions.

| 'The minimum' [Evidence that would be essential to either view] | |
| --- | --- |
| **'The straight path'** [Evidence supporting the idea of a long-term deliberate plan] | **'The twisted road to Auschwitz'** [Evidence supporting the idea of a confused response to short-term considerations] |

*Learning outcomes*

In this section you have examined the horrific events of the Holocaust from December 1941 to the end of the Nazi regime in 1945. You have gained an understanding of the bureaucratic nature of Nazi terror and the influence of ideological, political and economic factors on the implementation of the 'Final Solution'. You have also looked at the problem of responsibility, making an assessment of the relative importance of Adolf Hitler, key Nazi leaders and ordinary Germans in bringing about the mass murders of Jews and other 'racial enemies' during the Holocaust. You will have developed an overall understanding of the horrors of the Holocaust and of the complexities involved in studying it. These issues are investigated further in the conclusion.

# AQA Examination-style questions

a) Explain why concentration camp prisoners were sent on forced marches in 1945.

*(12 marks)*

In answering this question you will need to assemble a range of reasons why the forced marches took place in 1945. Decide which you consider the most important or over-riding reason, and then show how your other reasons link to this one. You might, for example, suggest that the Nazis knew they were losing the war and that they needed to retreat in the face of the advancing Russian army. Linked to this would be a concern that prisoners did not become swallowed up into the Russian army or workforce, a lack of concern as to what might happen to prisoners who had become a hindrance and too costly to look after and possibly an idea that Germany might have been able to rally somewhere in the West where these prisoners might once again have been put to work. A lack of guards, fear of a prisoners' revolt, sadism and a total lack of direction and policy have also all been suggested as possible reasons.

b) 'Hitler alone was responsible for the Holocaust.'
Explain why you agree or disagree with this statement.

*(24 marks)*

This question requires an understanding of Hitler's responsibility for the Holocaust, alongside alternative explanations – but it would not be enough to describe the rival interpretations. It is necessary to make a clear choice, assembling selected evidence to support a decisive argument. (The Activity above might be helpful in organising such an argument.)

You will need to think through a number of issues; the nature of Hitler's dictatorship; the extent to which Nazi ideology was coherent; the importance of war in shaping Nazi policies. Then you will need to decide the relative importance of long-term and short-term factors. An answer arguing that the key quotation is correct would need to be supported by appropriate evidence about Nazi ideology and Hitler's intentions from an early stage, perhaps even before 1933; an answer challenging this view would focus much more on short-term factors in the years 1939–42 to show how the origins of the 'Final Solution' lay in a rather chaotic response to the pressure of events.

# 6 Conclusion

**Fig. 1** *The Hall of Names. Yad Vashem memorial, Israel*

## The Hitler legacy

Adolf Hitler was a loser – after his suicide in the ruins of Berlin in May 1945, everything Hitler stood for was covered in failure and disgrace. His legacy to the German people was the opposite of all that he had promised them in his brief times of success.

- Hitler promised to wipe away the shame of Versailles and to restore the territorial unity of Germany – as a result of Hitler, post-war Germany was a divided nation, much reduced in size.

- Hitler promised to restore the pride of the German nation after defeat in the First World War – his legacy was a nation destroyed by bombing raids and invading armies, burdened with guilt for the Holocaust.

- Hitler promised to destroy communism – his legacy was the occupation of large parts of Germany by the Red Army, followed by 40 years of Communist rule in East Germany.

■ Hitler promised to destroy the 'weak' democracy of the Weimar Republic; his legacy was the emergence of the Federal Republic in West Germany from 1949, the strongest democratic system in German history and the embodiment of everything that Weimar stood for and of everything that Hitler hated.

■ Hitler promised to destroy 'Jewish decadence' and to establish a pure German culture; his legacy was the total rejection of Nazi culture and the raising of the cultural figures he had attacked to hero status.

This rejection of everything tainted by Nazism included anti-Semitism. Hitler had promised to destroy Europe's Jews; in terms of mass murder, he almost succeeded. But the legacy of the Third Reich was the total discrediting of anti-Semitism. The formation of the state of Israel as a Jewish national homeland was probably more due to Hitler than to any other factor. Nazi ideology was totally rejected in the post-war world. Anti-Semitism completely lost the political respectability it had, to a degree, possessed before 1933. Fascism and anti-Semitism seemed to have suffered permanent defeat.

## Anti-Semitism after 1945

There are few final victories in history. The Second World War did not really end in 1945. There was no final peace settlement. The temporary situation of 1945 was frozen in time and place by the Cold War and the division of Europe. West Germany became a key part of the western alliance – there was a strong motive to differentiate between the minority of 'evil Nazis' and the majority of 'good Germans'.

In post-war West Germany, notable efforts were made to counter anti-Semitism. From the 1960s, Holocaust education was compulsory in schools, including at least one visit to a former Nazi concentration camp. Some, though far from all, Nazi war criminals were hunted down and prosecuted. In 1969, the federal chancellor, Willy Brandt, made an emotive public gesture of apology by kneeling down at the memorial to the Warsaw ghetto. On the other hand, de-Nazification was far from complete and many former Nazis continued to hold influential positions in post-war society, including the security services. It has been claimed that West Germany 'pardoned itself at the cost of living memory'.

The record of East Germany was similarly mixed. The German Democratic Republic (GDR) was a state committed to anti-Fascism, opposed to everything the Nazis stood for; but the Communist regime never really faced up to the burden of guilt from the Third Reich and little was done in terms of historical education. In the early 1990s, there was a surge of neo-Nazi, 'skinhead' Nationalism in the former GDR, especially among young working-class men. These 'neo-Nazis' chanted anti-Semitic slogans and carried out numerous violent attacks against immigrants and asylum seekers.

One aspect of post-war anti-Semitism was the rise of the Holocaust deniers. Ever since 1945, a few cranks had spread their irrational claims that the Holocaust was simply Zionist propaganda – that it had been greatly exaggerated, or had never happened at all. A Canadian called Butz wrote *The Hoax of the Twentieth Century*; another Canadian, Fred Leuchter, used pseudo-scientific methods to 'prove' that poison gas had never been used at Auschwitz. Such claims were easily dismissed and their ideas remained on the lunatic fringe. From the 1980s, however, **Holocaust denial** began to gain more adherents.

The widespread advent of the internet provided fertile ground for conspiracy theories and racist computer games. The controversial British

### Key terms

**Holocaust denial:** politically-motivated campaigns to minimise the scale and importance of the Holocaust, or to deny that it ever took place at all.

historian David Irving lent his support to Holocaust denial. Irving was the author of numerous well-sourced books on the Nazi era and it was harder to dismiss him than cranks like Butz and Leuchter. In 1994, an American historian, Deborah Lipstadt, published *Denying the Holocaust: The Growing Assault on Truth and Memory*, to sound the alarm about the dangerous impact of Holocaust denial.

■ **Key profile**

### David Irving

Irving was a historical outsider – a self-taught enthusiast, determined to provoke and outwit the 'historical establishment'. He wrote several vivid and readable books on Nazi Germany, including biographies of Göbbels and Göring and a two-volumed history entitled *Hitler's War*. These were based on extensive, outwardly impressive research – but also contained deliberate distortions of the truth. Irving also frequently attended right-wing political meetings at which he supported Holocaust deniers. Irving was dangerous because he was talented and had massive knowledge of his subject. In 2001, however, he lost all his credibility (and all his money) when his libel trial against Deborah Lipstadt ended in total defeat.

The issue became an international sensation in 2001, when David Irving sued Deborah Lipstadt for libel. The trial at the Old Bailey became a duel between Irving, representing himself, and Professor Richard Evans, the historical expert witness for the defence. Irving was confident he could once again provoke and frustrate a professional historian, as he had often done in the past; but the outcome of the trial was a complete legal defeat that left him discredited and bankrupt. Later, Irving was convicted of Holocaust denial by a court in Austria and imprisoned. The sensational defeat of David Irving did not completely eliminate the problem of Holocaust denial, which has continued to feature on extremist websites.

Understandably, the unique horror of the Holocaust has convinced many people of the urgent need to prevent it from ever being forgotten, or misrepresented. The result has been a massive, ongoing focus of public attention on the Holocaust – museums and memorials, academic works of history, fictional and documentary films. The aim behind this mass of material is always: 'learn the lessons of history so that it is never repeated'.

However, there can be unhealthy ways of remembering as well as undesirable ways of forgetting. A constant obsession with the sufferings of the past can mean a distorted view of the present. History can be and has been used to claim that non-Jewish victims of the Nazi regime were of less importance; or that no other crime in history can ever be compared with what happened to the Jews between 1933 and 1945. But no one 'official view' of history should be allowed to silence other views. Concern about one terrible example of racial and religious hatred in the past should not deflect attention away from racial and religious hatreds in other places at other times.

### The moral problem

This brings us back to the moral and historical problems outlined in the introduction to this book. It is essential to steer a course through these problems – away from the dangers of denial, or trivialising, or forgetting without running into the opposite dangers of distortion and the misuse of history as propaganda. This is easier said than done. It requires balance and understanding, as well as remembering the past.

Such a balance includes understanding of the awful, exceptional suffering of the Jewish people – without ignoring the tragic suffering of others. It includes understanding of the unique importance of the personal role of Adolf Hitler; but always in the context of the role of others. It includes understanding why and how so many ordinary Germans actively or passively contributed to the Holocaust; but without making simplistic judgements about the 'collective guilt' of an entire nation. It includes understanding the need to come to terms with the past; but without forgetting.

On the subject of forgetting, we might leave the last words to Laurence Rees, in his conclusion to *Auschwitz: The Nazis and the Final Solution*.

> Soon, the last survivor and the last perpetrator will join those who were murdered at the camp. There will be nobody left alive who has personal experience of the place. And when that happens there is a danger that this history will merge into the distant past and become just one terrible event amongst many. But that should not be allowed to happen. Judged by the context of twentieth century, sophisticated European culture, the Nazis' Final Solution represents the lowest act in all history. By their crime, the Nazis brought to the world an awareness of what educated, technologically advanced human beings can do, as long as they possess a cold heart. Once in the world, knowledge of what they did must not be unlearnt. It lies there, ugly, inert, waiting to be discovered by each new generation. A warning for us, and for those who come after.

*L. Rees, **Auschwitz: The Nazis and The Final Solution**, 2005*

# Glossary

## A

**anti-Judaism:** hatred of the Jewish religion. In Europe, anti-Judaism led to traditional discrimination against Jews by Christians on the grounds of religion. Sometimes, Jews could escape from anti-Judaism by conversion or assimilation.

**anti-Zionism:** opposition to the idea of a separate homeland for the Jewish people. This included many Jews who believed in assimilation to European society; but it was also manipulated by people who used it as an excuse for outright anti-Semitism.

**Aryan race:** this term referred to people of 'pure' Nordic origins, supposedly superior to 'lesser' racial types such as Jews.

**Aryanisation:** Nazi policy of removing all Jews and other non-Aryans from key aspects of Germany's cultural and economic life. The policy was designed to lead ultimately to the complete expulsion of non-Aryans from Germany.

**'asocials':** term used to define 'social deviants' and 'un-German elements' imprisoned by the Nazi regime, including homosexuals, pacifists, Jehovah's Witnesses, jazz enthusiasts and others.

**assimilation:** the process by which Jews moved away from traditional customs, dress and religious observance to gain acceptance in mainstream society.

## B

**biological anti-Semitism:** anti-Jewish hatred on the grounds of race and blood. Unlike anti-Judaism, conversion or assimilation offered no protection; biological anti-Semitism demanded the extermination of all Jews and other 'racial undesirables' to bring about the 'purification' of the *Volk*.

***Blut und Boden***
**(Blood and Soil):** the idealised image of the supposedly sacred link between peasant farmers and the land. Work on the land was pure and noble, unlike the wicked and 'degenerate' life in the cities. The peasant farmer was racially pure and imbued with the spiritual values of the real Germany. Nazi propaganda did much to promote art and literature on Blood and Soil themes.

**boycott:** when a group of people purposely refuse to buy (and put pressure on others not to buy) goods and/or services in order to make a political protest.

**'Brown Revolution':** this was so-called because of the brown uniforms of the SA. Many leaders of the SA were impatient to let loose a 'revolution from below' that would overthrow the army and the ruling elites, paving the way for social revolution.

## C

**Communists:** revolutionary socialists, followers of the ideology put forward in the mid-19th century by the German-Jewish thinker Karl Marx – and thus often called Marxism. Together with Friedrich Engels, Marx published *The Communist Manifesto* in 1849. Marx's most famous book was *Das Kapital*, published in 1867. Marxism promised equality through a revolution that would overthrow the evils of Capitalism. It influenced all socialist movements in Europe, including the Bolsheviks, who seized power in Russia in 1917. To right wingers and anti-Semites, of course, the words 'Marxist' or 'Bolshevik' were terms of abuse.

**concentration camp:** (not to be confused with the death camps established during the Second World War) these were prison camps set up near major cities across Germany from 1933. The first was at Dachau near Munich. People such as socialists, pacifists, trade union officials and other 'unreliable elements' were held in the camps under hard conditions, though most were later released.

**cosmopolitanism:** term used by anti-Semites, attacking the cultural achievements of urban Jews (such as proficiency in foreign languages) seen as alien to traditional German values. It was also used to suggest Jews were 'un-German', linked to an international plot to take over the world.

## D

**DDP:** the German Democratic Party, formed in the early days of the Weimar Republic. It was a Liberal party that was slightly left of centre. Key members included Walther Rathenau, the German Jew who became foreign secretary but was later assassinated. The party was banned by the Nazis in 1933.

**death marches:** the forced marches of 1945, when thousands of prisoners in the camps were moved westwards as Soviet armies liberated the eastern territories of the Reich. Conditions were appalling and many died.

**DNVP:** the German National People's Party. A right-wing political party that was led by the press magnet Alfred Hugenberg. It was less extreme than the Nazi Party and was more successful than the Nazis during most of the Weimar Republic; this, however, changed in 1932–3. They joined the Nazis in a coalition in 1933 at Hitler's invitation. The party was dissolved by Hitler in June 1933.

## E

***Einsatzgruppen*:** these were 'special forces' of police and regular troops operating under SS commanders behind the frontline as German armies advanced through Poland and Soviet-controlled territories. According to their records, *Einsatzgruppen* killed 1.3 million Jews.

**eugenics:** the 'science' of selective breeding – applying scientific methods to improving the population. Eugenicists promote policies such as contraception and family planning, or the use of sterilisation to prevent the birth of mentally or physically-handicapped children.

**euthanasia:** sometimes described as 'mercy killing' – the painless ending of a life to free victims of terminal illness or severe disability from their suffering. The Nazi euthanasia programme put to death mentally ill or physically-disabled people whose condition was not necessarily terminal and without the consent of patients or their family.

**F**

**'Final Solution':** this 'solution' to the 'Jewish question' was a Nazi euphemism for the extermination of European Jews. It is also known as the Holocaust.

**Four Year Plan:** in 1936, Göring introduced a set of economic policies aimed at achieving self-sufficiency in Germany's agricultural and industrial production. The Plan involved the production of synthetic oil and rubber to avoid dependence of foreign imports. The challenge Göring faced was balancing rearmament and the need to ensure the availability of consumer goods.

*Freikorps:* unofficial armies that were formed out of the chaos of Germany's defeat in the First World War. These 'Free Corps' were led by experienced army commanders and played a key role in suppressing left-wing uprisings in 1919 and 1920. Those who joined the *Freikorps* were often violently nationalist, anti-Slav and anti-Semitic.

**G**

**Gauleiter:** the Nazis divided Greater Germany into 32 large administrative districts, known as a Gau – the leader of each Gau was a Gauleiter. Eleven more districts were added as the Reich expanded from 1938. These senior party bosses had considerable autonomy and reported directly to Hitler. Martin Bormann became Reichsleiter in 1941.

**General Government:** the area of Poland occupied by the Nazis in 1939 that was not incorporated into the German Reich but controlled as a semi-autonomous area under Governor Hans Frank. It became a dumping ground for Jews deported from the Reich. Most of the death camps that were built in 1941–2 were located within the General Government.

**genocide:** the deliberate attempt to destroy an entire race or people. This term can be very controversial – for example, many people have insisted that it should be applied to the Jewish Holocaust and nobody else; others have used the term for the mass killings of Armenians by Turks in 1915–16, or the massacres in Rwanda in 1994.

**gentile:** term used by Jews to define non-Jews. In some special cases, non-Jews (such as Oskar Schindler) who performed noble services on behalf of the Jewish people have been awarded the title 'Righteous Gentile'.

**Gestapo:** the *Geheimstaatspolizei* (Secret State Police). Formed in 1933, the Gestapo was originally controlled by Hermann Göring. In 1934, it was taken over by Heinrich Himmler and the SS.

**ghetto:** a controlled area of a town or city reserved for Jews. They had been a feature of life in Europe since medieval times and were especially numerous in Tsarist Russia before 1917. In the early stages of the conquest of the East, Nazi authorities herded Jews into overcrowded ghettos in cities such as Warsaw and Lodz.

**gypsies (Roma):** travelling communities of gypsies had been a prominent feature of life in central and Eastern Europe for centuries. Like Jews, and for similar reasons, they were often the victims of discrimination and persecution. Twenty thousand died in the Holocaust.

**H**

**Holocaust:** term derived from the Greek word for 'burnt offering', used to define the mass murders of the Third Reich. Some

historians claim it should refer exclusively to the Jews; in this book it refers to all the victims of Nazi racial extermination.

**Holocaust comparison:** historians or journalists who attempt to compare other acts of persecution with what the Nazis did between 1933 and 1945 are sometimes accused of the 'crime' of Holocaust comparison – minimising or trivialising the suffering of the Jews. These accusations are sometimes justified; but efforts to reject any form of Holocaust comparison have been termed 'moral blackmail' to silence critics of Israeli actions.

**Holocaust denial:** politically-motivated campaigns to minimise the scale and importance of the Holocaust, or to deny that it ever took place at all.

**I**

**Internal exile:** (sometimes called internal emigration) this was a mental process, not a physical one. People switched off from the Nazified outside world and retreated to a non-Nazi world inside their own homes or inside their own private thoughts.

**J**

**'Jewish-Bolshevism':** term used by anti-Semites to imply that Jews and Communists were closely associated and represented a danger to German values.

**'Jewish materialism':** the accusation that Jews lacked true spiritual values and were undermining German society through their influence over business and finance.

*Judenfrei:* literally means 'Jew-free'. The Nazis promised to remove not only Jewish people from Germany, but also to purge all Jewish cultural influences.

**K**

**KZ:** stands for *Konzentrationslager* (concentration camp).

**L**

*Lebensraum* **(living space):** the ambition for a 'Drang nach Osten' (drive to the East) to expand the Reich and find space for the intended massive increase of the German population. The idea of 'people without space' was a popular myth in right-wing circles. *Lebensraum* was closely linked to other Nazi ideological aims, such as Blood and Soil, racial purity and the inevitability of a war of annihilation against the Soviet Union.

**Liberal:** the economic and political ideas of Liberals in Germany reflected the views of the educated middle classes. Liberalism was strengthened by the 1848 revolution. Liberals believed in democracy and the rights of the individual; they also believed in science and progress.

## M

*Mischlinge*: a person of 'mixed race', who faced lesser discrimination than 'full Jews'. *Mischlinge* were defined as either 'half breeds of the 1st degree' (two Jewish grandparents), or 'half breeds of the 2nd degree' (one Jewish grandparent).

## N

**NSDAP:** National Socialist German Workers' Party, more commonly referred to as the Nazi Party. Originally founded as the German Workers' Party in 1919, it became the National Socialist Party in 1920, when Hitler became its leader. The NSDAP came to power in 1933 after many years in the political wilderness.

## O

**observant Jews:** Jews who resisted assimilation and continued to live by the principles of Jewish religion and customs.

**Orthodox Jews:** Jews whose religious observance was totally loyal to old ways of religious practice and daily life. Orthodox Jews were easily recognised by their forms of dress, such as black hats and prayer shawls. In Weimar Germany, they were outnumbered by Reform Jews.

## P

**Pan-German Nationalism:** Pan-German (All-German) nationalists defined the German identity by language, culture and race, not by citizenship. Pan-Germanism particularly appealed to German-Austrians before 1938 and to *Volksdeutsche* in central and Eastern Europe.

**Partisans:** bands of irregular forces fighting a guerrilla war against the Germans behind the front.

**Pogrom:** organised violence against Jews. Pogroms were a frequent occurrence in many parts of Europe, from the 12th century onwards.

**Polycratic regime:** this is a regime in which there are many different centres of authority, with competition between rival power bases. In the Nazi regime, there was constant infighting between the various Nazi 'barons', such as Hermann Göring, Josef Göbbels, Ernst Röhm, Heinrich Himmler, Reinhard Heydrich, Albert Speer and Martin Bormann.

**propaganda:** manipulation of information to influence public opinion. Propaganda emphasises the elements of information that support their position and plays down or leaves out bits that do not. Misleading statements and even lies may be used to create the desired effect in the public audience.

**Protocols of the elders of Zion:** a forged document concocted by the Tsarist secret police in 1902, claiming that there was a Jewish world conspiracy to overthrow the social order. The Protocols were widely used by Nazi ideologists such as Alfred Rosenberg in the 1920s to support their anti-Semitic propaganda.

**putsch:** an attempt to seize power by force. The two best-known examples in the early years of the Weimar Republic were the Kapp Putsch in 1920, when elements of the *Freikorps* attempted to take over in Berlin, and Hitler's so-called Beer Hall Putsch in Munich in 1923. Hitler's putsch got its name from the fact that its leaders launched their revolt from a large *Bierkeller* (beer-cellar) in the centre of Munich.

## R

**rabbi:** Jewish religious leader and teacher.

**'racial hygiene':** the aim to eliminate all 'racial degenerates' in order to 'purify' the German race.

**Red Army commissars:** these were put in place alongside army officers to ensure political obedience to the Communist regime.

**Reform Jews:** Jewish congregations who adapted to Western European ways. They continued to attend synagogues, but did not follow the strict requirements of Orthodox Jewry.

**Reichstag:** the Lower House of the German parliament (the Upper House was the Bundesrat).

**resettlement:** Nazi term for making Germany 'Jew-free' by removing Jews outside the Reich. This term was often meant and taken literally, to mean deportation to live somewhere else; but from 1941 it was merely as a euphemism to conceal the real aim of extermination.

**RSHA:** *Reichssicherheithauptamt* or Reich Security Head Office was formed on 22 September 1939 when the SD (Security Service) and Sipo (Security Police) merged. Between 1939 and 1941, it grew enormously under the control of Reinhard Heydrich and contained departments including the Gestapo and Criminal Police (Kripo). It played a major role in anti-Semitic policy in Germany and the Holocaust.

## S

**SA:** the Nazis' own 'private army', formed in 1921. Members of the SA, *Sturm Abteilung*, were often known as stormtroopers or Brownshirts. The SA played a major role in fighting the Communists during the Nazi rise to power and expanded to nearly 400,000 members after Hitler became chancellor. Ernst Röhm was its leader until he and other SA leaders were killed on the Night of the Long Knives in 1934.

**SS:** *(Schutzstaffel,* or Protection Force) this was a paramilitary organisation linked to the Nazi Party and led by Heinrich Himmler. Originally, the SS was only a small part of the SA *(Sturm Abteilung),* the main Nazi uniformed militia, but the SS steadily grew in power and influence until it took over from the SA after the Blood Purge of 1934.

**secularisation:** the process of moving away from religious observance. The majority of Jews in Weimar Germany were secular Jews, who had partly or wholly given up the outward forms of Jewish religious identity. Orthodox rabbis were very alarmed at the rate of secularisation in the 1920s, fearing that the religious core of Judaism might disappear altogether.

**selections:** the process of selecting which people would be sent to the gas chambers immediately on arrival at a death camp, as opposed to those who might have skills that would be useful for forced labour.

**Shoah:** a Hebrew word for suffering or sacrifice, often used as an alternative for 'Holocaust', partly because it refers exclusively to the fate of the Jews between 1933 and 1945. *Shoah* is the title of the very long but brilliant film documentary directed by Claude Lanzmann in 1985.

**shtetls:** traditional Jewish village communities in Eastern Europe. When the Nazis overran eastern Poland and the western USSR in 1941, they killed or deported millions of 'eastern Jews'; the Yiddish life and culture of the *shtetls* were permanently destroyed.

**Social Darwinism:** the ideological belief that Darwin's principle of 'natural selection' (the survival of the fittest) should be applied to human society.

**Soviet Jews:** those living within the borders of the USSR before June 1941. 'Polish Jews' were those living in Poland before the 1939 war; 'German Jews' were those living in Greater Germany. None

of these terms is very precise (some of the Jews living in Germany and in parts of the USSR were actually of Polish origin), but it is important to understand the different general categories.

**Spartacus:** the name (taken from the leader of a slave revolt against Ancient Rome) of the German Communists, led by Karl Liebknecht, who attempted to overthrow the temporary democratic government of Germany in 1918–19.

**'Special actions':** this was a Nazi euphemism for mass killings, almost always carried out by shooting at close range on the grisly principle 'one bullet, one Jew'.

**Strasserites:** the supporters of Gregor Strasser (profiled in Chapter 2, page 34) and his younger brother, Otto. The Strassers generally believed in the radical left-wing aspects of Nazi ideology. Strasserites tended to be concentrated in northern Germany and were not always happy with Hitler's personal domination of the NSDAP. They also tended to emphasise economic issues more than race.

### T

**T4 programme:** *Aktion T4* was the codename for the policy of euthanasia killings of disabled children, launched in 1939. It was this T4 programme that first used gas chambers for mass killings. Public protests led by Cardinal von Galen, the Catholic Archbishop of Munster, led to the programme being suspended in 1941.

### V

**Volk:** the word *Volk* means something much more than the literal English translation as folk, or people. To truly belong to the *Volk,* it was essential to be of the right racial stock and to hold all the right beliefs and values of Germanism. *Völkisch* Nationalism included many people who were not German citizens and excluded many people who were, including Jews.

**Völkisch:** this term means literally 'of the people', but the German word *Volk* implies much more than the people. Germany did not become a united state until 1871 and the idea of belonging to the German *Volk* involved deep feelings about national and racial identity.

**Volksdeutsche:** racially pure Germans who lived outside the Reich, for example in Poland, Romania or the Baltic States. Part of Nazi Germany was to bring these people back 'home to the Reich', giving them the lands and homes that became available when territories were 'Germanised' by expelling Jews and Slavs to the East.

**Volksgemeinschaft (National People's Community):** Nazism claimed to be a classless society, uniting all true Germans in one single mass, loyal to a single leader. The term was exclusive as much as inclusive, because many categories of people, including Jews, were defined as unfit to belong to the true *Volk.*

### Y

**Yiddish:** the language (partly German and partly Hebrew) used by Jewish communities in Eastern Europe.

### Z

**Zionists:** they believed in the idea of a national homeland for the Jewish people. Their dream was to create this homeland in Palestine, the historic home of Jews before they were driven out by the Romans in the 1st century AD. The founding father of modern Zionism was Theodor Herzl, the author of *The Jewish State* published in 1896.

**Zyklon B:** the poison gas that was used in the gas chambers of the death camps. Zyklon B was a form of cyanide, originally developed by a Jewish scientist as a weapon for use in the First World War. The role of the chief manufacturer, I. G. Farben, led to controversy after the war.

# Bibliography

## General

### Students

Engel, D. (2000) *The Holocaust: Hitler and the Jews*, Pearson.

Farmer, A. (2000) *Anti-Semitism and the Holocaust*, Hodder & Stoughton.

Neville, P. (1999) *The Holocaust*, Cambridge University Press.

### Teachers and extension

Adam, P. (1990) *The Arts In The Third Reich*, Thames & Hudson.

Aly, G. (1999) *Nazi Population Policy & the Destruction of European Jews*, Yale University Press.

Beller, S. (2007) *Antisemitism: A Very Short Introduction*, OUP.

Bergen, D. L. (2005) *War & Genocide: A Concise History of the Holocaust*, Littlefield.

Burleigh, M. and Wippermann, W. (1995) *The Racial State*, Longman.

Dawidowicz, L. (1988) *The War Against The Jews 1933–1945*, Penguin.

Gartner, L. P. (2001) *A History of the Jews in Modern Times*, OUP.

Kershaw, I. (2008) *Hitler, The Germans and the Final Solution*, Yale University Press.

Lacqueur, W. (2006) *The Changing Face of Antisemitism: From Ancient Times to the Present Day*, OUP.

Lipstadt, D. (1994) *Denying the Holocaust: The Growing Assault on Truth & Memory*, Penguin.

Marrus, M. (1986) *The Holocaust and History*, Penguin.

Niewyk, D. L. (2002) *The Holocaust: Problems & Perspectives of Interpretation*, Wadsworth.

Rees, L. (2005) *The Nazis: A Warning From History*, BBC Books.

Stone, D. (2006) *The Historiography of the Holocaust*, Palgrave Macmillan.

### Websites

Useful source material is provided on the following websites:

**www.spartacus.schoolnet.co.uk**

**www.wienerlibrary.co.uk**

## Section 1 Anti-Semitism in Germany, 1919–30

### Students

Bergen, D. L. (2005) *War & Genocide: A Concise History of the Holocaust*, Littlefield.

### Teachers and extension

Elon, A. (2002) *The Pity Of It All: A Portrait of Jews in Germany 1743–1933*, Penguin.

Evans, R. J. (2003) *The Coming of the Third Reich*, Penguin.

Gill, A. (1993) *A Dance Between Flames: Culture in Weimar Germany*, Bison.

Katz, J. (2000) *From Prejudice to Destruction: Antisemitism 1700–1933*, Oxford.

Niewyk, D. L. (2001) *The Jews in Weimar Germany*, Transaction Publishers.

Pulzer, P. (1992) *The Rise of Political Antisemitism in Germany & Austria*, Cambridge.

Slexhkine, Y. (2004) *The Jewish Century*, Princeton.

Watt, R. (1968) *The Kings Depart: Versailles and the German Revolution*, Simon & Schuster.

### DVD

Rees, L. (1996) *The Nazis: A Warning From History. I, Rise To Power*.

Wistrich, R. (1981) *The Longest Hatred: I. From the Cross to the Swastika*.

## Section 2 Hitler's anti-Semitic ideas

### Students

Engel, D. (2000) *The Holocaust: The Third Reich and the Jews*, Pearson.

Kershaw, I. (1991) *Hitler*, Longman.

### Teachers and extension

Abel, T. (1986) *Why Hitler Came Into Power*, Harvard University Press.

Haffner, S. (2002) *Defying Hitler: A Memoir*, Weidenfeld & Nicolson.

Hamann, B. (1999) *Hitler's Vienna: A Dictator's Apprenticeship*, Oxford University Press.

Kershaw, I. (1998) *Hitler: I Hubris*, Allen Lane.

Lane, B. M. and Rupp, L. (1990) *Nazi Ideology Before 1933*, Manchester University Press.

Noakes, J. and Pridham, G. (1988) *Nazism: I, Rise To Power 1919–1934*, Exeter University Press.

Stone, N. (1988) *Hitler*, Collins.

Turner, H. A. (1996) *Hitler's Thirty Days to Power: January 1933*, Bloomsbury.

*DVD*

Andrew, C. (1989) *Fatal Attraction*, BBC.

## ■ Section 3 The racial state, 1933–39

### Students

Farmer, A. (2000) *Anti-Semitism and the Holocaust*, Hodder & Stoughton.

### Teachers and extension

Evans, R. J. (2005) *The Third Reich in Power*, Penguin.

Friedländer, S. (2000) *Nazi Germany and the Jews: Years of Persecution 1933–1939*, Harper.

Kershaw, I. (1998) *Hitler: II Nemesis*, Allen Lane.

Klemperer, V. (2004) *I Shall Bear Witness: Diaries 1933–1941*, Weidenfeld & Nicolson.

Noakes, J. and Pridham, G. (1988) *Nazism: II State & Society 1933–1939*, Exeter University Press.

Read, A. (2001) *Kristallnacht*, Bison.

Welch, D. (1998) *The Third Reich: Politics & Propaganda*, Routledge.

*DVD*

People's Century (1996) *Master Race*.

Rees, L. (1996) *The Nazis: A Warning from History. 2, Chaos & Consent*.

World At War (1969) *16: Inside the Reich*.

*Websites*

Lively in-depth accounts of important events can be found on the BBC 'On This Day' site:

**www.news.bbc.co.uk/onthisday**

## ■ Section 4 The impact of war, 1939–42

### Students

Neville, P. (1999) *The Holocaust*, Cambridge University Press.

### Teachers and extension

Browning, C. (2005) *The Origins of the Final Solution*, Arrow.

Browning, C. (1992) *Ordinary Men: Reserve Police Battalion 101 & the Final Solution in Poland*, HarperCollins.

Evans, R. J. (2008) *The Third Reich At War*, Penguin.

Kershaw, I. (2008) *Fateful Choices: Ten Decisions That Changed The World*, Penguin.

Noakes, J. and Pridham, G. (1988) *Nazism: III, War & Racial Extermination*, Exeter University Press.

*DVD*

Pierson, F. (2001) *Conspiracy*, BBC Films.

Rees, L. (1996) *The Nazis: A Warning From History. 4, The Wild East*, BBC Films.

*Websites*

In-depth source material is presented by the Wannsee House Memorial Centre:

**www.ghwk.de/engl/kopfengl.htm**

## ■ Section 5 The Holocaust, 1941–45

### Students

Rees, L. (2005) *Auschwitz: The Nazis & The Final Solution*, BBC Books.

### Teachers and extension

Cohn-Sherbok, D. (1993) *Atlas Of Jewish History*, Routledge.

Finkelstein, N. (2000) *The Holocaust Industry*, Verso.

Finkelstein, N. and Birn, R. B. (1998) *Nation On Trial: The Goldhagen Thesis & Historical Truth*, Holt.

Friedländer, S. (2000) *Nazi Germany & The Jews: Years of Extermination 1939–1945*, Harper.

Herf, J. (2006) *The Jewish Enemy: Nazi Propaganda During World War II and the Holocaust*, Harvard University Press.

Keneally, T. (1993) *Schindler's List*, Touchstone.

Klemperer, V. (1999) *To The Bitter End: Diaries 1942–1945*, Weidenfeld & Nicolson.

Levi, P. (1986) *The Drowned and the Saved*, Vintage.

Roseman, M. (2002) *The Villa, The Lake, The Meeting: Wannsee and the Final Solution*, Penguin.

Steinberg, J. (1990) *All Or Nothing: The Axis and the Holocaust 1941–1943*, Routledge.

*DVD*

Isaacs, J. (1969) *World At War: 23 Genocide*, Thames TV.

Lanzmann, C. (1985) *Shoah*.

Rees, L. (1998) *Auschwitz*, BBC Films.

Rees, L. (1996) *The Nazis: A Warning From History, The Road To Treblinka*, BBC.

Spielberg, S. (1993) *Schindler's List*.

Stevens, G. (1985) *D Day to Berlin*.

# Acknowledgements

The author and publisher would like to thank the following for permission to reproduce material:

## Source texts:

P20 Quoted in Niewyk, D. L. *The Jews in Weimar Germany*, 200; (1) Elon, A. *The Pity Of It All: A Portrait of the Jews in Germany, 1743–1933*, 2002; (2) Quoted in Niewyk, D.L, *The Jews in Weimar Germany*, 2001; p22 (1) Kershaw, I. *Fateful Choices: Ten Decisions That Changed the World, 1940–41*, 2007, (2) Browning, C. quoted in Rees, L. *The Nazis: A Warning From History*, 2005; p24 Marx, J. quoted in Elon, A. *The Pity Of It All: A Portrait of the Jews in Weimar Germany, 1743–1933*, 2002; p28 Quoted in Abel, T. *Why Hitler Came Into Power*, 1938; p30 (5 and 6) Quoted in Abel, T. *Why Hitler Came Into Power*, 1938; p36 Rees, L. *The Nazis: A Warning From History*, 2005; p39 Laqueur, W. *The Changing Face Of Antisemitism*, 2006; p41 Longerich, P. *The Unwritten Order: Hitler's Role In The Final Solution*, 2001; p44 (7) quoted in Jäckel, E. and Kuhn, A. *Hitler: Sämtliche Aufzeichnungen 1905–1924*, 1980, (8) Hitler, A. *Mein Kampf*, British edition 1939 by Hurst & Blackett; p46 quoted in Jäckel, E. and Kuhn, A. *Hitler: Sämtliche Aufzeichnungen 1905–1924*, 1980; Kershaw, I. *Hitler, The Germans and the Final Solution*, 2008; p53 Speer, A. *Inside The Third Reich, The Memoirs of Albert Speer*, 1970; p58 (2) Roth, J. *What I Saw: Reports From Berlin 1920–33*, 2003, (A) Hitler, A. quoted in Hamann, B. *Hitler's Vienna: A Dictator's Apprenticeship*, 1999; p59 Hamann, B. *Hitler's Vienna: A Dictator's Apprenticeship*, 1999; p60 Hitler, A. quoted in Baynes, N.H. (ed) *The Speeches of Adolf Hitler, I*, 1942; p63 quoted in Smith, L. *Forgotten Voices of the Holocaust*, 2005; p64 Burleigh, M. *The Third Reich: A New History*, 2001; p65 quoted in Noakes, J. and Pridham, G. (eds) *A Documentary Reader: Nazism 1919–45, Volume 2, State, Economy and Society 1933–1939*, 1984; p67 Domarus, M. (ed) *Reden und Proklamationen 1932–1945 (Speeches and Proclamations 1932–1945)*, 1962; p73 Hitler, A. quoted in Baynes, N.H. (ed) *The Speeches of Adolf Hitler, I*, 1942; p74 quoted in Smith, L. *Forgotten Voices of the Holocaust*, 2005; p76 (2) quoted in Noakes, J. and Pridham, G. (eds) *A Documentary Reader: Nazism 1919–45, Volume 2, State, Economy and Society 1933–1939*, 1984, (3) quoted in Smith, L. *Forgotten Voices of the Holocaust*, 2005; p77 Rees, L. *Auschwitz, The Nazis and the 'Final Solution'*, 2005; p79 (Source 5 and in-text) quoted in Noakes, J. and Pridham, G. (eds) *A Documentary Reader: Nazism 1919–45, Volume 2, State, Economy and Society 1933–1939*, 1984; p80 Evans, R. *The Third Reich in Power*, 2005; p81 quoted in Noakes, J. and Pridham, G. (eds) *A Documentary Reader: Nazism 1919–45, Volume 2, State, Economy and Society 1933–1939*, 1984; p82 quoted in Noakes, J. and Pridham, G. (eds) *A Documentary Reader: Nazism 1919–45, Volume 2, State, Economy and Society 1933–1939*, 1984; p83 (in-text Hitler quote) Burleigh, M. *The Third Reich: A New History*, 2001; p84 quoted in Noakes, J. and Pridham, G. (eds) *A Documentary Reader: Nazism 1919–45, Volume 2, State, Economy and Society 1933–1939*, 1984; p93 quoted in Noakes, J. and Pridham, G. (eds) *A Documentary Reader: Nazism 1919–1945, Volume 3, Foreign Policy, War and Racial Extermination*, 1998; p94 quoted in Noakes, J. and Pridham, G. (eds) *A Documentary Reader: Nazism 1919–1945, Volume 3, Foreign Policy, War and Racial Extermination*, 1998; p95 quoted in Noakes, J. and Pridham, G. (eds) *A Documentary Reader: Nazism 1919–1945, Volume 3, Foreign Policy, War and Racial Extermination*, 1998; p96 quoted in Noakes, J. and Pridham, G. (eds) *A Documentary Reader: Nazism 1919–1945, Volume 3, Foreign Policy, War and Racial Extermination*, 1998; p98 (4 and 5) quoted in Aly, G. *'Final Solution': Nazi Population Policy and the Murder of the European Jews*, 1999; p104 Kershaw, I. *Fateful Choices: Ten Decisions that Changed the World 1940–41*, 2008; p109 (2 and 4) Rees, L. *Auschwitz: The Nazis and the 'Final Solution'*, 2005, (3) Rees, L. *The Nazis: A Warning From History*, 2005; p111 Kershaw, I. *Hitler: Nemesis 1936–1945*, 2001; p112 Rees, L. *Auschwitz: The Nazis and the 'Final Solution'*, 2005; p113 (B) quoted in Noakes, J. and Pridham, G. (eds) *A Documentary Reader: Nazism 1919–1945, Volume 3, Foreign Policy, War and Racial Extermination*, 1998, (C) Browning, C. *The Origins of the Final Solution 1939–1942*, 2004; p117 Roseman, M. *The Villa, The Lake, The Meeting: Wannsee and the Final Solution*, 2002; p123 (4 and 5) Herf, J. *The Jewish Enemy: Nazi Propaganda During World War II and The Holocaust*, 2006; p128 Herf, J. *The Jewish Enemy: Nazi Propaganda During World War II and The Holocaust*, 2006; p130 Speer, A. *Inside the Third Reich, The Memoirs of Albert Speer*, 1970; p132 Rees, L. *The Nazis: A Warning From History*, 2005; p143 Rees, L. *Auschwitz: The Nazis and The Final Solution*, 2005

## Photographs:

Cover photograph: Guy Harrop/Alamy

Ann Ronan Picture Library pp66, 124; David Shankbone p140; Edimedia Archive pp8, 9, 13, 17, 18, 25 (margin), 32, 36, 39, 55, 63, 64, 71, 72, 77, 78, 85, 93, 97, 101, 106, 111, 112, 117, 120 (top), 127; Mary Evans Picture Library p29 (both); Photos12 pp1, 19, 22, 50, 68, 74, 80, 129, 138; Public Domain: pp44, 54, 69; Samuel Wantman p122; Sante Archive pp120 (bottom), 133; The Literature Archive pp46, 57, 107 (bottom); Topfoto pp23, 28, 31, 51, 53, 70, 76, 79, 95, 100, 105, 107 (top), 116, 131, 136; World History Archive pp15, 25 (bottom), 27, 38, 41, 47, 56 (both), 60, 83, 91, 94

Photo research by Jason Newman and Alexander Goldberg of *www.uniquedimension.com*

Every effort has been made to contact the copyright holders and we apologise if any have been overlooked. Should copyright have been unwittingly infringed in this book, the owners should contact the publishers, who will make the corrections at reprint.

# Index